CompTIA Sec

MW01283426

Technology Workbook

Second Edition

---

www.ipspecialist.net

Document Control

Proposal Name	:	CompTIA Security+ Technology Workbook
Document Version	:	Second Edition
Release Date	:	25th-March-2019
Reference	:	SYO-501

Feedback:

If you have any comments regarding the quality of this book, or otherwise alter it to suit your needs better, you can contact us by email at info@ipspecialist.net

Please make sure to include the book title and ISBN in your message.

About IPSpecialist

IPSPECIALIST LTD. IS COMMITTED TO EXCELLENCE AND DEDICATED TO YOUR SUCCESS.

Our philosophy is to treat our learners like family. We want you to succeed, and we are willing to do everything possible to help you do it. We have all the proof to back up our claims. IPSpecialist strives to accelerate billions of careers by launching great courses with motives of providing accessibility and considering affordability of its readers. We believe that continuous learning and knowledge evolution are the most important things to revamp and rebuild skill set in the professional arena

Planning and creating a specific goal is where IPSpecialist helps. We help you choose a career track that suits your vision as well as develop the competencies you need to become a professional Network Engineer. We also assist you to evaluate and execute your proficiency level based on the career track chosen, as they are customized to fit your specific goals.

We help you STAND OUT from the crowd through our detailed IP training courses.

Course Features:

> Self-Paced learning
>   - Learn at your own pace and in your own time
> Covers Complete Exam Blueprint
>   - Prep-up for the exam with confidence
> Case Study Based Learning
>   - Relate the content to real-life scenarios
> Subscriptions that suits you
>   - Get more, pay less with IPS Subscriptions
> Career Advisory Services
>   - Let industry experts plan your career journey
> Virtual Labs to test your skills
>   - With IPS vRacks, you can testify your exam preparations
> Practice Questions
>   - Practice Questions to measure your preparation standards
> On Request Digital Certification
>   - On digital request certification from IPSpecialist LTD.

About the Authors:

This book has been compiled with the help of multiple professional engineers. These engineers specialize in different fields like Networking, Security, Cloud, Big Data, IoT, etc. Each engineer develops content in its specialized field that is compiled to form a comprehensive certification guide.

About the Technical Reviewers:

Nouman Ahmed Khan

AWS-Architect, CCDE, CCIEX5 (R&S, SP, Security, DC, Wireless), CISSP, CISA, CISM is a Solution Architect working with a major telecommunication provider in Qatar. He works with enterprises, mega-projects, and service providers to help them select the best-fit technology solutions. He also works closely with a consultant to understand customer business processes and helps select an appropriate technology strategy to support business goals. He has more than 14 years of experience working in Pakistan/Middle-East & UK. He holds a Bachelor of Engineering Degree from NED University, Pakistan, and M.Sc. in Computer Networks from UK.

Abubakar Saeed

Abubakar Saeed has more than twenty-five years of experience, Managing, Consulting, Designing, and implementing large-scale technology projects, extensive experience heading ISP operations, solutions integration, heading Product Development, Presales, and Solution Design. Emphasizing on adhering to Project timelines and delivering as per customers' expectations, he always leads the project in the right direction with his innovative ideas and excellent management skills

Muhammad Yousuf

Muhammad Yousuf is a professional technical content writer. He is a Certified Ethical Hacker (CEHv10) and Cisco Certified Network Associate (CCNA) in Routing and Switching, holding bachelor's degree in Telecommunication Engineering from Sir Syed University of Engineering and Technology. He has both technical knowledge and sound industry information, which he uses perfectly in his career.

Syeda Mashraba Batool Rizvi

Syeda Mashraba Batool Rizvi is a Technical Content Developer. She holds a bachelor's degree in Telecommunication Engineering from Dawood University of Engineering & Technology. She possesses great writing and researching skills and has an in-depth technical knowledge.

Free Resources:

With each workbook bought from Amazon, IPSpecialist offers free resources to our valuable customers. Once you buy this book, you will have to contact us at support@ipspecialist.net or tweet @ipspecialistnet to get this limited time offer without any extra charges.

Free Resources Include:

Exam Practice Questions in Quiz Simulation:

IP Specialists' Practice Questions have been developed keeping in mind the certification exam perspective. The collection of these questions from our technology workbooks is prepared keeping the exam blueprint in mind, covering not only important but necessary topics as well. It is an ideal document to practice and revise your certification.

Career Report:

This report is a step-by-step guide for a novice who wants to develop his/her career in the field of computer networks. It answers the following queries:

- Current scenarios and future prospects
- Is this industry moving towards saturation or are new opportunities knocking at the door?
- What will the monetary benefits be?
- Why to get certified?
- How to plan and when will I complete the certifications if I start today?
- Is there any career track that I can follow to accomplish specialization level?

Furthermore, this guide provides a comprehensive career path towards being a specialist in the field of networking and highlights the tracks needed to obtain certification.

IPS Personalized Technical Support for Customers:

Good customer service means helping customers efficiently, in a friendly manner. It is essential to be able to handle issues for customers and do your best to ensure that they are satisfied. Providing good service is one of the most important things that can set your business apart from the others of its kind.

Great customer service will result in attracting more customers and attain the maximum customer retention.

IPS is offering personalized TECH support to its customers to provide better value for money. If you have any queries related to technology and labs, you can simply ask our technical team for assistance via Live Chat or Email.

Become an Author & Earn with Us:

If you are interested in becoming an author and start earning passive income, IPSpecialist offers "Earn with us" program. We all consume, develop and create content during our learning process, certification exam preparations, and during searching, developing and refining our professional careers. That content, notes, guides, worksheets and flip cards among other material is normally for our own reference without any defined structure or special considerations required for formal publishing. IPSpecialist can help you craft this 'draft' content into a fine product with the help of our global team of experts. We sell your content via different channels as:

1. Amazon – Kindle
2. eBay
3. LuLu
4. Kobo
5. Google Books
6. Udemy and many 3rd party publishers and resellers

Our Products

Technology Workbooks

IPSpecialist Technology workbooks are the ideal guides to developing the hands-on skills necessary to pass the exam. Our workbook covers official exam blueprint and explains the technology with real life case study based labs. The content covered in each workbook consists of individually focused technology topics presented in an easy-to-follow, goal-oriented, systematic approach. Every scenario features detailed breakdowns and thorough verifications to help you completely understand the task and associated technology.

We extensively used mind maps in our workbooks to explain visually the technology. Our workbooks have become a widely used tool to learn and remember the information effectively.

vRacks

Our highly scalable and innovative virtualized lab platforms let you practice the IP Specialist Technology Workbook at your own time and your own place as per your convenience.

Quick Reference Sheets

Our quick reference sheets are a concise bundling of condensed notes of the complete exam blueprint. It is an ideal and handy document to help you remember the most important technology concepts related to the certification exam.

Practice Questions

IP Specialists' Practice Questions are dedicatedly designed from a certification exam perspective. The collection of these questions from our technology workbooks is prepared keeping the exam blueprint in mind covering not only important but necessary topics as well. It is an ideal document to practice and revise your certification.

Content at a glance

Table of Contents

About this Workbook

This workbook covers all the information you need to pass the CompTIA Security+ Exam that is SY0-501. The workbook is designed to take a practical approach to learning with real-life examples and case studies.

- Covers complete CompTIA Security+ SY0-501 blueprint
- Summarized content
- Case Study based approach
- Downloadable vRacks
- 100% pass guarantee
- Mind maps

CompTIA Certifications

CompTIA certification helps to establish and build your IT career. It benefits you in various ways either seeking certification to have a job in IT or want to upgrade your IT career with a leading certification, that is, CompTIA certification.

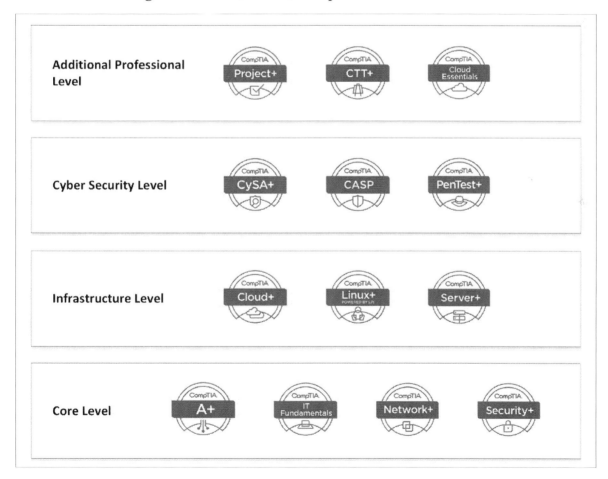

Figure 1. CompTIA Certifications Pathway

About Security+ Certification

The purpose of this certification is to make you a better IT Security Tech. All the essential principles for network security are covered in this Security+ certification.

The skills or techniques you will learn when you obtain Security+ certificate:

- Configuring a secure network for protection against threats, malware, etc.
- Identification of vulnerabilities in a network and provision of proper mitigation techniques.
- Knowledge of latest threats that harm your system intelligently.
- Implementation of secure protocols and appropriate security checks and the establishment of end-to-end host security.
- Implementation of access and identity management controls to have your data in legal hands.
- Ability to use encryption, configuring wireless security for information safety purpose.

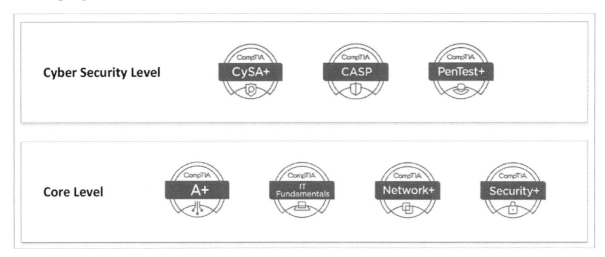

Figure 2. CompTIA Security Certifications Pathway

About the CompTIA Security+ Exam

- Exam Number: SY0-501 CompTIA Security+
- Duration: 90 minutes
- Number of Questions: Maximum 90
- Types of Questions: Multiple choice & performance based
- Passing Marks: 750
- Exam Price: $330 USD

The CompTIA Security+ Exam (SY0-501) is a 90-minute qualifying exam with a maximum of 90 questions for the CompTIA certification. The CompTIA Security+ Exam certifies the successful applicants that have the awareness and skills needed to configure and install the systems in order to secure the networks, devices, & applications. This Exam certifies that the successful applicant has the knowledge and skills of:

- Environmental and personal security and controls.
- Wireless, cloud and mobile security.
- Risk management.
- Authentication and authorization.
- Host, LAN, and application security.
- Cryptography.

The following topics are general guidelines for the content that is likely to be included in the exam:

Threats, Attacks, and Vulnerabilities	21%
Technologies and Tools	22%
Architecture and Design	15%
Identity and Access Management	16%
Risk Management	14%
Cryptography and PKI	12%

How to become Security+ certified?

Step 1: Choose a certification: Explore what is available and choose an IT certification that will benefit you in accomplishing your career target.

To study about various IT career tracks and to choose the best certification for yourself, you can use the "CompTIA Career Roadmap."

CompTIA has four core IT certifications that is; IT Fundamental, A+, Network+, and Security+ that examine your knowledge from the entry to the expert level.

If you have the skills to secure a network & deter hackers and want to become a highly efficient IT Security Tech, then CompTIA Security+ is the right type of certification for you.

Step 2: Learning & Training: Exam preparation can be done through self-study with textbooks, practice exams, and online classroom programs. However, this workbook provides you with all the information and offers complete assessments in one place to help you pass the CompTIA Security+ Exam.

IPSpecialist provides full support to the candidates in order for them to pass the exam.

Step 3: Familiarization with Exam: A great suggestion is to first understand what you are training for. For that, we are providing you not only the exam objectives but practice questions too, in order to give you a thorough idea about your final exam of certification.

Step 4: Register & Take Exam for Certification: After all the learning process, the next step is to take your test. Certification exams are offered at different locations all over the world. To register for an exam, contact the authorized test delivery partner of CompTIA, contact *Pearson VUE.*

The following are the steps for registration and scheduling an exam:

1. Buy the exam voucher from here "Buy a certification exam voucher."
2. Find and visit a testing center "testing center."
3. Create Pearson VUE account & Schedule your exam. Here is a link for that "Create a Pearson VUE testing account and schedule your exam."
4. You will receive a confirmation email having testing information after the registration process.
5. You are ready for the test.

Step 5: Results: After you complete an exam at an authorized testing center, you'll get immediate, online notification of your pass or fail status. If you have passed the exam, a congratulatory email will be forwarded to you with guidelines to access your record.

Make sure to keep a record of the email address you used for registration and score report with exam registration number. This information is required to log in to your certification account.

Congratulations! You are now CompTIA Security+ Certified.

Chapter 01: Threats, Attacks, and Vulnerabilities

An Overview of Malware

The term "Malware" can be defined as any malicious software that is intended to perform any suspicious activity in the network. These suspicious codes, scrips and softwares could degrade network's performance, steal information, unavailability, and loss of confidential data. Some of the most common forms of malware are:

- Virus
- Botnets
- Rootkits
- Crypto-Malware
- Ransomware
- Worms
- Trojan Horses
- Spyware
- Adware
- Keylogger
- Logic Bomb

How does Malware get in?

Malware takes advantage of the weaknesses and vulnerabilities in the operating system or the vulnerabilities introduced by accidentally clicking on the malicious links. A malware program starts running before the malware deploys itself on the system.

How to Keep Malware Away?

- Make sure to keep Operating Systems up to date.
- Update all the Applications.
- Avoid clicking unnecessary or malicious links.
- Use Anti-Virus / Anti-Malware software.

Malware Types

The following are the details of various kinds of Malware:

Virus

The term "Virus" in Network and Information security corresponds to the malicious software that in intended to harm the network. This malicious software is developed to spread, replicate itself, and attach itself to other files. By attaching the infected files with

other systems can result in the transfer of virus on the other system as well. These viruses require user interaction to trigger and initiate malicious activities on the resident system.

The virus is known for its "self-reproduction". Viruses replicate by attaching themselves with an executable file. For example, copying an infected file copies a virus. Some types of viruses do not cause problems; they are invisible, but some are obvious (provide pop-ups).

The first viruses created were of two types:

1. Boot sector viruses.
2. Program viruses.

<u>Working of Viruses</u>

Working of a virus involves two-phase process. in which a virus replicates onto an executable file and attacks on a system. Different phases are defined below:

1. *Infection Phase*

During an infection phase, a virus is planted on a target system which then replicates itself onto an executable file. By replicating into a legitimate software, it can be launched when a user runs the authentic application. These viruses spread by reproducing and infecting the programs, documents, or e-mail attachments. Similarly, they can be propagated through e-mails, file sharing or downloaded files from internet. They can enter into an operating system through CDs, DVDs, USB-drives and any other sort of digital media.

2. *Attack Phase*

In the attack phase, the infected file is executed either intentionally by the intruder or accidentally by the user. Viruses normally require a triggering action to infect the victim's system. This infection can completely destroy the system or may corrupt the program files and data. Some viruses can initiate an attack when they are executed, but they can also be configured to infect according to certain predefined conditions.

To prevent viruses, anti-virus programs are commonly used. This anti-virus software constantly scans the system, finds, and prevents the virus from getting into the system and ensures that no virus is executing into the system. One must maintain the signature list that is on the anti-virus software because a number of viruses are being discovered every day.

Worms

Unlike Viruses, Worms are capable of replicating themselves. This capability of worms makes them spread on a resident system very quickly. Worms are propagating in different

forms since the 1980s. Some types of emerging worms are very destructive and responsible for devastating DoS attacks. It can move without human action or intervention inside the network or computer. They spread and take over the system quickly. A well-known virus can be filtered through next-generation intrusion prevention system or firewall.

<u>Example of worm:</u>

- Sobig worm of 2003
- SQL Slammer worm of 2003
- 2001 attacks of Code Red and Nimba
- 2005 Zotob worm

Ransomware:

It takes the user data and encrypts it, and in return, it asks for money in order to decrypt the data back to its original form. Ransomware makes the system or computer encrypted. When a user attempts to access the files, a message is shown to him to pay a ransom to unlock your files. In case of ransomware, you need to take your system to a security professional to remove ransomware and decrypt your files and data, or you may need to follow the procedure through which you can send money for regaining access to the files or to have the decryption keys. The system of payment is not traceable, and also you cannot decrypt the data files because of the strong encryption method, i.e., Public Key Cryptography.

<u>Example of ransomware:</u>

- Crypto-Locker

Crypto-Malware:

It encrypts all the data or file either permanently or temporarily. It is more intended for denial of service by permanently encrypting the files or temporarily until a ransom amount is paid.

<u>How to prevent this infection?</u>

- Update Operating system and applications.
- Backup all data offline.
- Install anti-virus and update the anti-virus signature.

Trojans:

It damages the system by hiding its real functionality; this means that it pretends to be something else other than malware. It is easy for the malware to get inside the system. However, once they get inside, they open doors for other malware too, and that open

door is referred to as a back door. Remote Access Trojan commonly referred to as Remote Administrative Tools is a category of Trojan horse malware. It provides administrative access to the system and set up the back door.

Types of Trojans

- ■ ***Command Shell Trojans***

Command Shell Trojans are capable of providing remote control of command shell of a victim. Trojan server of command shell Trojan such as Netcat is installed on the target machine. Trojan server will open the port for command shell connection to its client application, installed on attacker's machine. This Client-Server based Trojan provides access to the Command line.

- ■ ***Defacement Trojans***

Using Defacement Trojan, an attacker can view, edit and extract information from any Windows program. By using this information, the attacker replaces the string, images, and logos often to leave their mark. Using User-Styled Custom Application (UCA), the attacker defaces programs. Website defacement is very popularly known; it is similar to the concept of applications running on the target machine.

- ■ ***HTTP/HTTPS Trojans***

HTTP and HTTPS Trojans bypass the firewall inspection and execute on the target machine. After execution, they create HTTP/ HTTPS tunnel to communicate with the attacker from the victim's machine.

- ■ ***Botnet Trojans***

Botnets are the number of compromised systems (zombies). These compromised systems are not limited to any specific LAN; they may be spread over a large geographical area. These Botnets are controlled by Command and Control Center. These botnets are used to launch attacks such as Denial of Service, Spamming, etc.

- ■ ***Proxy Server Trojans***

Trojan-Proxy Server is a standalone malware application which is capable of turning the host system into a proxy server. Proxy Server Trojan allows the attacker to use the victim's computer as a proxy by enabling the proxy server on the victim's system. This technique is used to launch further attacks by hiding the actual source of attack.

- ■ ***Remote Access Trojans (RAT)***

Remote Access Trojan (RAT) allows the attacker to get remote desktop access to a victim's computer by enabling Port which allows the GUI access to the remote system. RAT includes a back door for maintaining administrative access and control over the

victim. Using RAT, an attacker can monitor user's activity, access confidential information, take screenshots and record audio and video using a webcam, format drives and alter files, etc.

<u>How to prevent this malware?</u>

- You should examine the software before installing it. Install only what is trusted.
- You should have a backup of your data.
- You should update the antivirus software and operating system.

<u>Trojan Construction Kit</u>

Trojan Construction Kit allows attackers to create their own Trojans. These customized Trojans can be more dangerous for the target as well as the attacker if it backfires or is not executed properly. These customized Trojans created by using construction kits can avoid detection from virus and Trojan scanning software.

Some Trojan Construction Kits are:

- Dark Horse Trojan Virus Maker

- Senna Spy Generator

- Trojan Horse Construction Kit

- Progenic mail Trojan Construction Kit

- Pandora's Box

Rootkits:

A rootkit is a collection of software designed to provide privileged access to a remote user over the targeted system. Mostly, Rootkits are the collection of malicious software deployed after an attack, when the attacker has the administrative access to the target system to maintain its privileged access for future, it creates a backdoor for an attacker; Rootkits often mask the existence of its software, which helps to avoid detection.

> **Note:** It merges with another software to create malware and is mostly found in the kernel. *Example of Rootkit:* Zeus or Zbot. Rootkits are used for gaining administrative control over a machine.

<u>Types of Rootkits</u>

- **Application Level Rootkits**

    Application Level Rootkits perform manipulation of standard application files, modification of the behavior of the current application with an injection of codes.

- **Kernel-Level Rootkits**

  The kernel is the core of an OS. Kernel-Level Rootkits add additional codes (malicious); replaces the section of codes of original Operating system kernel.

- **Hardware / Firmware Level Rootkits**

  Type of Rootkits that hides in hardware such as hard drive, network interface card, system BIOS, which are not inspected for integrity. These rootkits are built into a chipset for recovering stolen computers, deleting data, or rendering them useless. Additionally, Rootkits have privacy and security concerns of undetectable spying.

- **Hypervisor Level Rootkits**

  Hypervisor Level Rootkits exploits hardware features like AMD-V (Hardware-assisted virtualization technologies) or Intel VT, which hosts the target OS as a virtual machine.

- **Boot Loader Level Rootkits**

  Bootloader Level Rootkits (Bootkits) replaces the legitimate boot loader with the malicious one, which enables the Bootkits to activate before an OS run. Bootkits are a serious threat to the system security because they can infect startup codes such as Master Boot Record (MBR), Volume Boot Record (VBR) or boot sector. It can be used to attack full disk encryption systems, hack encryption keys and passwords.

Rootkit Tools

- Avatar
- Necurs
- Azazel
- ZeroAccess

How to prevent this malware?

- Install a specific Rootkit Remover.
- Update anti-virus software.
- Take advantage of UEFI BIOS.

Keyloggers:

Keylogger saves the keystrokes you enter and then make a file and send it to the attacker, who wants to damage your system and want your personal information and data. It also saves information other than keystrokes.

How to prevent this malware?

- Update Anti-Virus Software.
- Use of exfiltration process.
- Set up firewall rules for the file transfer from the system.
- Use Keylogger scanner.

Detecting & Defending Rootkits

Integrity-Based Detection, using Digital Signatures, Difference-based detection, behavioral detection, memory dumps, and other approaches can be used for detecting Rootkits. In Unix Platform, Rootkit detection tools such as Zeppoo, chrootkit and other tools are available for detection. In Windows, Microsoft Windows Sysinternals, RootkitRevealer, Avast, and Sophos anti-Rootkit software are available.

Spyware:

Spywares are the specialized softwares that are designed for gathering user's interaction information with a system such as an email address, login credentials, and other details without informing the user of the target system. Mostly, Spyware is used for tracking internet interaction of the user. This gathered information is sent to a remote destination. Spyware hides its files and processes to avoid detection. The most common types of Spywares are -

- Adware
- System Monitors
- Tracking Cookies
- Trojans

Features of Spyware

There is a number of Spyware tools available on the internet providing several advanced features like

- Tracking Users such as Keylogging
- Monitoring user's activity such as Web sites visited
- Records conversations
- Blocking Application & Services
- Remote delivery of logs
- Email Communication tracking
- Recording removable media communication like USB
- Voice Recording
- Video Recording
- Tracking Location (GPS)

- Mobile Tracking

> Spywares are malicious software that scans the user activity like the website they visit and wait for their input to steal their personal information.

How does this get in?

It poses a security software which in reality, is a fake software which may be installed along with another software.

How does it work?

Once it is installed, it observes or monitors the user activity to scan the browsing history and use it for its own interest like when you log in to your bank account, it uses the scanned information to log in to your account and transfer the money into another account.

How to prevent it?

- Update the latest signature of the anti-virus.
- Be particular while installing the application.
- Backup all the data.

Adware:

A kind of malicious software that once installed on the system, shows advertisement and pop-up messages, and through this, the threat actors make money because they know it is one of the best ways to make money on the internet. The threat actor sometimes encapsulates the adware software inside some other application that people normally install and when they install that application, adware is installed along with it.

Adware removal - A Challenge

Removing adware is one of the most challenging process, because the attackers or threat actors are very clever, because they already know that people will definitely go for the adware removal tool when they come to know about the adware, and they present removal tool that contains more adware.

Botnets:

A kind of malware that stands for robot network. A robot is present inside the network and performs the tasks that are commanded to it and infect the device. Botnets are used for continuously performing a task. These botnets gain access to the systems using malicious script and codes. This alerts the master computer when the botnets start controlling the system. Through this master computer, an attacker can control the system and issue requests to attempt a DoS attack.

<u>Botnet Setup</u>

The Botnet is typically set up by installing a bot on a victim by using Trojan Horse. Trojan Horse carries a bot as payload, which is forwarded to the victim by phishing or redirecting to either a malicious website or a compromised genuine website. Once this malicious payload is executed, device gets infected and comes under the control of Bot Command and Control (C&C). C&C controls all the infected devices through Handler. Handler establishes the connection between infected device and C&S and waits for instructions to direct these zombies to attack on the primary target.

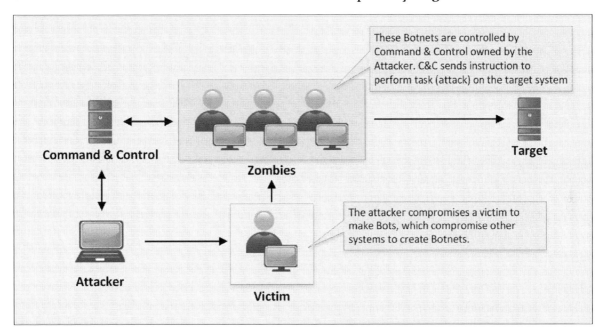

Figure 1-01: Typical Botnet Setup

Logic Bombs:

As the name implies, it is like a time bomb that waits for the right time for the event to occur. When the bomb goes off, something devastating happens like removal or deletion of information from the system. Identification of this malware is difficult because it is commonly installed by someone with administrative access and also because a known anti-malware signature does not match with it.

Types of Attacks

There are numerous types of attacks, and some of them are as follows:

1. Social Engineering Attacks
2. Phishing

Threat actor uses these techniques to convince the user to give their personal information like username & password or credit card number etc. Phishing attacks can be

implemented in various ways like through email or other electronic communication mediums. Spam emails are a very common way for phishing attacks. Malicious attachments are sent through phishing emails that masquerade or appear to come from a reputable source or entity and ask the user for their confidential information such as their credit card number, ID or Password, etc.

Tailgating and Impersonation

Impersonating is a human-based social engineering technique. Impersonation means pretending to be someone or something. Impersonating in Social engineering is where an attacker pretends to be a legitimate user or an authorized person. This impersonating may be either personal or behind a communication channel while communicating through email, telephone, etc.

Personal impersonating is performed through identity theft when an attacker has enough personal information about an authorized person. An attacker gathers information impersonating as a legitimate user, providing the personal information of a legitimate user. Impersonating as Technical support agent asking for the credential is another way to impersonate and gather information.

Piggybacking and Tailgating are similar techniques. Piggybacking is the technique in which an unauthorized person waits for an authorized person to gain entry in a restricted area, whereas Tailgating is the technique in which unauthorized person gain access to the restricted area by following the authorized person. By using Fake IDs and close following while crossing the checkpoint, tailgating becomes easy.

How Does It Work?

Threat actors are very clever and intelligent too; they search for the target through stalking and use various methods for identity theft like email phishing and eavesdropping. Once they get the identity, they try to gain access to the system or network so that they can do whatever they want.

Another technique used by the threat actor is *Tailgating*. This attack technique is done through which the attacker gains access to the restricted area by simply walking behind a legitimate person. Through this, they can use various tricks like showing fake identity token while carrying large pile of books and asks for other (legitimate person) to hold the door so that they can easily get inside the restricted area.

Dumpster Diving

Referred to as a rubbish skip or garbage bin, Dumpster diving is a technique used by the malicious actor to look for the information in the garbage bin because sometimes the information that is normally not available, can be found in the garbage bin of the

organization. The retrieved data from the garbage bin that might contain information like customer's record, phone number, etc. can help the threat actor to gain access to the system.

Shoulder Surfing

Accessing the information that is on the screen of the user. It is a very easy and very low-level hack because one can shoulder surf by using the webcam, telescope through which threat actor can easily see what someone is doing or what is on the screen of someone's computer.

Shoulder surfing is easily controllable because someone can easily control what people see on their screen, they just need to be aware of their surroundings. They can also use privacy filters like only allowing the person in front of the laptop or mobile to see the screen while all others (people on the left or right) can only see a blank screen.

Hoaxes

A type of threat that warns people about a particular problem and then asks for money to solve or remove the problem. These types of threat can be sent through email or through Facebook post or tweets, and its aim is to make money by fooling others.

Watering Hole Attacks

This is done when the security inside the organization is extremely strong, and there is no way for the threat actor to get inside the network and attack the security system. In this situation, the threat actors attack what the insiders visit instead of attacking the insider. For that, they just need to know about the sites that are commonly visited by the insiders, and then they attack inside the organization through attacking the third party. For the purpose of defense and security of the system, there should be multiple ways for the identification of attacks and for stopping them to penetrate into the network.

Application / Service Attacks

Denial of Service

Making services and network resources unavailable to the intended users is known as Denial of Service (DoS). The threat actors have multiple ways to do it, which are as follows:

- By taking advantage of Software vulnerabilities.
- Using Smokescreen method.
- Service overwhelming (too many users hitting the website at the same time).

It is not always a threat actor doing this. Sometimes, the user doesn't have enough bandwidth that is causing the Denial of Service or maybe he\she has created a loop and doesn't have span tree enabled, or it may even be a network-based denial of service.

Man in the Middle

As the name implies, Man in the Middle is the type of attack in which the attacker or the threat actor is present or relying on the communication path between the two parties and listen to the conversation. The goal of MITM attack is to steal personal data that can be used for identity theft, fund transfer or another purpose of attacker's interest.

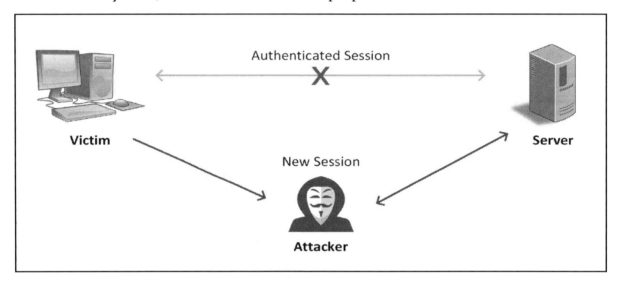

Figure 1-02: Man-in-the-Middle Attack

How to prevent it?

- Don't use Wi-Fi connection that is not password protected.
- Do pay attention to the notification of the browser that reports you about the unsecured website.
- Must log out of the application when not in use.
- For a sensitive transaction, don't use a public network.

How does it occur?

- Email hijacking
- Through Session hijacking
- Wi-Fi eavesdropping

Buffer Overflows

Also known as buffer overrun, Buffer Overflow is one of the major types of Operating System Attacks. It is related to software exploitation attacks. In Buffer overflow, a program or application does not have well-defined boundaries such as restrictions or pre-

defined functional area regarding the capacity of data it can handle or the type of data can be inputted. Buffer overflow causes problems such as Denial of Service (DoS), rebooting, achievement of unrestricted access and freezing.

How does it occur?

- Due to excess amount of data in the buffer.
- Buffer overflow is the vulnerability that creates an entry point for the threat actors.
- Coding errors are the cause of buffer overflow.

How to prevent it?

- The developers of application should avoid using standard functions of the library.
- Regular testing and fixing practice can help in decreasing the risk of buffer overflow attack.
- The language level automatic protection should be used.
- Data boundary checking at runtime also helps in preventing the Buffer overflow attacks.

Data Injection

Data injection means to cache malicious or untrusted data into the application or program. It is one of the most dangerous and oldest type of attack that results in loss and theft of data, data integrity loss, and DoS. In short, the full system is compromised due to this type of attack.

Data injection is due to bad programming and the attackers creep into the application through SQL (Structured Query Language).

How to prevent it?

- Proper input validation.
- Safe API usage.
- Contextually escape user data.

Cross Site Scripting

The acronym for Cross-site scripting is XSS. Cross-site Scripting attack is performed by an attacker by sending a crafted link with a malicious script. When the user clicks this malicious link, the script will be executed. This script may be coded to extract the Session IDs and send it to the attacker.

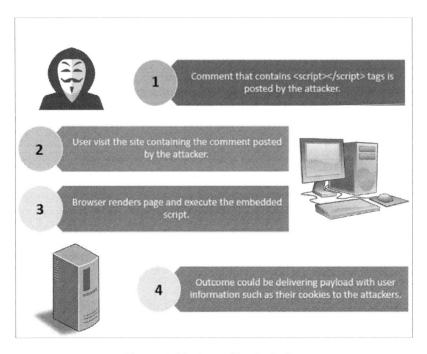

Figure 1-03: Cross Site Scripting

Cross-Site Request Forgery

Also known as Session riding attack and One-click attack. XSRF and CSRF (Sea Surf) are the acronyms used for Cross Site Request Forgery. Cross-Site Request Forgery (CSRF) attack is the process of obtaining the session ID of a legitimate user and exploiting the active session with the trusted website in order to perform malicious activities.

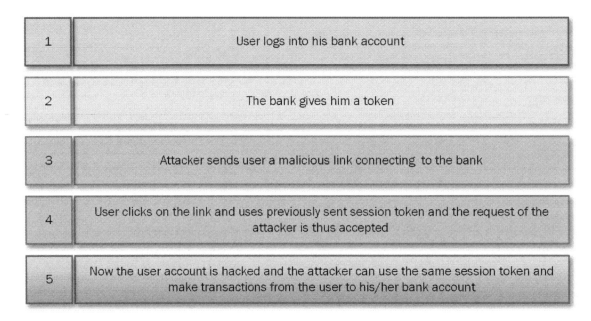

1	User logs into his bank account
2	The bank gives him a token
3	Attacker sends user a malicious link connecting to the bank
4	User clicks on the link and uses previously sent session token and the request of the attacker is thus accepted
5	Now the user account is hacked and the attacker can use the same session token and make transactions from the user to his/her bank account

Figure 1-04: Cross-Site Request Forgery

Privilege Escalation

This attack takes benefit of errors in programming and flaws in design. Privilege Escalation can be defined into two types Horizontal Privilege Escalation and Vertical Escalation. Through this attack, the Threat actor/ Attacker can become the administrator of the system and can do whatever he wants to do.

Horizontal Privileges Escalation

In Horizontal Privileges Escalation, an attacker attempts to take command over the privileges of another user having the same set of privileges for his account. Horizontal privileges escalation occurs when an attacker attempts to gain access to the same set of resources allowed to a particular user.

Consider an example of horizontal privileges escalation by supposing an operating system having multiple users including an Administrator, who has full privileges and User A, User B and so on with limited privileges to run application only (not allowed to install or uninstall any application). Each user is assigned the same level of privileges other than the administrator. By finding any weakness or exploiting any vulnerability, User A gains access to User B's account. Now, User A is able to control and access User B's account.

Vertical Privileges Escalation

In Vertical Privileges Escalation, an attacker attempts to escalate privileges to a higher level. Vertical privileges escalation occurs when an attacker attempts to gain access usually to the administrator account. Higher privileges allow the attacker to access sensitive information, install, modify and delete files and programs such as a virus, Trojans, etc.

How to prevent it?
Privilege escalation can be found and patched quickly.

- Update Operating system and anti-malware software.
- Through data execution prevention.
- Address Space Layout Randomization.

DNS Poisoning and Domain Hijacking

DNS poisoning is also known as DNS Spoofing. In DNS Poisoning attack the threat actor makes changes in the DNS server, and when the user visits any website, it directs the user to the wrong site (a malicious site) that they did not intend to visit (or to the site, they were not going).

Domain Name System (DNS) attacks include DNS Poisoning, Cybersquatting, Domain hijacking & Domain Snipping. An attacker may attempt to spoof by poisoning the DNS

server or cache to obtain credentials of internal users. Domain Hijacking involves stealing cloud service domain name. Similarly, through Phishing scams, users can be redirected to a fake website. DNS Hijacking is a type of attack in which the threat actor accesses the Domain registration and control the flow of traffic.

There is a slight difference between Hijacking and Poisoning. Through Spoofing the attacker poisons the cache of the DNS server whereas in Hijacking, the attacker hacks the DNS setting of the router or plant malware.

In case a DNS server receives a false entry, it updates its database. As we know, to increase performance, DNS servers maintain a cache in which this entry is updated to provide quick resolution of queries. This false entry causing poison in DNS translation continues until the cache expires. DNS poisoning is performed by attackers to direct the traffic towards the servers and computer owned or controlled by attackers.

How to prevent it?

- Don't visit every website you encounter.
- Make your password as strong as possible.
- Use anti-malware software.
- Being proactive can also save you from cyber-attack.

Zero-day Attacks

Many operating systems and applications have vulnerabilities. People are working hard to find those vulnerabilities before the hacker. In zero-day attack, the attacker finds the vulnerabilities that are not known to anyone and takes advantage of that before the security patches are made available. It means a zero-day attack exploits the vulnerabilities that are not known to anyone except the attacker.

Replay Attacks

When the information is transferred over the network the threat actors take advantage of it by replaying the information this is known as a replay attack. For replaying the information, the threat actors need raw network data (Network Packets). Malware is installed on the user's computer that captures the data and sends it to the threat actor for the purpose to use that information later. A replay attack is slightly similar to man in the middle attack, but in actual, it is not a MitM (Man in the Middle) attack.

Client Hijacking Attacks

- URL Hijacking
- Click Hijacking
- Browser Cookies and Session ID.
- Session Hijacking/Side-jacking.

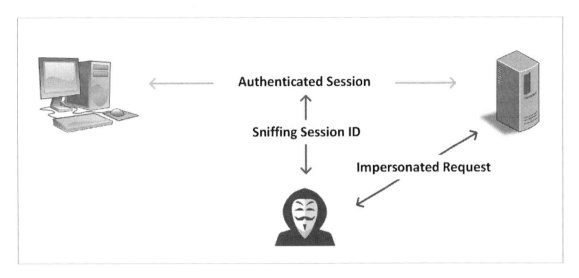

Figure 1-05: Session Hijacking

How to prevent it?

- Use session ID Monitor.
- Setup VPN connection (End to somewhere Encryption).
- End-to-End Encryption.

Spoofing

Spoofing is a very commonly used technique. In this type of attack, the device pretends to be the source that it is actually not. Such as pretending as a fake web server or DNS server. Spoofing can be implemented in various ways such as:

- Email Address Spoofing
- Caller ID Spoofing
- Man in the Middle Attack (ARP Spoofing)
- MAC (Media Access Control) Address Spoofing
- IP Address Spoofing

Wireless Attacks

Wireless Replay Attacks

In a wireless replay attack, the attacker spies the information being sent between the sender and the receiver and then gets the encryption key that is used later for replay attack for proving his identity or for authentication.

Wireless Jamming

It is the type of attack in which the attacker jams the radio frequency for communication. It is something like a denial of service, i.e., prevents wireless communication. The goal is to decrease Signal to Noise (SNR) ratio.

WPS Attacks

WPS is abbreviated as Wi-Fi Protected Setup. An example is the Pixie Dust-A WPS attack that occurred in 2014 (summer).

BlueJacking and BlueSnarfing

BlueJacking and BlueSnarfing are the two vulnerabilities associated with the Bluetooth.

- *BlueJacking* refers to the attack in which someone can send unsolicited messages over Bluetooth to the other devices and the person receiving it can't stop it.
- *BlueSnarfing* is the significant insecurity of Bluetooth, and through this type of attack, someone can access the Bluetooth enabled device and can easily transfer the data.

RFID and NFC Attacks

RFID (Radio Frequency Identification) attacks include multiple attacks like:

- Data Capture
- Spoof the Reader
- Denial of Service
- Decryption of Communication

NFC (Near field Communication) attack also includes various attacks that are as follows:

- Remote Capture
- Frequency Jamming
- Relay/Replay Attack
- Loss of RFC Devices

Cryptographic Attacks

Birthday

A type of cryptographic attack that takes its function and exploits through birthday problem in probability theory which states that in a class of 23 students, there is a 50 percent chance that 2 persons share the same birthday. Mathematically, the following equation can be used:

$$1.25k^{1/2}$$

k = the size of the set of possible values

Known plaintext/ciphertext

In this type of attack, the attacker has the encrypted information as well as some plain text. The plain text helps an attacker in breaking the cryptography, and this plaintext is known as "*crib.*" The remaining part of the plaintext is determined through this crib.

Rainbow Table

A table that contains every possible password and had done all the calculation is known as Rainbow Table. It may also be referred to as "*pre-built set of hashes.*" By performing a simple search, the password can be determined in few seconds by matching up the hashes, but it does not work with salted hash.

An example of offline attacks is comparing the password using a rainbow table. Every possible combination of character is computed for the hash to create a rainbow table. When a rainbow table contains all possible precomputed hashes, attacker captures the password hash of target and compares it with the rainbow table. The advantage of Rainbow table is all hashes are precomputed. Hence it takes few moments to compare and reveal the password. Limitation of a rainbow table is that it takes a long time to create a rainbow table by computing all hashes.

To generate rainbow tables, the utilities you can use to perform this task are **winrtgen**, GUI-based generator, rtgen, and command line tool. Supported hashing formats are the following:

- MD2
- MD4
- MD5
- SHA1
- SHA-256
- SHA-384
- SHA-512 and other hashing formats

Exercise

Open **Winrtgen** application, Click Add table button  to add new Rainbow table

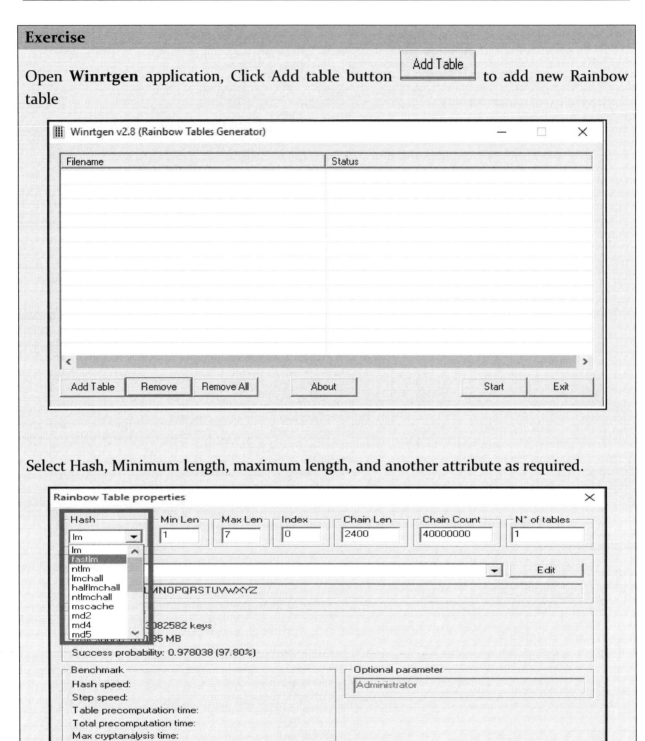

Select Hash, Minimum length, maximum length, and another attribute as required.

Select the Charset value; Available options are Alphabets, Alphanumeric, and other combination of characters as shown in the figure below.

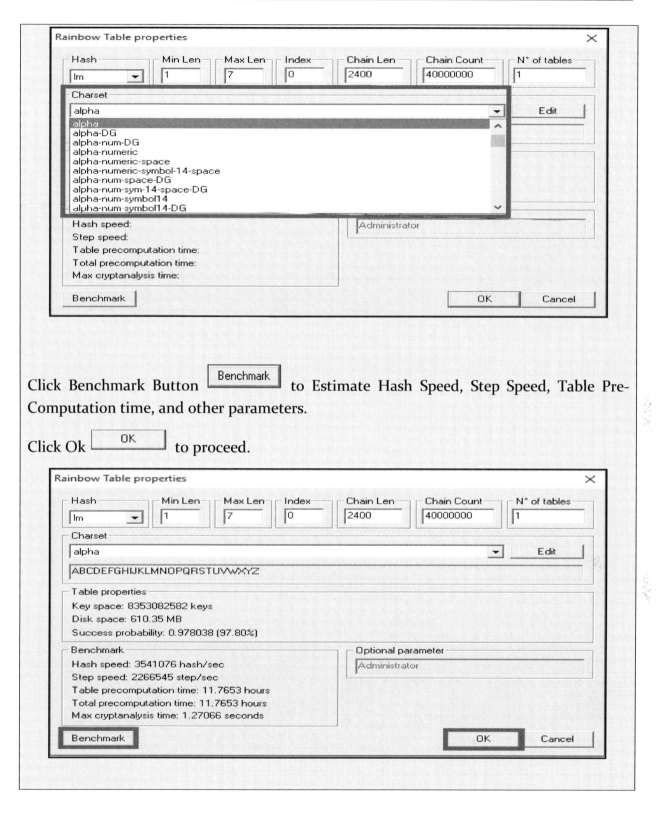

Click Benchmark Button [Benchmark] to Estimate Hash Speed, Step Speed, Table Pre-Computation time, and other parameters.

Click Ok [OK] to proceed.

Click Start to Compute.

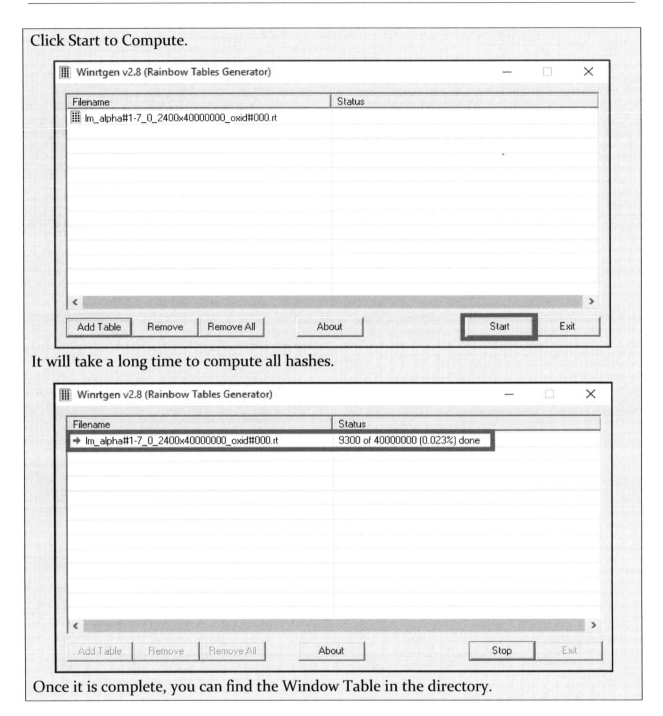

It will take a long time to compute all hashes.

Once it is complete, you can find the Window Table in the directory.

Dictionary

Dictionary attacks are used to reverse engineer the password. Generally, common words are used as passwords. Thus, if the attackers try those most common words first, they would be able to determine the password quickly. These common words can be found in the dictionary or on the internet.

Brute Force

In brute force attack, the attacker tries every possible combination of numbers, letters, and special characters in order to determine the password.

Online/Offline

Online brute force attack is difficult as well as a slow process. The system mostly detects when the wrong password is put again and again, and they disable the account. If the file containing the hash is accessed by the attackers, it will be easier for them to brute force offline.

Collision

Collision refers to the hash collision, which means two different plaintexts have the same hash value. This is a rare condition which is not supposed to be in a hash algorithm. Hashing process accepts infinite input length and produces a finite output. Consider a scenario where an attacker finds the hash collusion of among legitimate document and altered document. Now the attacker can fool the target easily being undetected.

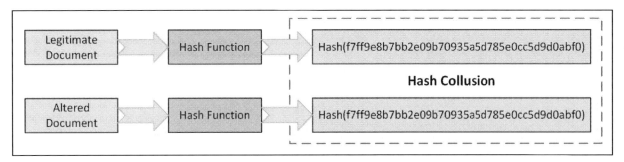

Figure 1-06: Hash Collision

Downgrade

Use of some weak cryptographic algorithm instead of a strong algorithm which may result in downgrade attack. Example: A downgrade attack was used in 1995 with web servers

Replay

When the information is transferred over the network, the threat actors take advantage of it by replaying the information is known as a replay attack. For replaying the information, the threat actors need raw network data (Network Packets). Malware is installed on the user's computer that captures the data and sends it to the threat actor for the purpose to use that information later. A replay attack is slightly similar to man in the middle attack, but in actual it is not MITM (Man in the Middle) attack.

Weak implementation

Another issue linked with backward compatibility is weak implementation. Whenever an older version is granted to proceed operation, there is a risk of weak implementations.

Introduction to Threat Actors

Threat actors are miscreants who use your personal information against you. These people are also known as malicious actors. There are various types of malicious actors that are as follows:

- Script Kiddie
- Hacktivist
- Organized Crime
- Nation states/ APT (Advance Persistence Threat)
- Insiders
- Competitors

Types of Threat Actors

Script Kiddie

Script kiddie usually an individual, not a group, is the type of malicious actor who finds vulnerabilities in the system by running pre-made script (not created by them) in order to exploit your data. They could be inside or outside of the network looking for easily exploitable vulnerabilities.

Hacktivist

Hacktivist (usually outside of the network) is a compound word for Hacker and Activist. They may have a political agenda, or maybe a political goal to bring down a website or get other hacks including DoS (Denial of Service), Releasing of personal documents, etc.

Organized Crime

A professional, well-organized state of crime. They usually work in a group; in which one is for hacking, other is for managing, one is for gathering data, and possibly a selling team also whose work is to sell the hacked data accordingly. Their main goal is to make money through an organised medium of action.

Nation-State

Hackers who work for government agencies against external governments or organizations, for national security purpose. They are usually assigned to attack large security sites like of an external military organization.

Insider

The threat actors within the network are referred to as insiders, and they are difficult to guard. They can easily pass through various security paths because they have primary knowledge of security as an insider, related to things like the IP addressing scheme or the location of the server and possibly have access to a number of things. For example, a disgruntled employee of an organization is a type of insider threat.

Competitor

Significant threat actors are the competitors in the organization. They have multiple intents for attacking; maybe they want to corrupt or steal the data or to bring someone's system down. Competitive Intelligence gathering is a method of collecting information, analyzing and gathering statistics regarding the competitors. Competitive Intelligence gathering process is non-interfering as it is the process of collection of information through the resources such as the internet, target organization's website, advertisements, press releases, Annual Reports, Product Catalogues, analyst reports and well as agent and distributors.

Vulnerability Assessment

Vulnerability analysis or assessment is a procedure to find out loopholes (security holes) in our network infrastructure that can be risky for it. This process helps in preventing your computer or network from attacks, by stopping/blocking threats from entering or spreading into the network. Vulnerability assessment mainly focuses on exposing as many security weaknesses as possible. To make your system or network attacks free and totally secure, vulnerability assessment is needed, and all the possibilities of security attacks must be fixed. Any defects exposed to security attacks or hacking, the tests will figure them out.

Vulnerability Assessment Process:

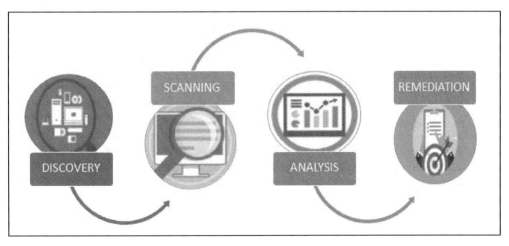

Figure 1-07: Vulnerability Assessment Process

The steps through which the assessment process is carried out are as follows:

- **Network Discovery** - It is the identification of assets (resources) in a network and collection of key information about an application and its infrastructure
- **Vulnerability Scanning** - Is a step for discovering security vulnerabilities and possible theft to each asset.
- **Result Analysis** - Refers to carry out a comprehensive report of the assessment of the company's security position and a list of vulnerabilities, which may include false or positive.
- **Remediation** - In this step the tester recommends proper remediation or mitigation to eliminate or reduce risk.

LAB 01-1: Installing and Using Vulnerability Assessment Tool

Main Objective: In this lab, you will learn how to install and use vulnerability assessment tool. There are many tools available for vulnerability scanning. The one I am going to install and use is "Nessus".

> Go to the browser and type 'Nessus Home'. Click on the Nessus home link that I have marked.

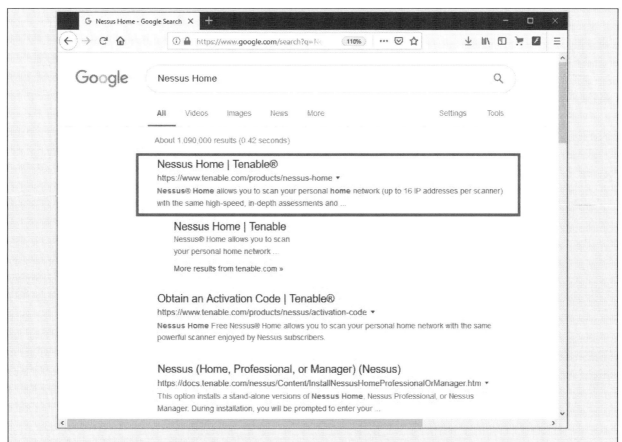

This is going to take you to the Nessus registration page. You need to register in order to get the activation code which you are going to need to activate Nessus.

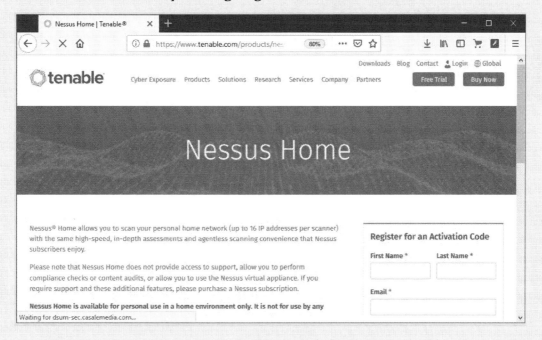

For registration, you need to put in your first name, last name, email address. Check the checkbox and click on register.

Register for an Activation Code

First Name *   Last Name *

Email *

☐ Check to receive updates from Tenable

Register

Now to download Nessus, click on the download link.

Thank You for Registering for Nessus Home!
Check Your Email for the Activation Code

Thank you for registering for Nessus® Home. An email containing your activation code has been sent to you at the email address you provided.

Please note that Nessus Home is available for non-commercial, home use only. If you will use Nessus at your place of business, you must purchase a Nessus subscription.

Download Nessus

To download Nessus, visit the Nessus Download page.

Download

Select the Operating system on which you are going to install Nessus. I am going to install it on Windows 8 machine (64 bit), therefore I am going to download the first link which is for the 64-bit version of Windows.

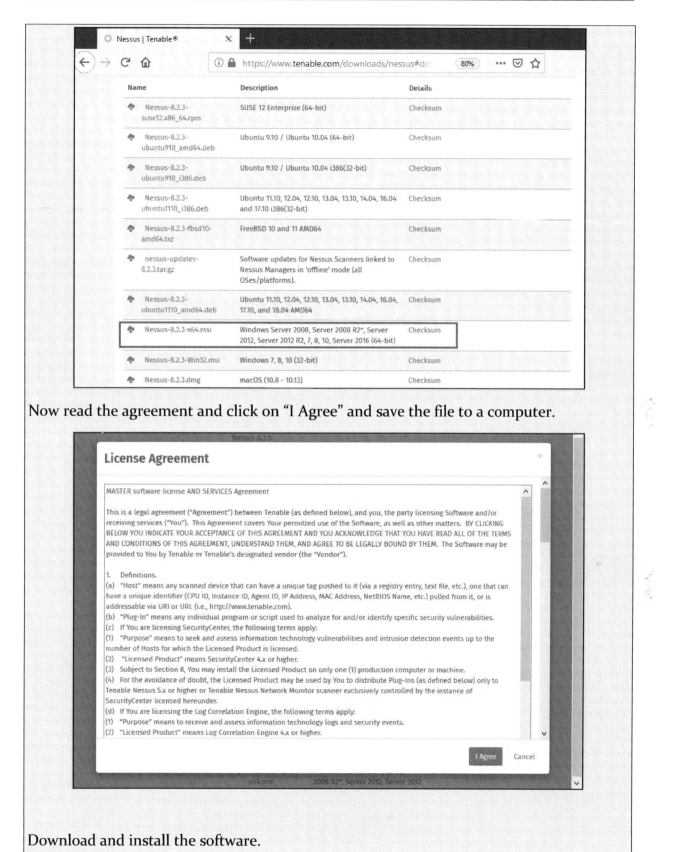

Now read the agreement and click on "I Agree" and save the file to a computer.

Download and install the software.

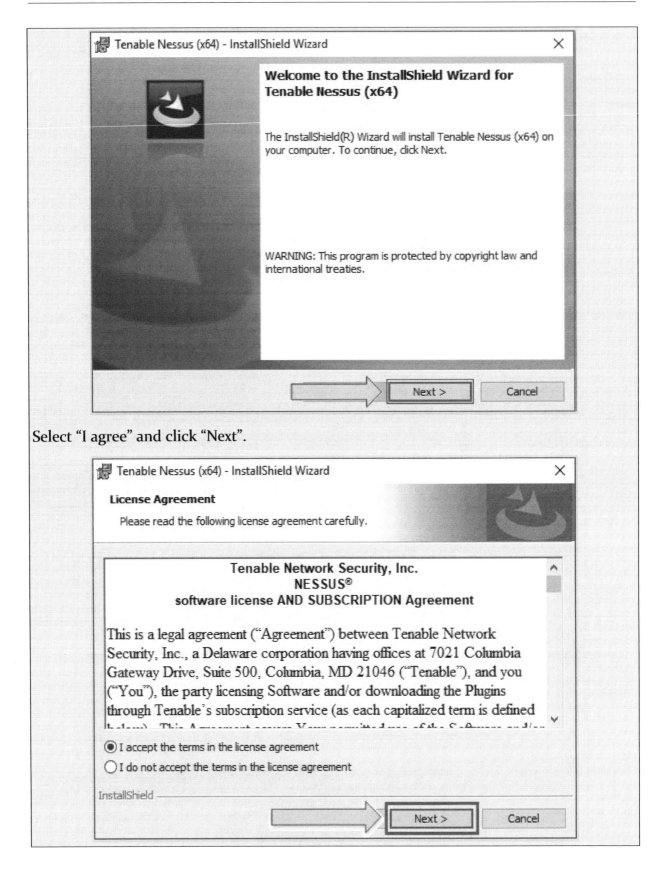

Select "I agree" and click "Next".

Now if you want to change the file destination, you can change it by clicking on the 'change' button or else just click click "Next".

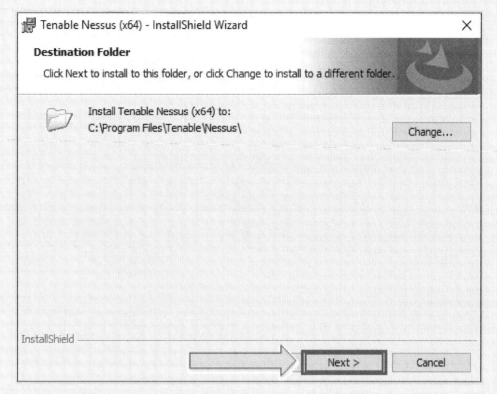

Now click on 'Install" button.

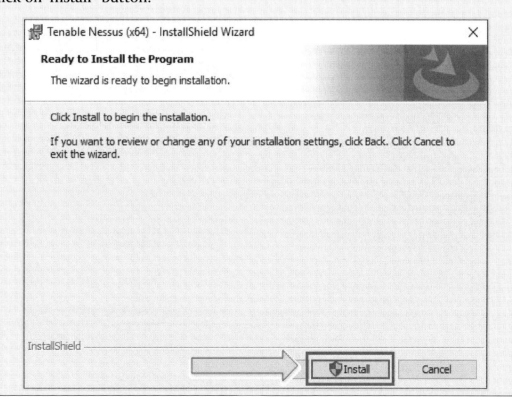

Once you click the 'install'. The installation process will start.

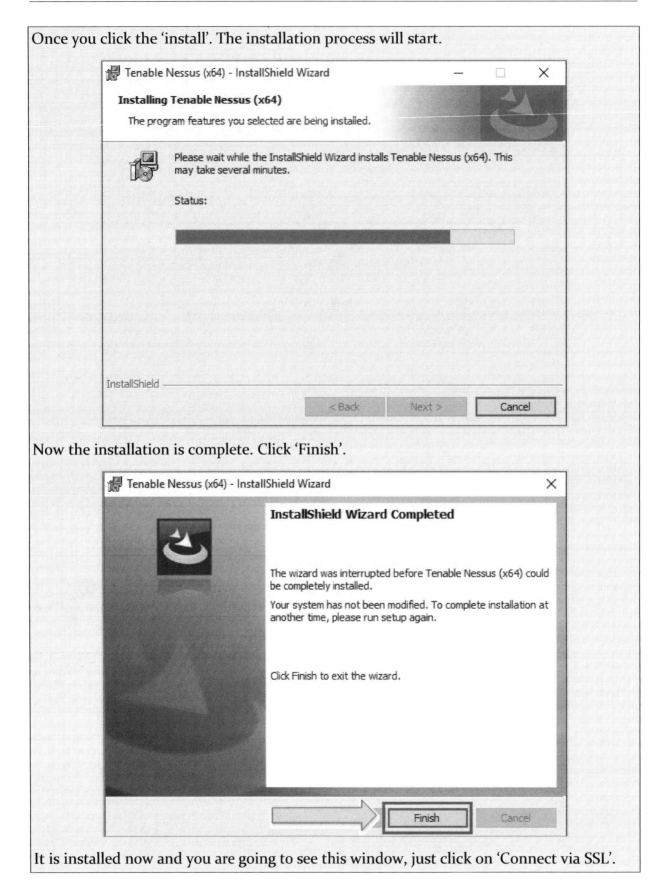

Now the installation is complete. Click 'Finish'.

It is installed now and you are going to see this window, just click on 'Connect via SSL'.

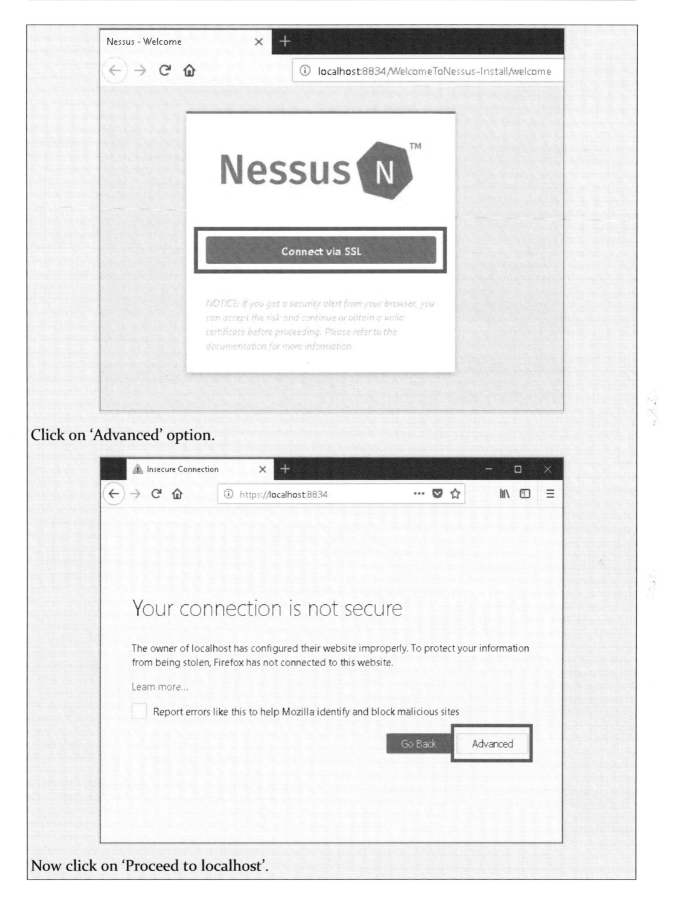

Click on 'Advanced' option.

Now click on 'Proceed to localhost'.

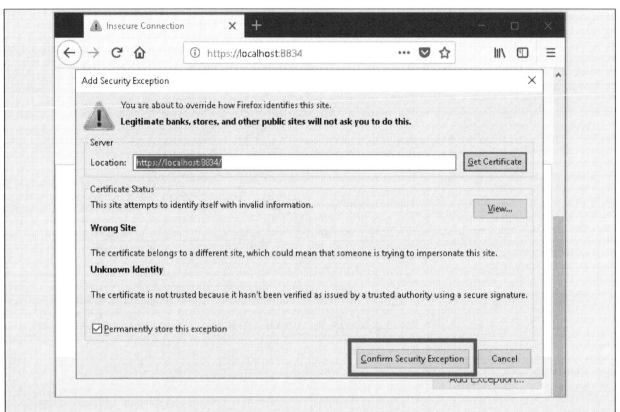

Now you have to create an account for Nessus server. here you are going to choose a login name and password and make sure you remember it because this is what you going to use to log in to Nessus from now on. After inserting username and password, click on 'Continue' button.

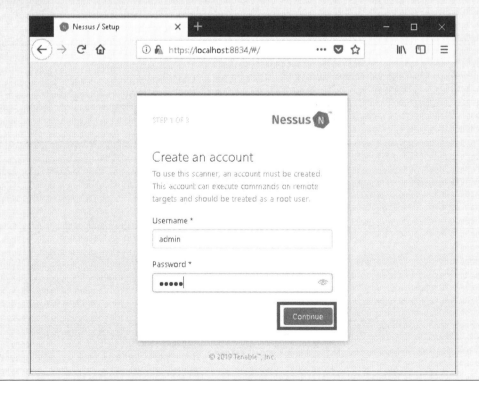

Now choose the scanner type that you want. I have selected the first one which is 'Home, professional or manager'.

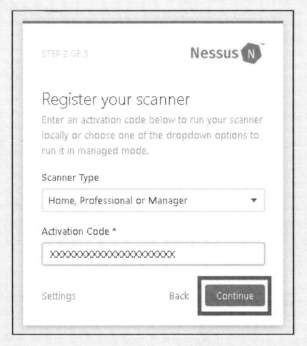

Now go to the email and copy the activation code that was forwarded to you and paste it here and click 'Continue'.

After that, you are going to see this 'Initializing' window. It basically fetching all the plugins for Nessus and this can take about 15 to 20 minutes.

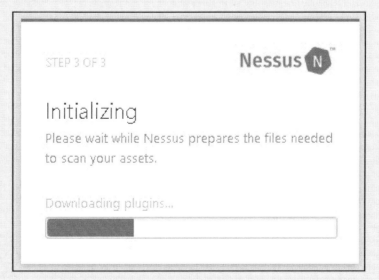

Once all the plugins are installed, this Window will appear and this is what Nessus looks like. Now the first thing you have to do is to create a policy. So click on 'Policies'

Now click on 'Create new policy'.

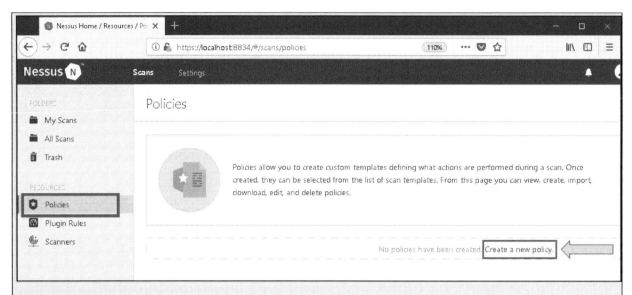

Here you have multiple scanner options available. What I am going to do is 'Basic Network Scan'. So for this click on Basic network scan option

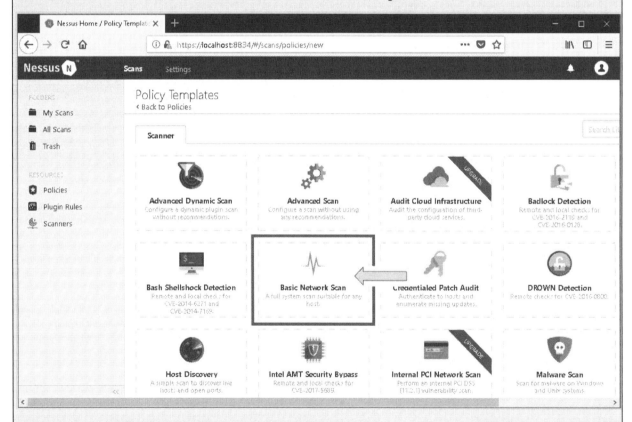

Now you are going to see this window. Here you have to name the policy. You can name it anything you want; I am going to name it 'Basic Scan'.

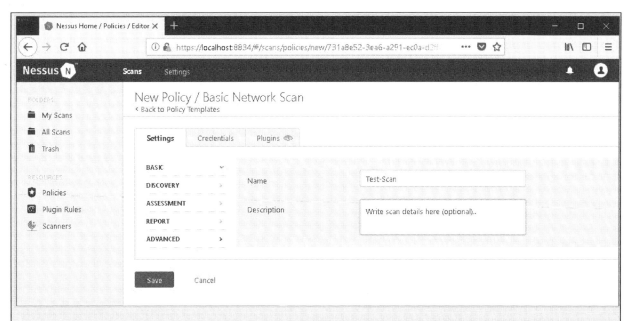

In basic setting, you have another setting option that is 'Permission' setting. In this you have two option, one is 'No Access' and other is 'Can Use'. I am going to leave it as default. Now click on 'Discovery' option.

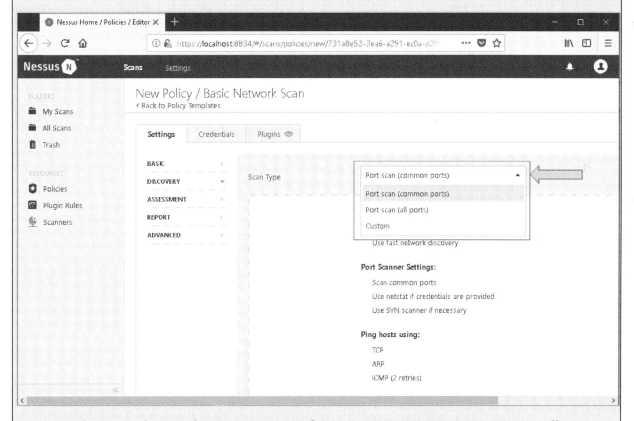

Here you have to choose the Scan Type. Either you want scan common ports, all ports or you want to customize it. After selecting your desired option, click on 'Assessment'.

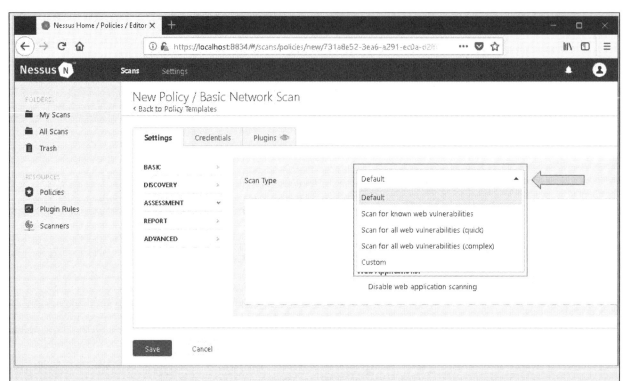

Here you are going to see 3 scanning option, choose whatever you want and then click on 'Report'.

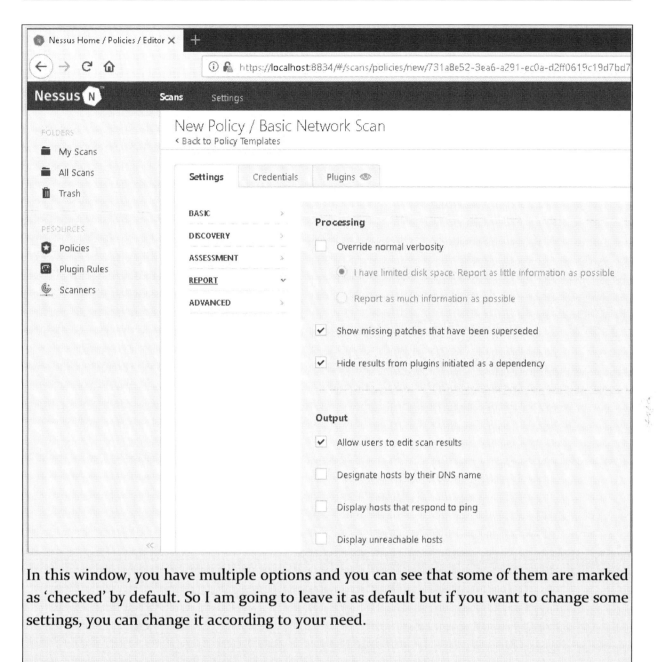

In this window, you have multiple options and you can see that some of them are marked as 'checked' by default. So I am going to leave it as default but if you want to change some settings, you can change it according to your need.

Here in the 'advanced' setting option, you have 3 options to choose from. Select any of them and click on 'Credentials' button.

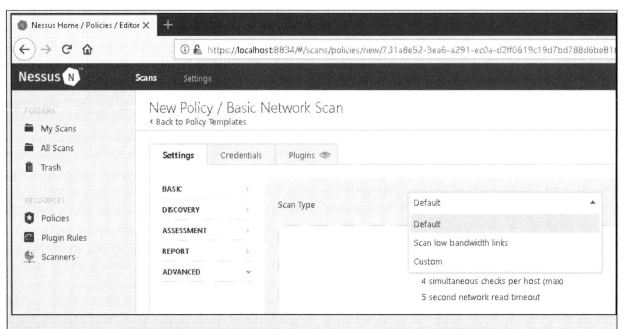

Here I am going to select 'Windows' as I have Windows OS but if you have Mac or Linux then you have to select SSH.

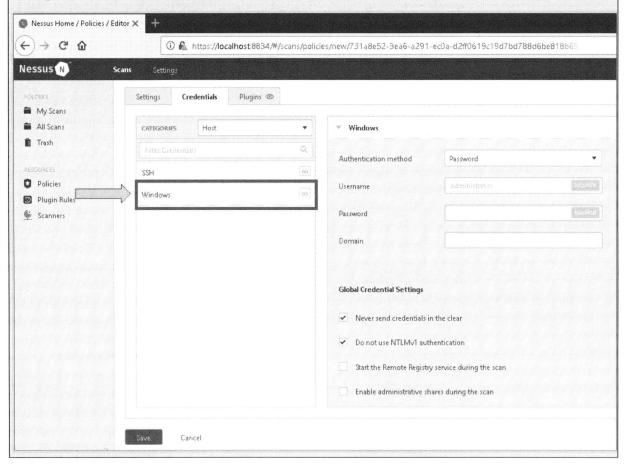

Go ahead and insert your credentials and authentication method. If you have a domain, you can insert that, in my case I don't so I am going to leave it blank. Check the below boxes and click on Save button at the bottom.

And that is it, the policy has been created. Now in order to scan, you have to click on 'Scan' button up on top.

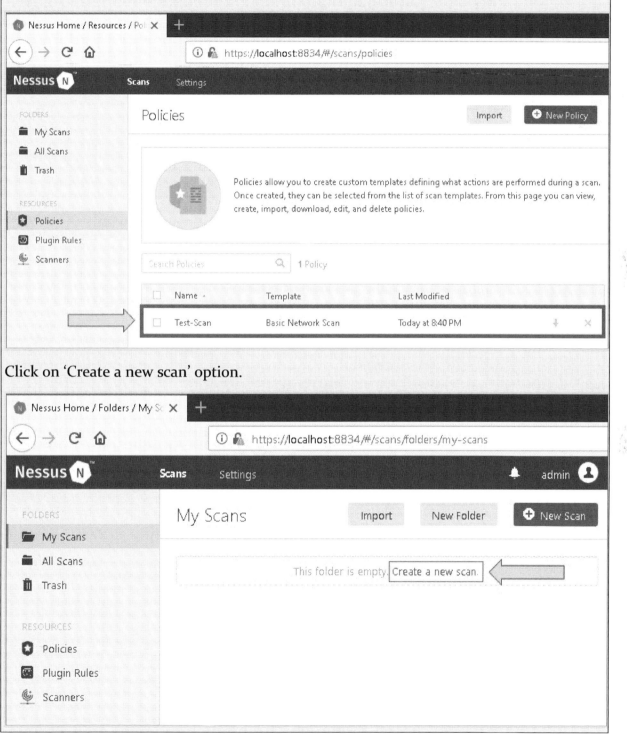

Click on 'Create a new scan' option.

Go to 'User Defined' option. Click on 'Basic Scan'.

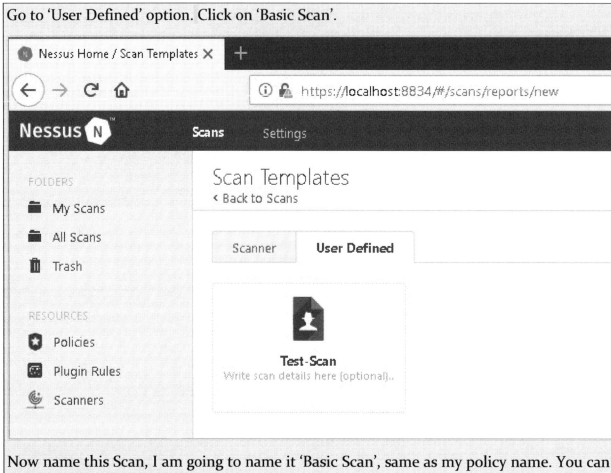

Now name this Scan, I am going to name it 'Basic Scan', same as my policy name. You can also add a description if you want.

Select the folder where you want to save a scan and at last insert the IP address of the target.

You can insert the target in different ways. Example: 192.168.1.1, 192.168.1.1/24, & test.com

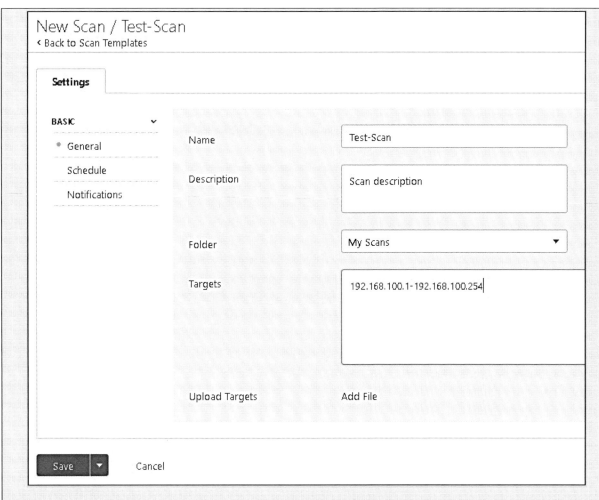

You can also schedule your scan. For this, click on 'Enabled', now select the frequency, start time and Time zone.

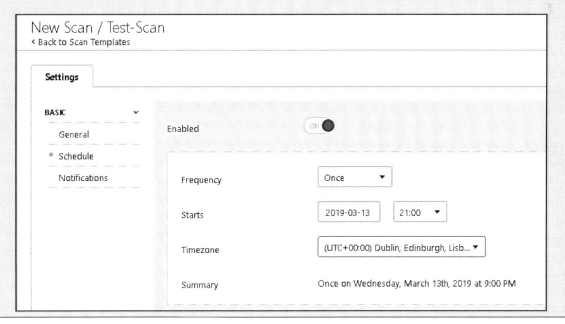

And if you want to get a notification, you can add your email address. After doing all the settings click on 'Save' button.

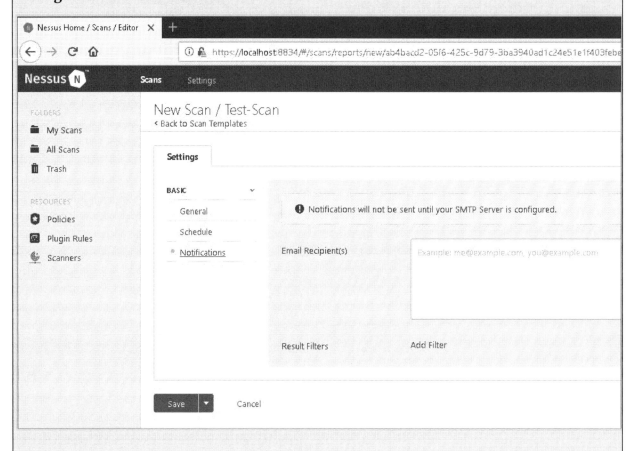

Here you can see that the scanning process is started. Once the scanning process is completed. You can see the result by clicking on the section that I have marked.

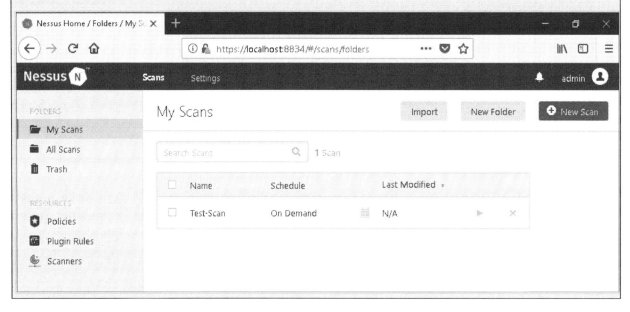

Here is the scan result. The result is shown in multiple colors. The red represents the Critical Vulnerability, the Orange one is for High, Yellow is for Medium, Green is for Low and Blue one is for Info.

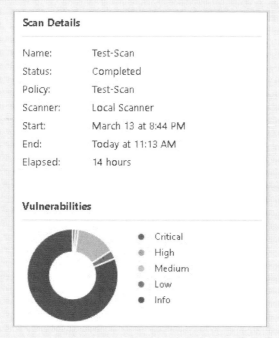

Now click on the 'Vulnerability' next to 'Host' option. And here you are going to see the vulnerabilities that have been found. Now click any of that.

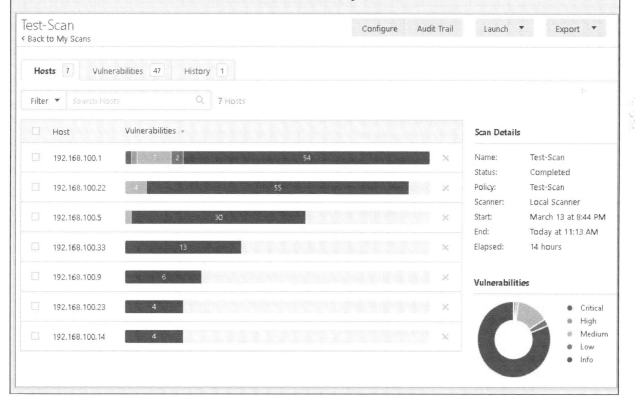

Now you can see the description of a particular vulnerability as well as a solution for it.

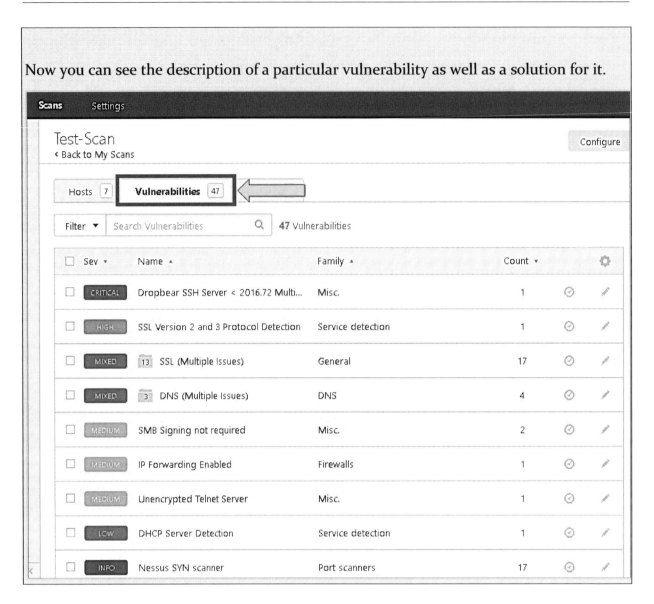

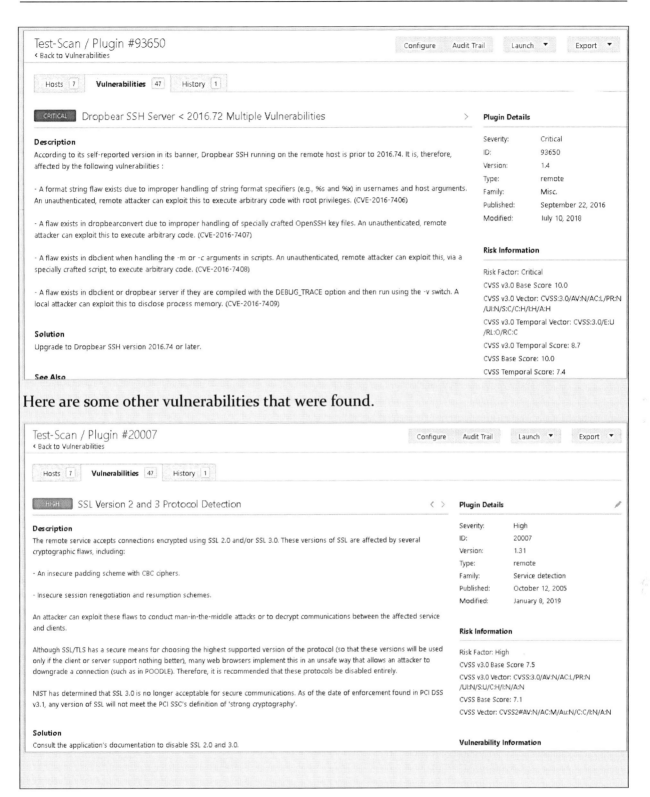

Here are some other vulnerabilities that were found.

LAB 01-2: Malware Scanning using Nessus Vulnerability Scanning tool

Now I am going to do a Malware Scan. Here, I am going to do all the settings that are required for creating a policy. First, I have to name the policy. You can name it whatever you want.

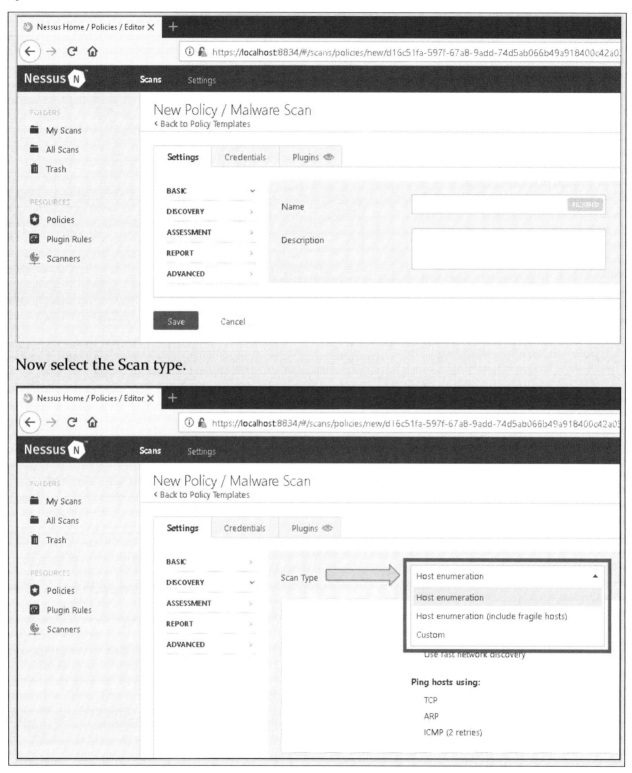

Now select the Scan type.

Enable the 'Scan for Malware' option and leave everything as default.

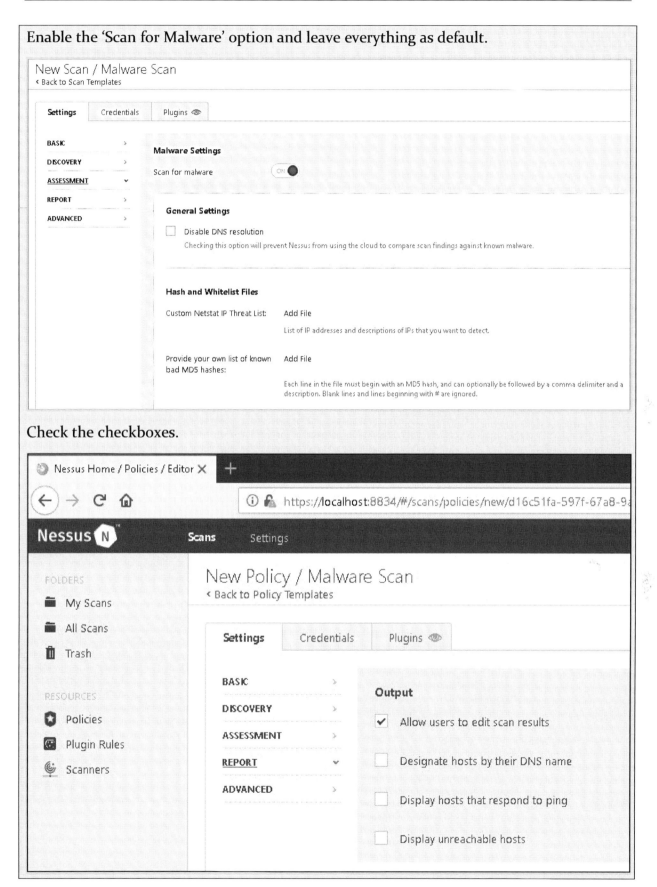

Check the checkboxes.

Select any option you want.

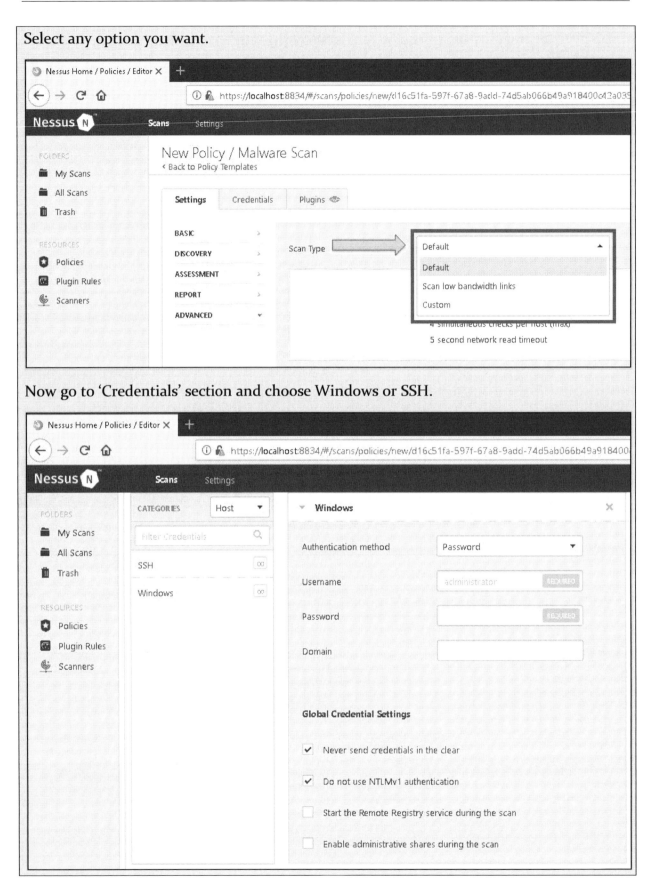

Now go to 'Credentials' section and choose Windows or SSH.

Fill out the credential section and click on the 'Save' button.

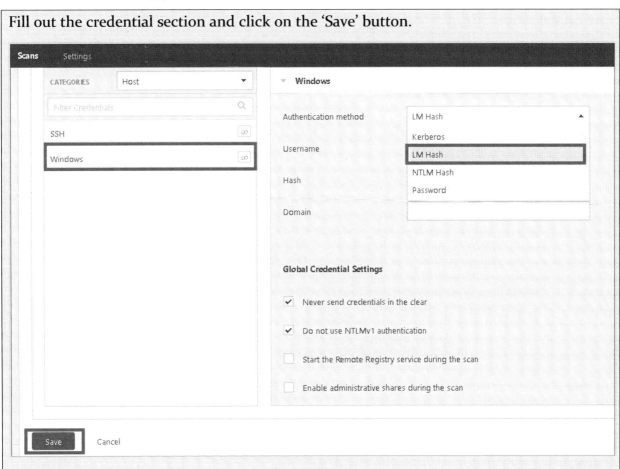

Now the policy has been created. Click on the scan button at the top then click on the 'New scan'.

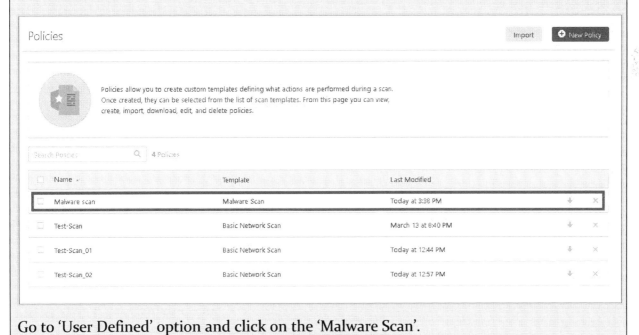

Go to 'User Defined' option and click on the 'Malware Scan'.

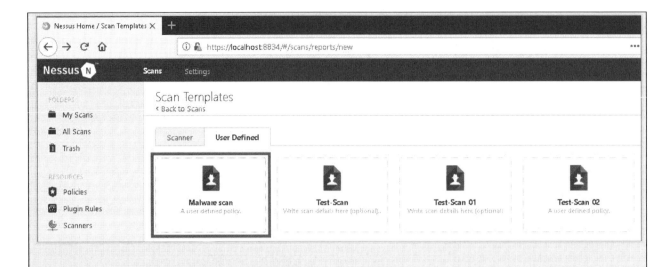

Here you have to name the scan. Choose a folder to save it and insert the target in the target section and click on the 'Save' button.

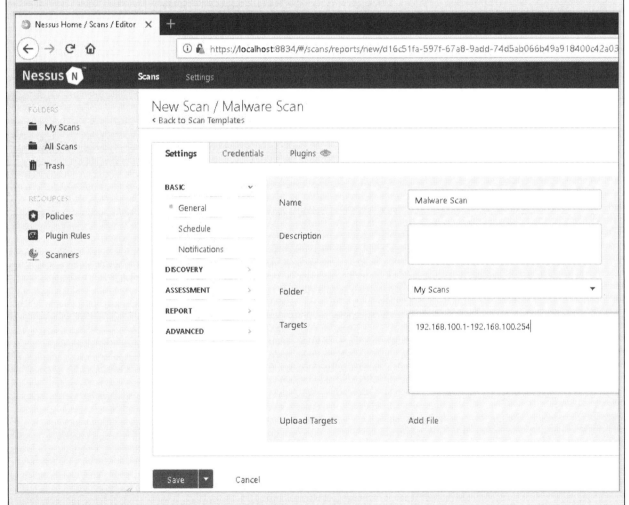

Here you can see that the scan has been created. Now when you click on the launch button, it will start to run. Launch button looks like this

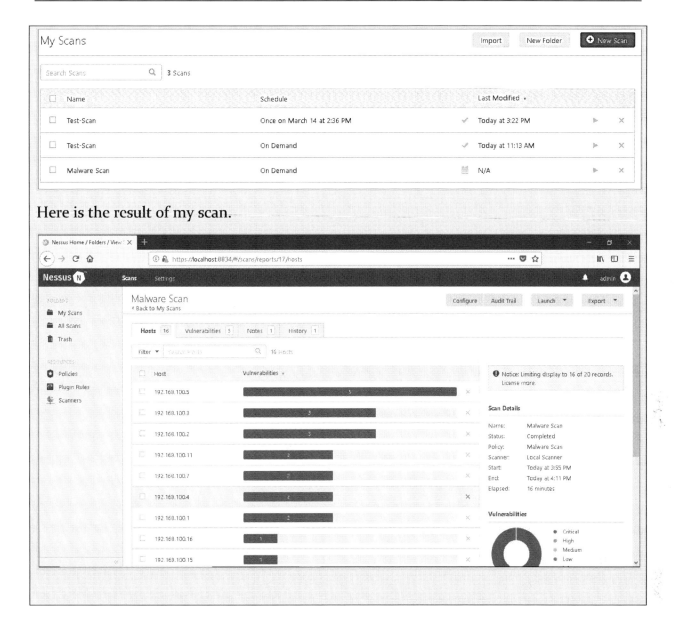

Here is the result of my scan.

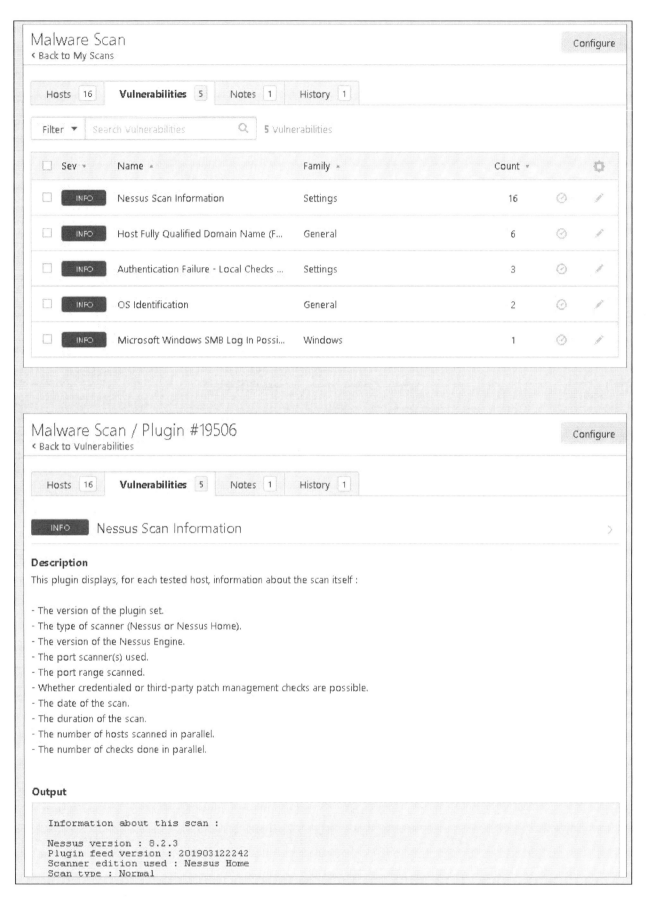

Threat Actor Attributes

Internal/External

One considerable superiority of internal threat actors over external threat actors is that they have an approach to the system which is limited as compared to the user but it gives them strength to continue their attack. On the other hand, external threat actor has to do an extra step, that is, to first establish access to the system that is targeted.

Level of Sophistication

The stronger the skill level, the better a threat actor will lead and plan the attacks. One prominent thing that is linked to the level of sophistication is that strong skills result in the adoption of minimum methods.

Resources/Funding

A criminal organization has large team and budgets to continue operation for the long time period. Advanced Persistence Threats require considerable resources to involve in this type of actions, so long-term resources are desired that large organizations or states can manage.

Intent/Motivation

Behind any attack, the motivation or intention can be simple or can be multi fold. For instance, the threat actor just wants to carry out a technique work or want to steal something valuable.

Use of Open Source Intelligence

Open source intelligence is also called open source threat intelligence. OPSIT refers to the intelligence data that is gathered from open or public sources. Used primarily in law enforcement, national security and for business intelligence functions.

One of the biggest decision is where one's resources can be applied to the compound environment of cybersecurity defenses. Threat intelligence refers to the gathering of information from multiple sources in order to allow a system to concentrate well on their defenses against possible threat actors.

Penetration Testing

Penetration testing often-called pen test can have a great deal of overlap with a vulnerability assessment. In fact, a penetration tester often performs as a vulnerability assessment to some extent. A penetration test has less to do with uncovering vulnerabilities and is rather more focused on how an attacker is able to breach defenses.

It identifies if one can access the system without authorization. It tries to carry out a vulnerability in the system and thus regulate unauthorized access situation.

The difference is, the penetration tester will then take things further and try to exploit a site within the bounds of an agreed-upon test. The vulnerability assessment will often just check to see where the problems exist but a good penetration test would not only show where they exist but also how to actually attack them.

Reconnaissance

The first step that is performed in penetration test is reconnaissance. The purpose of it is to have a knowledge of the system and the components of it that the attackers may choose to attack. Reconnaissance is of two types: Active and Passive.

Active reconnaissance

In an active reconnaissance testing, the use of tools can be viewed by the defenders (defenders get alert) means the tools actually collaborate with the system & network. Active reconnaissance provides a lot of effective information.

Passive reconnaissance

In a passive reconnaissance, when tools are used, the information is not provided to the system or network that is under investigation.

Pivot

A method that enables attacker or penetration tester to move or flow across a network is called Pivot. The first step in pivoting is obtaining access to a machine and moving tools to that machine and controlling them remotely. The penetration tester then examines the system or network using the IP address of the machine that is accessed remotely.

Initial Exploitation

The initial exploitation is destined to indicate only the presence of vulnerability and that the vulnerability is exploitable, but it does not indicate whether the target of the pen test is attainable or not.

Persistence

Persistence is a key element of attack which is also referred to as Advanced Persistence Threat that places two factors at the lead edge of all the actions, i.e., persistence and invisibility from defenders. Persistence can be accomplished through multiple methods, from agents that beacon back out, to malicious accounts, to vulnerabilities introduced to enable reinfection.

Escalation of Privilege

Escalation of privilege is transferring from a low-level account into an account that permits activity of root level. An ordinary account is used by the attacker for the exploitation of vulnerability on the processes that are operating from the root and this permits the attackers to assume the privileges of the process that is exploited.

Types of Penetration Tests

There are three types of penetration tests:

1. Black box penetration test
2. Grey box penetration test
3. White box penetration test

Let's discuss these in detail.

Black box

This is a common type most people probably visualize when they think of hacking. In a black box penetration test, the tester does not know about the internal system, he/she only is given a single URL and no further information.

Gray box

Gray box, is a type of penetration testing in which the pen tester has very limited prior knowledge of the system or any information of targets such as IP addresses, operating system or network information is very limited. Gray box is designed to demonstrate an emulated situation as an insider might have this information and to counter an attack as the pen tester has basic, limited information regarding the target.

White box

Refers to the test where an attacker is provided with the whole range of information of the system, in other words, keys to the kingdom. The tester can have any information they want including; the ability to log into any system with any level of access can get the diagram of the infrastructure and can have the source code for review. Everything about the system is wide open for the tester's review.

Pen Testing Process

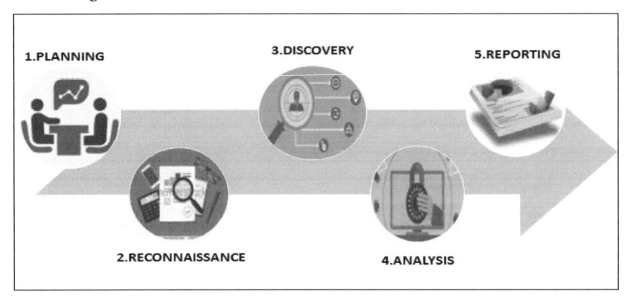

Figure 1-08: Penetration Testing Process

- **Planning** - In this step the penetration test goals and objectives are decided by the client and the tester.
- **Reconnaissance** - The tester obtains complete information of the system from the client. Analyzes available information and requests for more if required.
- **Discovery** - A tester discovers; Network (servers and other devices), Host (determine open ports on these devices) and Services (interrogate ports to determine actual services running on them). In this step, tester uses tools to scan target assets to find vulnerabilities.
- **Analysis** - It refers to the analysis of information and vulnerabilities identified which possess the actual risks and eliminate the weaknesses in the system or recommend fixing them.
- **Reporting**-In this step a complete report containing the summary of the penetration test, that is, the detail of all vulnerabilities discovered, information about cleaning the system and suggestion for future security is generated.

Difference between Vulnerability Assessment and Penetration Testing

Both are used to assess weaknesses in a company's physical and IT system. Most companies frequently test their own security, and in some companies, it is ongoing every minute of every day, and all changes are immediately run through a vulnerability scanner and others may just check periodically.

Vulnerability assessment discovers weaknesses and tries to resolve them whereas pen test also assesses if anyone can break into the system and if yes, then what damage can he/she do.

Penetration test also determines whether an identified vulnerability is authentic or not. If tester manages to exploit that, it is considered authentic.

Here are some common differences:

PENETRATION TEST	VULNERABILITY ASSESSMENT
Focuses on depth over breadth approach- when the network security defenses are strong but want to check if they can withstand an attack from the advanced attacker.	Focuses on breadth over depth approach- when the organizations are not security mature and want to know all possible security weak points.
Combination of automated and manual techniques.	Usually automated.
Performed by only high maturity level clients	Does not require high-level expertise.

Table 1-01: Pen Test and Vulnerability Assessment Differences

Why Is Pen Testing and Vulnerability Assessment Necessary?

The reason that VAPT (Vulnerability assessment and Penetration testing) is needed because it protects us from harm, secures us from intrusion, keeps our confidential data confidential and keeps our information away from prying eyes. Every corporate manager or network administrator needs to know their weak points, so they can address them. We all know that networks are vulnerable, but we do not all know where and how, that is where a vulnerable assessment comes in.

It is a comprehensive check of physical weaknesses in computers and networks. It identifies potential risks and threats at any exposure and develops strategies for dealing with them.

"Prevention is better than the cure."

Another reason for VAPT is Hacks prevention. We are very much aware of hacks such as:

- Loss of sensitive data
- Account numbers
- Email addresses
- Personal information

These things happen every day in networking. This is why we need to look at our network from the outside and see as an attacker would see it. Learn its strength, its weaknesses and then plug the gaps. Your infrastructure may be secure, your servers lock down the firewall on strong policies but what about attached devices including printers, scanners, fax machines, default configuration. They are adorned to your network vulnerability often neglected, thus a vulnerability assessment and penetration testing would highlight it in seconds. Any network that has users, is not as secure as we would expect. Protecting our network should be our priority. Therefore, to summarize, the reasons to perform VAPT are:

- To protect the network from attack
- Learn its strength and weaknesses
- Safeguard information from theft
- To comply with data security standards
- To add reliability and value to services

Vulnerability Scanning Concepts

Passively test security control

A side effect of using an automated vulnerability scanner is *security control's passive testing*. In passive testing, the *system* is the target of a scanner, not the controls. Effective security control resists the scanner in identifying the vulnerabilities

Identify Vulnerability

Vulnerability scanner goes through a list that is well-defined of known vulnerabilities. It provides as much information as it can, but the scanner does not perform an exploit (it is performed in penetration test).

Identify lack of security control

The result of vulnerability scan provides information about making system secure. It may provide information about lack of security like *no firewall is running, signatures of anti-virus are outdated*, etc.

Identify common misconfiguration

The vulnerability scanner also helps you to identify common misconfigurations like open shares or guest access into the parts of Operating System.

Intrusive vs. Non-intrusive

A method of scanning in which information that we see on the network collected, is called Non-Intrusive Scanning. It is like a simple packet capturing process in which the conversation is determined by looking through the packets. This is a type of scanning in

which you will try out the vulnerability to see if it works, without taking any advantage of the vulnerability.

Credential vs. Non-credentials

Credential scanning is something in which the scanner is provided with the credential to get into the system and then find ways to run around the existing security. Another type of scanning is Non-credential scanning in which the scanner does not have any credential that could be used for authentication and try to get into the system.

False Positive

False positive can also be called as wrong alert. It is something that is reported falsely as a vulnerability which means the scanner alerts you that there is an issue but in reality, there is no issue.

Impact associated with Types of Vulnerabilities

Race Condition

Race condition refers to a coding problem. When multiple functions are performed by multiple users at the same time, and the coding is not done properly because of it, then it results in an error called race condition. The impact associated with this type of vulnerability is generally the 'System Failure.'

Vulnerability due to:

End of Life System: When the system no longer operates or works as expected, it is called an 'End of life system'. There are many reasons behind the end of life system, like lack of vendor support or incompatibility with the other features of systems. The impact of this vulnerability is that the system becomes easy to target for the attacker as the vendor no longer helps it with patches and updates.

Embedded System: Embedded system is a system that uses embedded operating system, and the user does not have any direct access to that operating system, and it is simply accessed through the user interface. One of the impacts associated with this embedded system is that if it is not updated or patched, it can develop hidden vulnerabilities into the system.

Lack of Vendor Support: When the devices, components or software are no longer under the vendor's support, the condition is known as End of life system. It typically increases the risk factor and makes the system more vulnerable.

Improper Input Handling

The main cause of injection attack, memory overflow, or structure error is Improper Input Handling. While handling input, trust nobody and handle all the input properly because allowing inputs that are invalid, can be devastating. Impact of improper input handling is the increase of attacker's privilege level.

Improper Error Handling

The improper handling of errors can drive to a variety of disclosures like SQL errors, can reveal data elements or structures. The impact of it is that the attackers can utilize the information that is collected from the errors to facilitate their attack.

Weak Configuration

Weak configuration is the type of vulnerability that resists the system from achieving all the required security objectives. The type of vulnerability opens the gate for attackers and advances their privilege level.

Default Configuration

Default configuration needs to be secured from the start because no security against default configuration can make the system vulnerable. Just like weak configuration, this type of vulnerability also opens the gate for attackers and advances their privilege level.

Resource Exhaustion

When the system does not have all the necessary resources required for the function to work, is called Resource exhaustion. The impact related to this type of vulnerability is a system failure.

Untrained Users

Untrained users are those who do not have any training related to the capability of the system, and they do not know how to properly operate a system. The impact of this vulnerability is the addition of risk to a system.

Improperly Configured Accounts

The improperly configured account can cause improper allowance and access. An account that is not configured correctly makes it easy for the attacker to access the account and steal valuable information.

Vulnerable Business Processes

If the organization does not have necessary check and balance for handling business processes, then it could benefit the attackers and can result in failure of a business process. Like if the invoice of payment is processed by the organization without any verification, then it is clearly a failure of a business process.

Weak Cipher Suites and Implementations

Weak cipher suites are those that were once regarded as secure, but they are no longer considered secure. The impact of this type of vulnerability is the lack of security (the security that was granted no longer exists).

Buffer Vulnerability

Buffer vulnerability which is also referred as a memory vulnerability is divided into following types:

- Memory Leak.
- Memory Overflow.
- Pointer Dereference.
- DLL Injection.

Memory Leak

When memory is assigned during program execution and is never unassigned after being used. Eventually uses all memory that is available and as a result, crashes the system or application.

Overflow

Also known as a buffer overrun. Reasons behind buffer overflows are:

- An excessive amount of data in the buffer.
- Coding errors

The impact associated with buffer overflow is that it creates an entry point for the threat actors and also cause the system to crash or abort the program.

DLL Injection

DLL (Dynamic Link Library) injection is the adding of the library to a program containing the specific vulnerability. DLL injection also creates an entry point for the threat actors.

Pointer Dereference

Dereferencing a pointer is the process of querying the value stored in the memory located by the pointer. The program can potentially dereference a null pointer, thereby raising a Null Pointer Exception. Null pointer errors are usually the result of one or more programmer assumptions being violated. The attacker might be able to use the resulting exception to bypass security logic or to cause the application to reveal debugging information that will be valuable in planning subsequent attacks.

System Sprawl/Undocumented Assets

System sprawl takes place when the system is improved constantly by adding functionality but not periodically updated and these added elements become undocumented assets. Impact of these types of vulnerabilities is that they become unknown.

Design Weaknesses

Any weakness in architecture or design, adds vulnerability and increase the risk factor and makes it easy for the threat actor to approach the sensitive data.

The zero-day attack is the type of vulnerability that is unknown (that is not yet addressed) and since it is unknown, therefore its effect or risk is also unknown. However, the compensating control usage can mitigate the risk.

Improper Certificate and Key Management

The cryptographic keys are transferred and managed through the certificates. Therefore, the improper management of certificate can cause cryptographic failure and key issues, and the improper management of key can cause failure to secure the data.

Practice Question

1. A harmful program which disrupts operation, gathers sensitive information, or gains unauthorized access to computer systems are commonly referred to as?

2. A self-replicating computer program containing malicious segment is called:

3. Which of the terms listed below refers to an example of a crypto-malware?

   A. Virus

   B. Ransomware

   C. Worm

   D. Adware

4. Malware that restricts the access by encrypting files or locking the entire computer system down until the user performs requested action is known as?

5. A standalone malicious computer program that typically propagates itself over a computer network to adversely affect system resources and network bandwidth is called?

6. A type of software that performs unwanted and harmful actions in disguise of a legitimate and useful program is known as a Trojan horse. This type of malware may act like a legitimate program and have all the expected functionalities, but apart from that it will also contain a portion of malicious code that the user is unaware of? (True/False)

7. A collection of software tools used by a hacker to mask intrusion and obtain administrator-level access to a computer or computer network is known as?

8. Which of the following terms is an example of spyware?

   A. Keylogger

   B. Vulnerability Scanner

   C. Worm

9. What is adware?

10. Malicious software collecting information about users without their knowledge/consent is known as?

11. A malware-infected network host under the remote control of a hacker is commonly referred to as?

12. Which of the terms listed below applies to a collection of intermediary compromised systems that are used as a platform for a DDoS attack?

Chapter 02: Technologies and Tools

An Overview of Security Components

Firewall

Firewall is used to control traffic flow, i.e., usually controlling malicious incoming traffic from outside the network, or we can say inappropriate or undesired traffic and content. Firewall lets you filter all unwanted traffic, in order to protect your system from threats.

Firewalls are usually classified into two types:

Host-based Firewalls: Host-based firewalls are usually software-based firewalls installed on the endpoint host to protect it. It is installed on each server to filter incoming and outgoing network traffic.

Network-based Firewalls: A Network-based firewall is a network security device that monitors and filters the incoming and outgoing traffic, either allow or block the filtered traffic based on a defined set of security rules.

There are various types of the firewall by their functions and features:

- Stateless Firewall
- State-full Firewall
- Application-Aware Security Device

Stateless Firewall

Initially the firewalls analysed data packets just to see if they match the particular sets of rules, and then decides how to forward or drop the packets accordingly. This type of packet filtering is referred to as stateless filtering. This type of filtering does not care either a packet is part of an existing data flow or not. Each packet is analysed individually based solely on the values of certain parameters in the packet header, this is somehow similar to ACLs packet filtering.

Stateless firewall monitors network traffic and allow, restrict or block packets based on static values like source and destination addresses. They are not aware of data flows and traffic patterns.

A stateless firewall filter, sometimes also known as an access control list (ACL), because it does not state-fully analyse traffic and they are not aware of communication path. The basic purpose of a stateless firewall filter is to use of packet filtering to enhance security. Packet filtering lets you to take the decision and actions based upon the policies you applied. Stateless firewalls are faster and can perform better under heavier traffic loads.

Stateless firewall works like a packet filter. It does not keep the track of the currently active session. It looks at the traffic going by, and then compare it to a list of access control and then either allows or restricts traffic to flow.

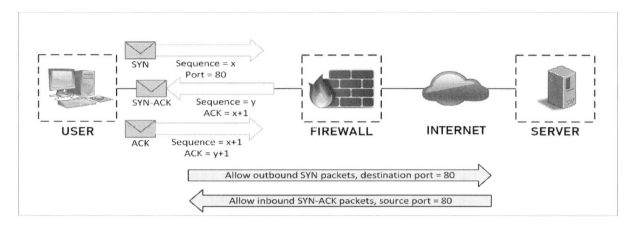

Figure 2-01: Stateless Firewall

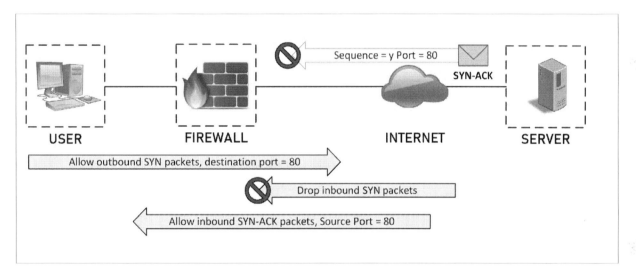

Figure 2-02: Stateless firewall-traffic blocking

State-full Firewall

Stateful firewalls analyse the state of connections in data flows during packet filtering. They analyse either the packet belongs to an existing flow of data or not. Stateful firewalls can see traffic streams from one end to another. They know about the communication paths and they can apply different IP Security (IPsec) functions such as encryption and tunnelling. Stateful firewalls lets you know about different TCP connections or port states either open, open sent, synchronized, synchronization acknowledge or established. Stateful firewalls are better at identifying unauthorized access from somewhere.

<u>Operation</u>

Stateful firewall is able to maintain the state of every connection either incoming or outgoing, through the firewall and thus replaced long lines of configuration. When the traffic wants to go out through a firewall, the packet will be first matched against a firewall rules list to check either the packet allowed or not. If this packet type is allowed to go out through the firewall, then the process of stateful filtering will begin.

Usually, stateful firewall uses the traffic that is using the Transport control protocol (TCP). TCP is stateful to begin with because TCP maintains a track of its connections by using source and destination address, port number and IP flags. Three-way handshake will begin a connection (SYN, SYN-ACK, ACK) and a two-way exchange (FIN, ACK) will sum up the connection. This process makes keeping track of the connection's state easier.

State-full is a bit intelligent firewall. It keeps track of the flow of traffic and remembers the 'state' of the session. It only allows the valid traffic to flow.

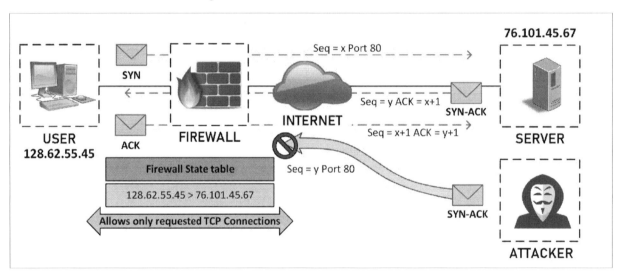

Figure 2-03: Stateful Firewall

<u>Difference between Stateless and Stateful firewall</u>

Stateless Firewall	Stateful Firewall
No session	Session
No login	Login
No basket	Basket
Static Content	Dynamic Content

Table 2-01: Difference between Stateless and Stateful Firewall

Application-Aware Security Device

As the name implies, it filters the traffic based on the application, which is a modern firewall technique. It is also named as Application Layer Gateway, State-full Multilayer Inspection, and Deep Packet Inspection.

Firewall Rules

Access Control List (ACL): A series of rules through which the firewall determines whether to allow or restrict the traffic flow. It can also be called the group of variables (tuples) or security policies.

Logical Path: Matches the traffic with the policies in the checklist from the top to bottom in series. Alternatively, in short, examines the rules in the list.

Specific or General: Firewall rule can be very specific or can be very general.

Implicit Deny: Once every rule in the list is examined, and the firewall has gone through the entire list, but if any of the rules does not match the traffic, it is dropped by the firewall, this is known as implicit deny.

Risks	Protection by firewall
Access by untrusted entities	Firewalls try to categorize the network into different portions. One portion is considered as a trusted portion of internal LAN. Public internet and interfaces connected to are considered as an untrusted portion. Similarly, servers accessed by untrusted entities are placed in a special segment known as a demilitarized zone (DMZ). By allowing only specific access to these servers, like port 90 of the web server, firewall hide the functionality of network device which makes it difficult for an attacker to understand the physical topology of the network.
Deep Packet Inspection and protocols exploitation	One of the interesting features of the dedicated firewall is its ability to inspect the traffic more than just IP and port level. By using digital certificates, Next Generation Firewalls available today can inspect traffic up to layer 7. A firewall can also limit the number of established as well as half-open TCP/UDP connections to mitigate DDoS attacks.
Access Control	By implementing local AAA or by using ACS/ISE servers, the firewall can permit traffic based on AAA policy.
Antivirus and protection from infected data	By integrating IPS/IDP modules with firewall, malicious data can be detected and filtered at the edge of the network to protect the end-users

Table 2-02: Firewall protection against risks

LAB 2-1: Configuring Zone-based Policy Firewall

Case Study: Consider a scenario in which a small private network is connected to Internet. Requirement for the private network is to configure Zone-based policy which only permits the traffic requested from the inside interfaces & return traffic of these requests. Any incoming traffic originated from the outside zone will be denied.

Topology Diagram:

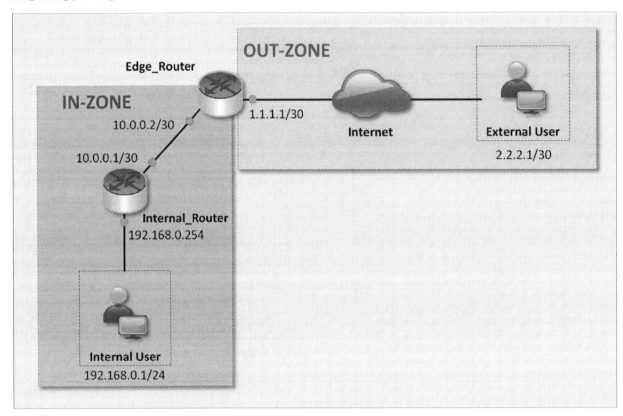

Configuring Edge Router:
Edge_Router(config)# **interface FastEthernet0/0** Edge_Router(config-if)# **ip address 1.1.1.1 255.255.255.252** Edge_Router(config-if)# **no shutdown** Edge_Router(config-if)# **exit** Edge_Router(config)# **interface FastEthernet0/1** Edge_Router(config-if)# **ip address 10.0.0.2 255.255.255.252** Edge_Router(config-if)# **no shutdown** Edge_Router(config-if)# **exit**

```
Edge_Router(config)# ip route 0.0.0.0 0.0.0.0 1.1.1.2
Edge_Router(config)# ip route 192.168.0.0 255.255.255.0 10.0.0.1


Edge_Router(config)# zone security IN-ZONE
Edge_Router(config-sec-zone)# exit
Edge_Router(config)# zone security OUT-ZONE
Edge_Router(config-sec-zone)# exit


Edge_Router(config)# access-list 101 permit ip 192.168.0.0 0.0.0.255
any
Edge_Router(config)# class-map type inspect match-all IN-NET-CLASS-MAP
Edge_Router(config-cmap)# match access-group 101
Edge_Router(config-cmap)# exit


Edge_Router(config)# policy-map type inspect IN-2-OUT-PMAP
Edge_Router(config-pmap)# class type inspect IN-NET-CLASS-MAP
Edge_Router(config-pmap-c)# inspect
%No specific protocol configured in class IN-NET-CLASS-MAP for inspection. All
protocols will be inspected
Edge_Router(config-pmap-c)# exit
Edge_Router(config-pmap)# exit


Edge_Router(config)# zone-pair security IN-2-OUT-ZPAIR source IN-ZONE
destination OUT-ZONE
Edge_Router(config-sec-zone-pair)# service-policy type inspect IN-2-
OUT-PMAP
Edge_Router(config-sec-zone-pair)# exit


Edge_Router(config)# interface fastEthernet 0/1
Edge_Router(config-if)# zone-member security IN-ZONE
Edge_Router(config-if)# ex


Edge_Router(config)# interface fastEthernet 0/0
Edge_Router(config-if)# zone-member security OUT-ZONE
Edge_Router(config-if)# ex
```

Configuring Internal Router:

```
Router(config)# hostname Internal_Router

Internal_Router(config)# interface FastEthernet0/0
Internal_Router(config-if)# ip address 10.0.0.1 255.255.255.252

Internal_Router(config)# interface FastEthernet0/1
Internal_Router(config-if)# ip address 192.168.0.254 255.255.255.0

Internal_Router(config)# ip route 0.0.0.0 0.0.0.0 10.0.0.2
```

Configuring Internal User:

```
VPC> ip 192.168.0.1/24 192.168.0.254
VPC> Save
```

Configuring External User:

```
VPC> ip 2.2.2.1/30 2.2.2.2
VPC> Save
```

Simulated Internet Configuration

```
ISP(config)# interface FastEthernet0/0
ISP(config-if)# ip address 2.2.2.2 255.255.255.252
ISP(config-if)# no shutdown
ISP(config-if)# exit

ISP(config)# interface FastEthernet0/1
ISP(config-if)# ip address 1.1.1.2 255.255.255.252
ISP(config-if)# no shutdown
ISP(config-if)# exit

ISP(config)# ip route 0.0.0.0 0.0.0.0 1.1.1.1
```

Verification:

Edge_Router# **show policy-map type inspect zone-pair IN-2-OUT-ZPAIR sessions**

```
Edge_Router#show policy-map type inspect zone-pair IN-2-OUT-ZPAIR sessions
 Zone-pair: IN-2-OUT-ZPAIR

  Service-policy inspect : IN-2-OUT-PMAP

    Class-map: IN-NET-CLASS-MAP (match-all)
      Match: access-group 101
      Inspect
        Established Sessions
         Session 66E5C1E8 (192.168.0.1:8)=>(2.2.2.1:0) icmp SIS_OPEN
          Created 00:00:03, Last heard 00:00:00
           ECHO request
          Bytes sent (initiator:responder) [224:224]

    Class-map: class-default (match-any)
      Match: any
      Drop (default action)
        0 packets, 0 bytes
```

VPC# **Ping 2.2.2.1**

//pinging External User (2.2.2.1) from Internal User (192.168.0.1)

```
VPC>ping 2.2.2.1

Pinging 2.2.2.1 with 32 bytes of data:

Reply from 2.2.2.1: bytes=32 time<1ms TTL=125
Reply from 2.2.2.1: bytes=32 time<1ms TTL=125
Reply from 2.2.2.1: bytes=32 time<1ms TTL=125
Reply from 2.2.2.1: bytes=32 time=10ms TTL=125

Ping statistics for 2.2.2.1:
    Packets: Sent = 4, Received = 4, Lost = 0 (0% loss),
Approximate round trip times in milli-seconds:
    Minimum = 0ms, Maximum = 10ms, Average = 2ms
```

As configured, Policy is passing the traffic generating from inside zone towards outside zone.

VPC# **Ping 192.168.0.1**

//pinging Internal User (192.168.0.1) from External User (2.2.2.1).

```
External_User                                          —    □    ×

VPC>ping 192.168.0.1

Pinging 192.168.0.1 with 32 bytes of data:

Request timed out.
Request timed out.
Request timed out.
Request timed out.

Ping statistics for 192.168.0.1:
    Packets: Sent = 4, Received = 0, Lost = 4 (100% loss),
```

As configured, Policy is blocking the traffic from outside zone destined towards outside zone.

VPN Concentrator

One of the challenges with the communication through internet is that we do not know who might be in the middle of the communication path and able to see the traffic in flow. For this, we need *Encryption method*. VPN (Virtual Private Network) is used to encrypt data traversing, a public network and make traffic useless for the attacker. The encryption is done through VPN Concentrator. It is sometimes integrated into a firewall and designed specifically for encryption and decryption of data or traffic.

Common VPN

- SSL VPN
- Site to Site VPN
- IP Sec

Remote Access VPN

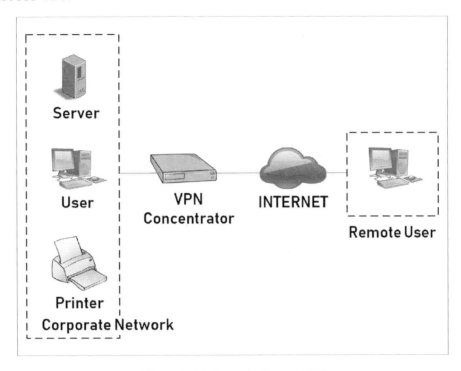

Figure 2-04: Remote Access VPN

LAB 2-2: IPSEC Site-to-Site VPN Configuration

Case Study: In this lab, we will learn how to configure IPSEC site-to-Site VPN on routers. We know that IPSEC is used to transmit data securely over unsecured network. In this lab R1 and R2 is participating in IPSEC peers, therefore, these two routers are required to be configured in order to support IPSEC site to site VPN for the traffic transmitting from their LANs. We have used two routers (R1 and R2), two switches (SW3 and Sw4), and two Virtual PCs (VPC5 and VPC6).

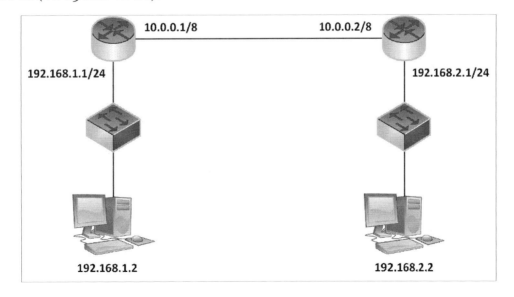

Let's start the lab.

The following are screenshots that will help you understand how to configure and verify the IPsec site to site VPN.

Step 1: Configure all the devices in the topology

Assign IP address with Subnet mask and Gateway to virtual PCs. The IP assigned to VPC5 is 192.168.1.2/24 and the gateway is 192.168.1.1.

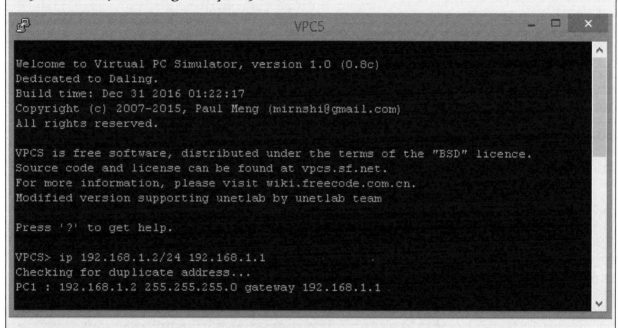

The IP address assigned to VPC6 is 192.168.2.2/24 and the gateway 192.168.2.1.

Now assign IP address to all the interfaces of Router 1 and Router 2 as shown in the next page.

```
R1                                                          _ □ ✕

*Jun  7 22:44:55.804: %CRYPTO-6-ISAKMP_ON_OFF: ISAKMP is OFF
*Jun  7 22:44:55.804: %CRYPTO-6-GDOI_ON_OFF: GDOI is OFF
Router>en
Router#config t
Enter configuration commands, one per line.  End with CNTL/Z.
Router(config)#hostname R1
R1(config)#interface e0/0
R1(config-if)#ip address 10.0.0.1 255.0.0.0
R1(config-if)#no shut
R1(config-if)#exit
*Jun  7 22:46:29.320: %LINK-3-UPDOWN: Interface Ethernet0/0, changed state to up
*Jun  7 22:46:30.324: %LINEPROTO-5-UPDOWN: Line protocol on Interface Ethernet0/
0, changed state to up
R1(config-if)#exit
R1(config)#interface e0/1
R1(config-if)#ip address 192.168.1.1 255.255.255.0
R1(config-if)#no shut
R1(config-if)#exit
R1(config)#
*Jun  7 22:47:22.249: %LINK-3-UPDOWN: Interface Ethernet0/1, changed state to up
*Jun  7 22:47:23.253: %LINEPROTO-5-UPDOWN: Line protocol on Interface Ethernet0/
1, changed state to up
R1(config)#
```

```
R2                                                          _ □ ✕

Router>en
Router#config t
Enter configuration commands, one per line.  End with CNTL/Z.
Router(config)#hostname R2
R2(config)#interface e0/0
R2(config-if)#ip address 10.0.0.2 255.0.0.0
R2(config-if)#no shut
R2(config-if)#exit
R2(config)#
*Jun  7 22:54:28.080: %LINK-3-UPDOWN: Interface Ethernet0/0, changed state to up
*Jun  7 22:54:29.080: %LINEPROTO-5-UPDOWN: Line protocol on Interface Ethernet0/
0, changed state to up
R2(config)#interface e0/1
R2(config-if)#ip address 192.168.2.1 255.255.255.0
R2(config-if)#no shut
R2(config-if)#exit
R2(config)#
*Jun  7 22:55:08.414: %LINK-3-UPDOWN: Interface Ethernet0/1, changed state to up
*Jun  7 22:55:09.418: %LINEPROTO-5-UPDOWN: Line protocol on Interface Ethernet0/
1, changed state to up
R2(config)#
```

```
*Jun  7 22:47:22.249: %LINK-3-UPDOWN: Interface Ethernet0/1, changed state to up
*Jun  7 22:47:23.253: %LINEPROTO-5-UPDOWN: Line protocol on Interface Ethernet0/
1, changed state to up
R1(config)#router rip
R1(config-router)#network 10.0.0.0
R1(config-router)#network 192.168.1.0
R1(config-router)#exit
R1(config)#
```

Step 2: ISAKMP policy

Configure the parameters which will be used for IKE phase 1 tunnel.

```
R1(config-router)#exit
R1(config)#crypto isakmp policy 10
R1(config-isakmp)#authentication pre-share
R1(config-isakmp)#encryption aes 256
R1(config-isakmp)#group 2
R1(config-isakmp)#lifetime 86400
R1(config-isakmp)#exit
R1(config)#
```

Step 3: Transform Set

Configure the parameters which will be used for IKE phase 2 tunnel

```
R1(config-isakmp)#exit
R1(config)#crypto isakmp key redhat address 10.0.0.2
R1(config)#crypto ipsec transform-set TSET esp-aes esp-sha-hmac
R1(cfg-crypto-trans)#
```

Step 4: ACL-Access Control List

Now, we create ACL in order to define what traffic will be sent over the Virtual Private Network.

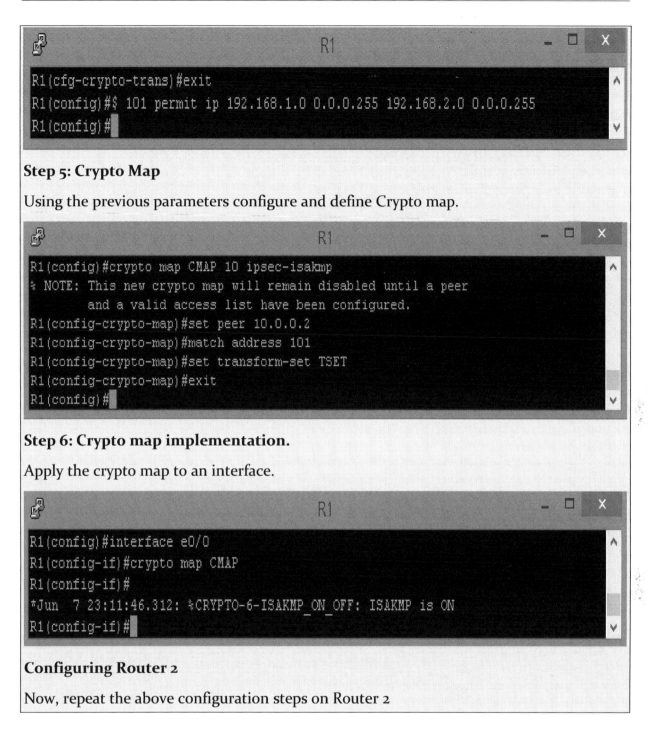

Step 5: Crypto Map

Using the previous parameters configure and define Crypto map.

Step 6: Crypto map implementation.

Apply the crypto map to an interface.

Configuring Router 2

Now, repeat the above configuration steps on Router 2

R2
```
*Jun  7 23:05:09.647: %SYS-5-CONFIG_I: Configured from console by console
R2>en
R2#config t
Enter configuration commands, one per line.  End with CNTL/Z.
R2(config)#router rip
R2(config-router)#network 10.0.0.0
R2(config-router)#network 192.168.2.0
R2(config-router)#
```

Step 1. ISAKMP policy

R2
```
R2(config-router)#crypto isakmp policy 10
R2(config-isakmp)#authentication pre-share
R2(config-isakmp)#hash sha
R2(config-isakmp)#encryption aes 256
R2(config-isakmp)#group 2
R2(config-isakmp)#lifetime 86400
R2(config-isakmp)#exit
R2(config)#
```

Step 2: Transform Set

R2
```
R2(config)#crypto isakmp key redhat address 10.0.0.1
R2(config)#crypto ipsec transform-set TSET esp-aes esp-sha-hmac
R2(cfg-crypto-trans)#
```

Step 3: ACL-Access Control List

R2
```
R2(config)#$ 101 permit ip 192.168.2.0 0.0.0.255 192.168.1.0 0.0.0.255
R2(config)#
```

Step 4: Crypto Map

R2
```
R2(config)#crypto map CMAP 10 ipsec-isakmp
% NOTE: This new crypto map will remain disabled until a peer
        and a valid access list have been configured.
R2(config-crypto-map)#set peer 10.0.0.1
R2(config-crypto-map)#match address 101
R2(config-crypto-map)#set transform-set TSET
R2(config-crypto-map)#exit
R2(config)#
```

Step 5: Crypto map implementation.

```
R2(config-crypto-map)#exit
R2(config)#interface e0/0
R2(config-if)#crypto map CMAP
R2(config-if)#
*Jun  7 23:43:12.233: %CRYPTO-6-ISAKMP_ON_OFF: ISAKMP is ON
R2(config-if)#
```

Verification (Test and Verify IPSEC Configuration)

Ping VPC6 and gateway from VPC5 to check and verify the connectivity.

```
VPCS> ping 192.168.1.1

84 bytes from 192.168.1.1 icmp_seq=1 ttl=255 time=2.324 ms
84 bytes from 192.168.1.1 icmp_seq=2 ttl=255 time=2.074 ms
84 bytes from 192.168.1.1 icmp_seq=3 ttl=255 time=1.496 ms
84 bytes from 192.168.1.1 icmp_seq=4 ttl=255 time=3.179 ms
84 bytes from 192.168.1.1 icmp_seq=5 ttl=255 time=2.654 ms

VPCS> ping 192.168.2.2

192.168.2.2 icmp_seq=1 timeout
84 bytes from 192.168.2.2 icmp_seq=2 ttl=62 time=6.205 ms
84 bytes from 192.168.2.2 icmp_seq=3 ttl=62 time=4.578 ms
84 bytes from 192.168.2.2 icmp_seq=4 ttl=62 time=4.326 ms
84 bytes from 192.168.2.2 icmp_seq=5 ttl=62 time=5.253 ms

VPCS> ping 192.168.2.1

84 bytes from 192.168.2.1 icmp_seq=1 ttl=254 time=2.337 ms
84 bytes from 192.168.2.1 icmp_seq=2 ttl=254 time=3.021 ms
84 bytes from 192.168.2.1 icmp_seq=3 ttl=254 time=3.397 ms
84 bytes from 192.168.2.1 icmp_seq=4 ttl=254 time=2.143 ms
84 bytes from 192.168.2.1 icmp_seq=5 ttl=254 time=2.389 ms

VPCS>
```

Now, Ping VPC5 and gateway from VPC6.

Now for verification, use command 'crypto isakmp policy' on both routers, it will show you the encryption algorithm we have configured and other details as shown in the screenshot.

Now TEST and VERIFY the IPsec configuration on R1 also.

```
                                    R1                          _  □  ×
R1>en
R1#show crypto isakmp policy

Global IKE policy
Protection suite of priority 10
        encryption algorithm:   AES - Advanced Encryption Standard (256 bit keys)

        hash algorithm:         Secure Hash Standard
        authentication method:  Pre-Shared Key
        Diffie-Hellman group:   #2 (1024 bit)
        lifetime:               86400 seconds, no volume limit
R1#
```

Use also 'show crypto isakmp sa' and 'show crypto ipsec sa' command for verification.

```
                                    R1                          _  □  ×
R1#show crypto ipsec sa

interface: Ethernet0/0
    Crypto map tag: CMAP, local addr 10.0.0.1

    protected vrf: (none)
    local  ident (addr/mask/prot/port): (192.168.1.0/255.255.255.0/0/0)
    remote ident (addr/mask/prot/port): (192.168.2.0/255.255.255.0/0/0)
    current_peer 10.0.0.2 port 500
      PERMIT, flags={origin_is_acl,}
    #pkts encaps: 9, #pkts encrypt: 9, #pkts digest: 9
    #pkts decaps: 9, #pkts decrypt: 9, #pkts verify: 9
    #pkts compressed: 0, #pkts decompressed: 0
    #pkts not compressed: 0, #pkts compr. failed: 0
    #pkts not decompressed: 0, #pkts decompress failed: 0
    #send errors 0, #recv errors 0

     local crypto endpt.: 10.0.0.1, remote crypto endpt.: 10.0.0.2
     plaintext mtu 1438, path mtu 1500, ip mtu 1500, ip mtu idb Ethernet0/0
     current outbound spi: 0x10E077B0(283146160)
     PFS (Y/N): N, DH group: none

     inbound esp sas:
      spi: 0x2162715B(560099675)
        transform: esp-aes esp-sha-hmac ,
        in use settings ={Tunnel, }
        conn id: 1, flow_id: SW:1, sibling_flags 80004040, crypto map: CMAP
        sa timing: remaining key lifetime (k/sec): (4263383/3571)
        IV size: 16 bytes
        replay detection support: Y
        ecn bit support: Y status: off
        Status: ACTIVE(ACTIVE)

     inbound ah sas:

     inbound pcp sas:

     outbound esp sas:
      spi: 0x10E077B0(283146160)
        transform: esp-aes esp-sha-hmac ,
        in use settings ={Tunnel, }
        conn id: 2, flow_id: SW:2, sibling_flags 80004040, crypto map: CMAP
        sa timing: remaining key lifetime (k/sec): (4263383/3571)
```

```
                                    R1                        —  □  ×

plaintext mtu 1438, path mtu 1500, ip mtu 1500, ip mtu idb Ethernet0/0
current outbound spi: 0x10E077B0(283146160)
PFS (Y/N): N, DH group: none

inbound esp sas:
 spi: 0x2162715B(560099675)
   transform: esp-aes esp-sha-hmac ,
   in use settings ={Tunnel, }
   conn id: 1, flow_id: SW:1, sibling_flags 80004040, crypto map: CMAP
   sa timing: remaining key lifetime (k/sec): (4263383/3571)
   IV size: 16 bytes
   replay detection support: Y
   ecn bit support: Y status: off
   Status: ACTIVE(ACTIVE)

inbound ah sas:

inbound pcp sas:

outbound esp sas:
 spi: 0x10E077B0(283146160)
   transform: esp-aes esp-sha-hmac ,
   in use settings ={Tunnel, }
   conn id: 2, flow_id: SW:2, sibling_flags 80004040, crypto map: CMAP
   sa timing: remaining key lifetime (k/sec): (4263383/3571)
   IV size: 16 bytes
   replay detection support: Y
   ecn bit support: Y status: off
   Status: ACTIVE(ACTIVE)

outbound ah sas:

outbound pcp sas:
R1#
```

```
                                    R1                        —  □  ×

R1#show crypto isakmp sa
IPv4 Crypto ISAKMP SA
dst              src              state            conn-id status
10.0.0.2         10.0.0.1         QM_IDLE             1001 ACTIVE

IPv6 Crypto ISAKMP SA

R1#
```

LAB 2-3: VPN configuration

Case Study: In this lab, we will learn how to configure VPN and how to create VPN tunnel between routers for safe communication. For showing VPN configuration on routers, I have taken 3 Routers and total 5 networks are used as shown in the topology.

Network 192.168.1.0/24

Network 192.168.2.0/24

Network 1.0.0.0/8

Network 2.0.0.0/8

Network 172.16.1.0/16 (For VPN tunnel)

Topology:

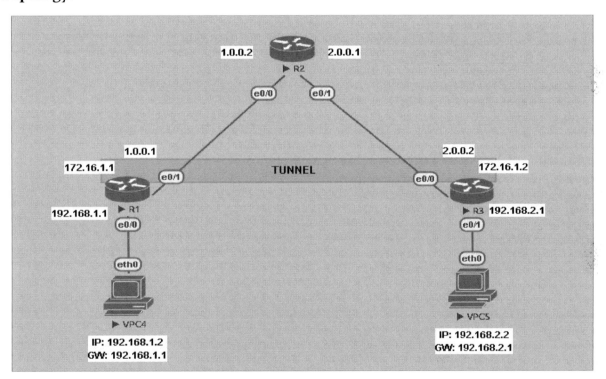

Let's start the lab.

The first thing to do in this lab is to assign IP address on the PCs and on each interface of the Routers. The following are screenshots that will help you in configuring VPN step by step.

Step 01: Configure all routers

Assign IP address on each interface of router 1.

```
                              R1                          _  □  ×
Router>en
Router#config t
Enter configuration commands, one per line.  End with CNTL/Z.
Router(config)#hostname R1
R1(config)#interface e0/0
R1(config-if)#ip address 192.168.1.1 255.255.255.0
R1(config-if)#no shut
R1(config-if)#
*Jun 12 18:37:31.139: %LINK-3-UPDOWN: Interface Ethernet0/0, changed s
tate to up
*Jun 12 18:37:32.143: %LINEPROTO-5-UPDOWN: Line protocol on Interface
Ethernet0/0, changed state to up
R1(config-if)#exit
R1(config)#interface e0/1
R1(config-if)#ip address 1.0.0.1 255.0.0.0
R1(config-if)#no shut
R1(config-if)#
*Jun 12 18:38:15.404: %LINK-3-UPDOWN: Interface Ethernet0/1, changed s
tate to up
*Jun 12 18:38:16.406: %LINEPROTO-5-UPDOWN: Line protocol on Interface
Ethernet0/1, changed state to up
R1(config-if)#
```

Now assign IP address on router 2

```
                              R2                          _  □  ×
Router>en
Router#config t
Enter configuration commands, one per line.  End with CNTL/Z.
Router(config)#hostname R2
R2(config)#interface e0/0
R2(config-if)#ip address 1.0.0.2 255.0.0.0
R2(config-if)#no shut
R2(config-if)#
*Jun 12 18:43:08.796: %LINK-3-UPDOWN: Interface Ethernet0/0, changed state to up
*Jun 12 18:43:09.800: %LINEPROTO-5-UPDOWN: Line protocol on Interface Ethernet0/
0, changed state to up
R2(config-if)#exit
R2(config)#interface e0/1
R2(config-if)#ip address 2.0.0.1 255.0.0.0
R2(config-if)#no shut
R2(config-if)#
*Jun 12 18:43:46.737: %LINK-3-UPDOWN: Interface Ethernet0/1, changed state to up
*Jun 12 18:43:47.741: %LINEPROTO-5-UPDOWN: Line protocol on Interface Ethernet0/
1, changed state to up
R2(config-if)#
```

And now configure router 3

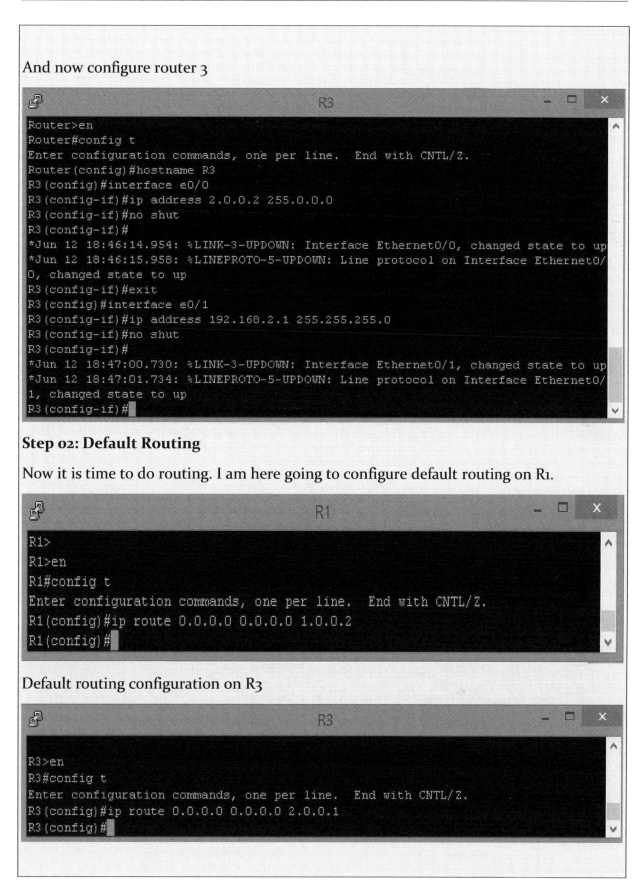

```
Router>en
Router#config t
Enter configuration commands, one per line.  End with CNTL/Z.
Router(config)#hostname R3
R3(config)#interface e0/0
R3(config-if)#ip address 2.0.0.2 255.0.0.0
R3(config-if)#no shut
R3(config-if)#
*Jun 12 18:46:14.954: %LINK-3-UPDOWN: Interface Ethernet0/0, changed state to up
*Jun 12 18:46:15.958: %LINEPROTO-5-UPDOWN: Line protocol on Interface Ethernet0/
0, changed state to up
R3(config-if)#exit
R3(config)#interface e0/1
R3(config-if)#ip address 192.168.2.1 255.255.255.0
R3(config-if)#no shut
R3(config-if)#
*Jun 12 18:47:00.730: %LINK-3-UPDOWN: Interface Ethernet0/1, changed state to up
*Jun 12 18:47:01.734: %LINEPROTO-5-UPDOWN: Line protocol on Interface Ethernet0/
1, changed state to up
R3(config-if)#
```

Step 02: Default Routing

Now it is time to do routing. I am here going to configure default routing on R1.

```
R1>
R1>en
R1#config t
Enter configuration commands, one per line.  End with CNTL/Z.
R1(config)#ip route 0.0.0.0 0.0.0.0 1.0.0.2
R1(config)#
```

Default routing configuration on R3

```
R3>en
R3#config t
Enter configuration commands, one per line.  End with CNTL/Z.
R3(config)#ip route 0.0.0.0 0.0.0.0 2.0.0.1
R3(config)#
```

Step 03: Check Connectivity

Now check the connectivity by pinging each other. First go to router 1 and ping with R3

```
                                    R1                        _  □  ×
R1(config)#exit
R1#
*Jun 12 18:53:41.178: %SYS-5-CONFIG_I: Configured from console by console
R1#ping 2.0.0.2
Type escape sequence to abort.
Sending 5, 100-byte ICMP Echos to 2.0.0.2, timeout is 2 seconds:
!!!!!
Success rate is 100 percent (5/5), round-trip min/avg/max = 1/1/1 ms
R1#
```

Now go to R3 and test network by pinging R1 interface. You can clearly see both routers pinging each other successfully.

```
                                    R3                        _  □  ×
R3(config)#exit
R3#
*Jun 12 18:54:54.515: %SYS-5-CONFIG_I: Configured from console by console
R3#ping 1.0.0.1
Type escape sequence to abort.
Sending 5, 100-byte ICMP Echos to 1.0.0.1, timeout is 2 seconds:
!!!!!
Success rate is 100 percent (5/5), round-trip min/avg/max = 1/1/1 ms
R3#
```

Step 04: VPN tunnel between R1 and R3

First create VPN tunnel on R1

```
                                    R1                        _  □  ×
R1#config t
Enter configuration commands, one per line.  End with CNTL/Z.
R1(config)#interface tunnel 10
R1(config-if)#ip addr
*Jun 12 18:56:31.651: %LINEPROTO-5-UPDOWN: Line protocol on Interface Tunnel
10, changed state to down
R1(config-if)#ip address 172.16.1.1 255.255.0.0
R1(config-if)#tunnel source e0/1
R1(config-if)#tunnel destination 2.0.0.2
R1(config-if)#no
*Jun 12 18:57:28.388: %LINEPROTO-5-UPDOWN: Line protocol on Interface Tunnel
10, changed state to up
R1(config-if)#no shut
R1(config-if)#
```

Create VPN tunnel on R3

```
┌─────────────────────────────────────────────────────────────────────────┐
│ 🖥                                  R3                         — □ ✕       │
├─────────────────────────────────────────────────────────────────────────┤
│ Success rate is 100 percent (5/5), round-trip min/avg/max = 1/1/1 ms  ^  │
│ R3#config t                                                              │
│ Enter configuration commands, one per line.  End with CNTL/Z.            │
│ R3(config)#interface tunnel 100                                          │
│ R3(config-if)#ip add                                                     │
│ *Jun 12 18:59:23.196: %LINEPROTO-5-UPDOWN: Line protocol on Interface Tunnel100, │
│  changed state to down                                                   │
│ R3(config-if)#ip address 172.16.1.2 255.255.0.0                          │
│ R3(config-if)#tunnel source e0/0                                         │
│ R3(config-if)#tunnel destination 1.0.0.1                                 │
│ R3(config-if)#                                                           │
│ *Jun 12 19:00:43.240: %LINEPROTO-5-UPDOWN: Line protocol on Interface Tunnel100, │
│  changed state to up                                                     │
│ R3(config-if)#no shut                                                    │
│ R3(config-if)#█                                                       ∨  │
└─────────────────────────────────────────────────────────────────────────┘
```

Step 05: Test communication

Now test communication between these two routers again by pinging each other

```
┌─────────────────────────────────────────────────────────────────────────┐
│ 🖥                                  R1                         — □ ✕       │
├─────────────────────────────────────────────────────────────────────────┤
│ R1(config-if)#exit                                                    ^  │
│ R1(config)#exit                                                          │
│ R1#                                                                      │
│ *Jun 12 19:01:46.456: %SYS-5-CONFIG_I: Configured from console by console │
│ R1#ping 172.16.1.2                                                       │
│ Type escape sequence to abort.                                           │
│ Sending 5, 100-byte ICMP Echos to 172.16.1.2, timeout is 2 seconds:      │
│ !!!!!                                                                     │
│ Success rate is 100 percent (5/5), round-trip min/avg/max = 1/1/1 ms     │
│ R1#█                                                                  ∨  │
└─────────────────────────────────────────────────────────────────────────┘
```

```
┌─────────────────────────────────────────────────────────────────────────┐
│ 🖥                                  R3                         — □ ✕       │
├─────────────────────────────────────────────────────────────────────────┤
│ R3(config-if)#no shut                                                 ^  │
│ R3(config-if)#exit                                                       │
│ R3(config)#exit                                                          │
│ R3#pin                                                                   │
│ *Jun 12 19:02:49.310: %SYS-5-CONFIG_I: Configured from console by console │
│ R3#ping 172.16.1.1                                                       │
│ Type escape sequence to abort.                                           │
│ Sending 5, 100-byte ICMP Echos to 172.16.1.1, timeout is 2 seconds:      │
│ !!!!!                                                                     │
│ Success rate is 100 percent (5/5), round-trip min/avg/max = 1/1/1 ms     │
│ R3#█                                                                  ∨  │
└─────────────────────────────────────────────────────────────────────────┘
```

Step 06: Routing for VPN tunnel

Now do routing for created VPN tunnel on R1 and R3 using command 'ip route'.

```
R1                                                    _  □  X
R1#config t
Enter configuration commands, one per line.  End with CNTL/Z.
R1(config)#ip route 192.168.2.0 255.255.255.0 172.16.1.2
R1(config)#
```

```
R3                                                    _  □  X
Success rate is 100 percent (5/5), round-trip min/avg/max = 1/1/1 ms
R3#config t
Enter configuration commands, one per line.  End with CNTL/Z.
R3(config)#ip route 192.168.1.0 255.255.255.0 172.16.1.1
R3(config)#
```

Step 07: Test VPN tunnel configuration.

Go to R1 and test whether VPN tunnel is created or not using command 'show interface tunnel 10'.

```
R1                                          _  □  ✕

R1#show interfaces tunnel 10
Tunnel10 is up, line protocol is up
  Hardware is Tunnel
  Internet address is 172.16.1.1/16
  MTU 17916 bytes, BW 100 Kbit/sec, DLY 50000 usec,
     reliability 255/255, txload 1/255, rxload 1/255
  Encapsulation TUNNEL, loopback not set
  Keepalive not set
  Tunnel source 1.0.0.1 (Ethernet0/1), destination 2.0.0.2
   Tunnel Subblocks:
      src-track:
         Tunnel10 source tracking subblock associated with Ethernet0/1
          Set of tunnels with source Ethernet0/1, 1 member (includes iterato
rs), on interface <OK>
  Tunnel protocol/transport GRE/IP
    Key disabled, sequencing disabled
    Checksumming of packets disabled
  Tunnel TTL 255, Fast tunneling enabled
  Tunnel transport MTU 1476 bytes
  Tunnel transmit bandwidth 8000 (kbps)
  Tunnel receive bandwidth 8000 (kbps)
  Last input 00:06:17, output 00:06:17, output hang never
  Last clearing of "show interface" counters 00:12:55
  Input queue: 0/75/0/0 (size/max/drops/flushes); Total output drops: 0
  Queueing strategy: fifo
  Output queue: 0/0 (size/max)
  5 minute input rate 0 bits/sec, 0 packets/sec
  5 minute output rate 0 bits/sec, 0 packets/sec
     10 packets input, 1240 bytes, 0 no buffer
     Received 0 broadcasts (0 IP multicasts)
     0 runts, 0 giants, 0 throttles
     0 input errors, 0 CRC, 0 frame, 0 overrun, 0 ignored, 0 abort
     10 packets output, 1240 bytes, 0 underruns
     0 output errors, 0 collisions, 0 interface resets
     0 unknown protocol drops
     0 output buffer failures, 0 output buffers swapped out
R1#
```

Now go to R3 and do the same.

```
R3                                          _  □  X

*Jun 12 19:11:18.387: %SYS-5-CONFIG_I: Configured from console by console
R3#show interface tunnel 100
Tunnel100 is up, line protocol is up
  Hardware is Tunnel
  Internet address is 172.16.1.2/16
  MTU 17916 bytes, BW 100 Kbit/sec, DLY 50000 usec,
      reliability 255/255, txload 1/255, rxload 1/255
  Encapsulation TUNNEL, loopback not set
  Keepalive not set
  Tunnel source 2.0.0.2 (Ethernet0/0), destination 1.0.0.1
   Tunnel Subblocks:
      src-track:
         Tunnel100 source tracking subblock associated with Ethernet0/0
          Set of tunnels with source Ethernet0/0, 1 member (includes iterators),
on interface <OK>
  Tunnel protocol/transport GRE/IP
    Key disabled, sequencing disabled
    Checksumming of packets disabled
  Tunnel TTL 255, Fast tunneling enabled
  Tunnel transport MTU 1476 bytes
  Tunnel transmit bandwidth 8000 (kbps)
  Tunnel receive bandwidth 8000 (kbps)
  Last input 00:08:24, output 00:08:24, output hang never
  Last clearing of "show interface" counters 00:12:10
  Input queue: 0/75/0/0 (size/max/drops/flushes); Total output drops: 0
  Queueing strategy: fifo
  Output queue: 0/0 (size/max)
  5 minute input rate 0 bits/sec, 0 packets/sec
  5 minute output rate 0 bits/sec, 0 packets/sec
     10 packets input, 1240 bytes, 0 no buffer
     Received 0 broadcasts (0 IP multicasts)
     0 runts, 0 giants, 0 throttles
     0 input errors, 0 CRC, 0 frame, 0 overrun, 0 ignored, 0 abort
     10 packets output, 1240 bytes, 0 underruns
     0 output errors, 0 collisions, 0 interface resets
     0 unknown protocol drops
     0 output buffer failures, 0 output buffers swapped out
R3#
```

Step 08: Testing and Verification

Now if you want to check what path VPN tunnel is using, just go to any of the PC and then ping another PC located in different and then trace the path using 'trace' command. Its result will show the path followed by VPN tunnel that you created.

In the picture below, you can see that I have successfully pinged VPC5 from VPC4 and the trace command have shown the path followed.

```
VPC4                                              _  □  ×

VPCS> ping 192.168.2.2

84 bytes from 192.168.2.2 icmp_seq=1 ttl=62 time=2.114 ms
84 bytes from 192.168.2.2 icmp_seq=2 ttl=62 time=1.125 ms
84 bytes from 192.168.2.2 icmp_seq=3 ttl=62 time=1.017 ms
84 bytes from 192.168.2.2 icmp_seq=4 ttl=62 time=1.239 ms
84 bytes from 192.168.2.2 icmp_seq=5 ttl=62 time=1.078 ms

VPCS> trace 192.168.2.2
trace to 192.168.2.2, 8 hops max, press Ctrl+C to stop
  1    192.168.1.1   0.338 ms   0.261 ms   0.271 ms
  2    172.16.1.2    1.139 ms   0.923 ms   0.906 ms
  3   *192.168.2.2   2.118 ms  (ICMP type:3, code:3, Destination port

VPCS>
```

```
VPC5                                              _  □  ×

VPCS> ip 192.168.2.2/24 192.168.2.1
Checking for duplicate address...
PC1 : 192.168.2.2 255.255.255.0 gateway 192.168.2.1

VPCS> ping 192.168.1.2

84 bytes from 192.168.1.2 icmp_seq=1 ttl=62 time=1.943 ms
84 bytes from 192.168.1.2 icmp_seq=2 ttl=62 time=1.178 ms
84 bytes from 192.168.1.2 icmp_seq=3 ttl=62 time=1.397 ms
84 bytes from 192.168.1.2 icmp_seq=4 ttl=62 time=1.550 ms
84 bytes from 192.168.1.2 icmp_seq=5 ttl=62 time=1.228 ms

VPCS>
```

```
VPC4                                              —  □  ✕

VPCS> ip 192.168.1.2/24 192.168.1.1
Checking for duplicate address...
PC1 : 192.168.1.2 255.255.255.0 gateway 192.168.1.1

VPCS> ping 192.168.2.2

84 bytes from 192.168.2.2 icmp_seq=1 ttl=62 time=2.114 ms
84 bytes from 192.168.2.2 icmp_seq=2 ttl=62 time=1.125 ms
84 bytes from 192.168.2.2 icmp_seq=3 ttl=62 time=1.017 ms
84 bytes from 192.168.2.2 icmp_seq=4 ttl=62 time=1.239 ms
84 bytes from 192.168.2.2 icmp_seq=5 ttl=62 time=1.078 ms

VPCS>
```

Network Intrusion Detection and Prevention

Network Intrusion Detection

It is used to monitor traffic at selected points in a network in real-time. It examines Application, Transport, or Network level protocol activities. The network traffic pattern analysis and detect based on library of known attacks. Behavioral, anomaly and signature based monitoring & detection of NIDS strengthen the security across the network.

<u>Functions of NID</u>

- The main function of NID is to filter out the IP Address of the intruder by configuring the firewall.
- It launches a separate program to handle the event.
- It can terminate the TCP session by forging a TCP FIN packet to force a connection to terminate.
- It sends an entry to the system log file.

Network Intrusion Prevention

It is an "inline" NIDS that can terminate TCP connection and can discard packets.

<u>Functions of NIPS</u>

It can identify malicious packets using the following methods:

- Pattern Matching
- Stateful Matching
- Protocol Anomaly
- Statistical Anomaly
- Traffic Anomaly

It can also provide flow data protection through:

- Monitoring full application flow content
- Re-assembling whole packets

Difference between NIDS and NIPS

The major difference between NIDS and NIPS is in their location:

- NIPS would be located 'inline' on the firewall itself to allow NIPS to take action more quickly against the attack.
- NIDS has sensors that monitor traffic entering and leaving firewall, and report back to the central device for analysis.

The placement of sensor within a network differentiates the functionality of IPS over the IDS. When sensor is placed in line with the network, i.e., the common in/out of specific network segment terminates on hardware or logical interface of the sensor and goes out from second hardware or logical interface of the sensor, then every single packet will be analyzed and pass through sensor only if it does not contain anything malicious. By dropping the malicious traffic, the trusted network or a segment of it, can be protected from known threats and attacks. This is the basic working of Intrusion Prevention System (IPS). However, the inline installation and inspection of traffic may result in a slighter delay. IPS may also become a single point of failure for the whole network. If 'fail-open' mode is used, the good and malicious traffic will be allowed in case of any kind of failure within IPS sensor. Similarly, if 'fail-close' mode is configured, the whole IP traffic will be dropped in case of sensor's failure.

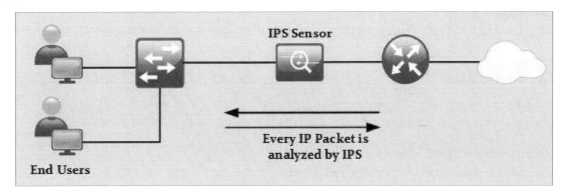

Figure 2-05: In-line deployment of IPS sensor

If a sensor is installed in the position as shown below, a copy of every packet will be sent to the sensor to analyze for any malicious activity.

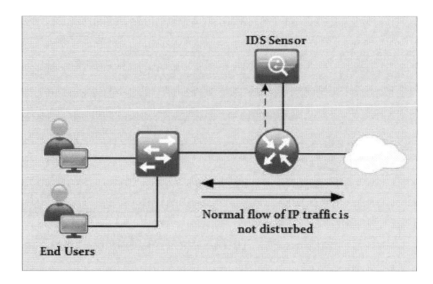

Figure 2-06: Sensor deployment as IDS

In other means, the sensor, running in promiscuous mode will perform the detection and generate an alert if required. As the normal flow of traffic is not disturbed, no end-to-end delay will be introduced by implementing IDS. The only downside of this configuration is that IDS will not be able to stop malicious packets from entering the network because IDS is not controlling the overall path of traffic.

This table summarizes and compares various features of IDS and IPS.

Feature	IPS	IDS
Positioning	In-line with the network. Every packet goes through it.	Not in-line with the network. Receives the copy of every packet.
Mode	In-line/Tap	Promiscuous
Delay	Introduces delay because every packet is analyzed before forwarded to the destination	Does not introduce delay because it is not in-line with the network.
Point of failure	Yes. If the sensor is down, it may drop as well as well as malicious traffic from entering the network, depending on one of the two modes configured on it, namely fail-open or fail-close	No impact on traffic as IDS is not in-line with the network
Ability to mitigate an attack?	Yes. By dropping the malicious traffic, attacks can be readily reduced on the network. If deployed in TAP mode, then it will receive a copy of each packet but cannot mitigate the attack	IDS cannot directly stop an attack. However, it can assist some in-line device like IPS to drop certain traffic to stop an attack.
Can do packet manipulation?	Yes. Can modify the IP traffic according to a defined set of rules.	No. As IDS receive mirrored traffic, so it can only perform the inspection.

Table 2-03: IDS/IPS Comparison

Router and Switch Security

Router

The router is specifically designed to route traffic and not to serve as a security device, but some of the router's functions facilitate security. There are different hardening techniques that are applicable to the router, such as following:

- Disable unused router interfaces
- Disable unused services such as CDP, FTP, etc.
- Disable management protocols that you are not using such as SNMP etc.
- Disable features that are techniques for re-directing your traffic such as ICMP Redirects & IP Source routing
- Disable features that are techniques for probes and scans in reconnaissance attacks like Finger, ICMP unreachable, ICMP mask reply
- Ensure security of terminal connections such as IP identification service & TCP keep alive
- Disable gratuitous ARP and proxy ARP
- Disable IP-directed broadcasts
- Enable SSH for Access to the Router
- Enable Unicast RPF on Outside Interfaces
- Set Users
- Enable Logging
- Set Enable Secret Password
- Disable IP Source Route
- Enable Password Encryption Service
- Use Secure Protocols

Switches

Switches are OSI layer 2 devices that have more than one ports and high bandwidth. Its function is to bridge traffic in hardware. NAC (Network Access Control) is used to control the security of switches. Following are some basic hardening techniques for switches.

- Change default passwords
- Enable Logging
- Using Secure Protocols
- Configure AAA
- Configuring Management VLAN
- Network Segmentation
- Enabling SSH
- Configuring Management IP addresses
- Configuring Port Security

Proxies

Proxies are the intermediary requests between the client and the servers. Proxy server acts as a gateway between client on a local network and the larger-scale network such as internet. Proxies are used to increase performance and security. Proxy server intercepts the connection between sender and receiver by blocking the direct access between them, all ingress traffic from one port is forwarded via another port.

There are two modes of operation in proxies:

- Explicit Proxy
- Transparent Proxy

Explicit Proxy

The user needs to configure his operating system to use the proxy explicitly to communicate over the network or internet.

Transparent Proxy

No configuration is required to do on the operating system, as the users do not have any idea about the proxy residing in the middle of the network.

Network-Based Proxies

Application Proxy

One of the most common network-based proxy is Network Address Translator (NAT). Application proxies are most commonly used which determine the way application works. Some proxies know only one application. Advanced or modern proxies are multi-purpose proxies, that can use multiple kinds of application.

Forward Proxy

This proxy is enabled inside the network to help the user to protect and control themselves from accessing the internet are known is "Forward Proxy".

Reverse Proxy

This proxy is enabled outside the network and controls the traffic flow that is coming inside the network.

Open Proxy

A proxy that is set up and configured by the third party and can be a significant security concern. This uncontrolled proxy is used to circumvent existing security controls.

Load Balancer

Load Balancer takes the load and distributes it among various resources without the user being informed. The load balancer is able to provide fault tolerance and have very fast convergence.

A load balancer is something that takes the load of traffic and distributes it among multiple resources or servers. This process of distributing load is invisible to the user. A benefit of the load balancer is that it provides fault tolerance.

Scheduling

It is the scheduling algorithm on the basis of which the load balancer determines how to distribute the traffic load among various internal servers. There are many different scheduling algorithms, some of them are discussed below.

Affinity

The affinity is the characteristic of a load balancer, which means that for a particular application or user, the load balancer will use the same server.

Round Robin

Round Robin is the kind of schedule in which every new request is sent over to the next server in a cycle or rotation, and all these requests are forwarded in equal amount despite server load. The modified Round-Robin scheme involves a weight factor that considers servers load and other principles when forwarding the request to the next server in turn.

Active-Passive

In active-passive load balancing scheme, there are two load balancers, one for doing active balancing and another load balancer passively observes the system and functions when the primary load balancer fails.

Active-Active

In the active-active type of load balancing scheme, both the load balancer are active means both of them are sharing the duty of load balancing.

Virtual IP Addresses (VIP or VIPA)

Virtual IP addresses are those IP addresses that are not corresponding to any actual physical network interface card. For example, pool of IP addresses for Network Address Translation (NAT) are not directly associated to any NIC. Similarly, VIPs are used for fault tolerance, fail-over, mobility and redundancy.

These VIP addresses have several variations and implementation scenarios, including Common Address Redundancy Protocol (CARP) and Proxy ARP. In addition, if there are

multiple actual IP addresses, load balancing can be performed as part of NAT. You can use virtual IP and proxy ARP to achieve load balancing across multiple interfaces.

Access Points

SSID

SSID is an acronym for Service Set Identifier that refers to the name associated with the wireless network. The SSID of a wireless network can be determined by performing packet captures, therefore disabling it does not mean that it becomes secure.

MAC filtering

MAC (Media Access Control) filtering is used to limit access to some certain devices on the network. Typically, it is used for keeping neighbours out or to ensure that only the people of a company can connect to the network. The disadvantage of MAC filtering is that it is easy to circumvent.

Signal Strength

Some WAP permits the user to set the level of power to be used by the network. This allows the user to limit the signal strength to the premises of a building and stop the signals from going out of it.

Band Selection

A number of frequencies are there that you can configure on WAPs. Configuring frequencies on the network also depends on the standard type being used for the wireless network. Some access point support 2.4 GHz spectrum and some support 5 GHz spectrum.

Antenna types

Multiple types of antennas are available that can be connected to the WAP. Most common type of antenna that usually comes with most WAP is 'Omnidirectional antenna' which projects signals equally on all sides. Another type of antenna is 'Directional antenna' which is the best to be used for long distance projection. 'Yagi antenna' is the type of directional antenna that provides high gain. 'Parabolic antenna is also a directional antenna type that projects the signals to a single point.

Fat vs. Thin

There are two types of Wireless Access Points (WAP). Thick APs deals with most of the advance wireless tasks and are intelligent for managing, control and restricting the inside and outside communication using advance protocols. Thin APs are not as intelligent as compared to the thick access points having no or minimum capability of configuration.

Controlled based vs. Stand alone

The fat access point is standalone access point whereas thin access point is controlled based access point. The standalone access point has significant skills in terms of encryption, authentication, channel and degree management. Controlled based access point supports centralized management that has multiple benefits like better management of channels, better load balancing, and easy patch deployment.

Wireless Access Points (WAP)

Wireless Access point is a device that allows us to connect to the internet over the air interface. Hotspot is commonly confused with the term wireless access point. Wireless access point covers an area with Wi-Fi signal whereas the area in which one can connect to the internet over the air interface is called a hotspot.

The setup procedure should emphasize security above everything. The essential solution to the wireless access point is encryption.

SIEM (Security Information and Event Management)

Security Information and Event Management (SIEM) is an industry standard term used to monitor and manage networks. SIEM is a combination of two related technologies; Security Event Management (SEM) and Security Information Management (SIM).

SEM deals with the real-time monitoring and notifying the security events such as authentication failures and intrusion events generated by the security systems while SIM is responsible for collecting and managing security-related log data from firewalls, antivirus software, network routers, DNS servers, databases and another origin. Therefore, SIEM is referred to as the System Information and Event Management which strengthens the effect on the whole system, particularly on security.

Some popular SIEM options include:

- ArcSight Express

- McAfee ESM (Enterprise Security Manager)

- IBM Security QRadar

- Splunk Enterprise Software or Virtual Machines

- LogRhythm's appliance, Software and Virtual Machines

Some common features offered by SIEM are:

Logging Device

SIEM is a centralized logging device.

Common Database

Collects data from all the devices and bring it to a single database.

Security Alerts

It can also provide security alerts as the user is getting real-time information.

Storage

The storage of SIEM is long term.

Data Correlation

SIEM also includes additional feature of data correlation.

How SIEM works

SIEM provides reports on security-related events and incidents like failed and successful logins, malicious activities, etc. It sends alerts if analysis shows any that activity runs against predetermined rule sets and thus indicates a potential security issue.

Challenges

One of the most occurring challenge during log collection against all the devices that are connected to a network like switches, workstations, routers, servers, workstations, etc. is *Time Synchronization*.

Every device has its own clock, and if the user wants to synchronize all the devices to a single clock, then a standard protocol is required that is NTP (Network Time Protocol). This allows all the devices to automatically synchronize all these clocks to one single clock. It is a flexible and accurate method.

Log Transfer

A standard method to transfer logs between devices to gather log data from the devices. There is a central receiver, which is often integrated into a SIEM.

An organization that is focused on the security of logs and needs storage method that cannot be changed, uses WORM devices technology which, in short, protect important security logs. *Example*: DVD-R

DLP

DLP is an acronym for Data Loss Prevention. It basically stops the data before the threat actor receives it. The endpoint DLP tool on the computer observes the data and prevents

its unauthorized access. DLP appliance on the network connection looks constantly all the confidential information like credit card number that should not be in the form of clear text. The DLP system that is on the server watches the data and prevents it from getting into the hands of threat actor.

USB blocking

DLP on the workstation can be implemented through preventing data transfer on the workstation and also resist certain tasks to occur on the workstation. In November 2008, the US DoD (Department of Defense) received a worm on the USB device and as a result, the DoD banned removable flash media in order to prevent it from happening again. The DLP agent is the responsible of handling USB blocking.

Cloud-based

Cloud-based DLP is used by many organizations, which is between the users and the internet. Every bit goes through the DLP tool means it watches every bit of network traffic. Everything takes place in the cloud, and no hardware or software is required for this purpose.

Email

A major risk factor is the email system. Therefore, DLP appliance is used by many organizations that monitor, track and filter all the inbound and outbound emails.

Network Access Control (NAC)

NAC is an acronym for Network Access Control. With NAC, the traffic flow from inside or outside the network is controlled. Access control is based on different rules like the type of user, their location, application, etc. One of the advantages of access control is that it can be enabled or disabled easily.

Dissolvable/Permanent

Dissolvable agents are those agents that are deployed upon demand and removed later after use. On the other hand, permanent agents are those that are pre-deployed to the endpoints, and they function as the gateway to the functionality of NAC.

Host health check

A major advantage of NAC solution is the capability of carrying out the definite level of checks (Host health Checks) on the client before they enter a network. Common host health checks involve the verification of the presence of antivirus and the verification of patched application and operating system.

Agent vs. Agentless

In agent-based network access control, the code is kept on the system of host for activation, and it runs at the time of connection. Agentless network access control is integrated with Windows Active Directory. In agentless access control, checks are performed during login & log out, and it cannot be scheduled.

Mail Gateways

Unsolicited email: Unsolicited email or spam email is stopped at the email gateway before it reaches the user. It can be On-site or Cloud-based.

Identification of Spam: Multiple methods are used by the email gateway to identify spam messages some of them are as follows:

Whitelist: This allows email from only trusted users and known locations.

SMTP Standard Checking: This blocks everything that does not match RFC standards.

rDNS: rDNS or Reverse DNS is used to check spam. This only allows emails whose senders' domain matches with its IP address and blocks all other emails whose IP address does not match its sender's domain.

Tarpitting: This slows down the server conversation that the threat actor does not like and give up.

Recipient Filtering: This block emails that are not from a valid recipient's email address.

Bridges

A bridge may also be referred to as network segregation device, and it works at OSI layer 2. It joins two separate network sectors and support communication between them.

SSL/TLS accelerator

When there are hundreds of servers, the SSL accelerator is used to maintain encryption and security of data moving across the network, and it also improves the efficiency of the application.

SSL decryption

SLL decryption is also a common security technique used between the third-party site and the browser. Its purpose is to decrypt the information in order to check for anything malicious and then again re-encrypt it to forward it on its path.

Media gateway

The use of media gateway has also become common in organizations. Media gateway connects from PSTN and converts that to VOIP, in order to be used internally with VOIP telephones.

Hardware Security Module

A hardware security module implementation is necessary for managing a large group of servers and certificates. It is a high-end hardware piece that performs cryptographic functions. A place where the keys can also be backed up and secured.

Security Software

Security tools are of two different types that are Passive Security tools and active Security tools.

Protocol Analyzer

- To capture packets.
- To solve complex application issues.
- Allow the user to view traffic pattern.

Network Scanner

- To determine what services are being used or running on remote devices. Like FTP services, Web services, etc.
- To determine what operating system might be running.
- Can visually graph all the identified devices.
- Detect rogue system.
- *Example*: N-map, Zen-map, and angry IP scanner.

Password Cracker

In most of the applications and operating systems, the passwords are stored as hashes because it is a 'one-way function.' Some old OS or applications that are poorly developed, store the hashes in a straightforward way which makes easy for the attackers to brute force weak hashes and gain access to the password. Password cracker is, therefore used to find weak passwords.

Vulnerability Scanner

Staying up to date with recent security patches is essential before the threat actor takes any advantage of vulnerabilities in a system. Vulnerability scanner helps you in finding vulnerabilities in a system. There are many vulnerability scanners available like Nikto, Tenable Nessus, etc.   Configuration Compliance Scanner

To see if the system meets the minimum security configuration requirement, there is scanner available called configuration compliance scanner. It gives you a detailed report about all of the system's configurations.

Exploitation Framework

For gaining access to the system, the threat actor uses every possible tool. The threat actor looks for vulnerabilities in the browser, OS, applications, etc. and take advantage of it by writing an exploit. For this purpose, the threat actors use 'exploitation framework' instead of writing exploits every time from scratch. Example of some common frameworks includes BeEF and RouterSploit.

Data Sanitization Tools

Data Sanitization primarily focuses on sanitizing the data i.e. securely discarding the data of hard drives or other storage media to avoid recovery. In the process of sanitization, the data is simply overwritten irreversibly. Overwriting the data once makes it unavailable forever but overwriting it multiple times can make the data unrecoverable.

Steganography Tools

Using steganography, the data can be stored in plain sight but still hidden.

Honeypot

A honeypot is a system that is set for the threat actors for the purpose of attracting and trapping them. A honeypot is usually a virtual organization structure, that looks exactly like a real organization.

Backup Utilities

Backup utilities helps you through the unexpected disruption in the system like the failure of system, when it gets infected and also at the time of data loss. At Such crucial times, the backed up utilities become lifesavers. Banner Grabbing

A technique used for the collection of information from services that advertise information using banner is called Banner grabbing. It can be used for the identification of service by version, type, etc.

Passive vs. Active

The interaction of *active tools* in a system can be detected like network scanning through Nmap (an active tools). Whereas the interaction of passive tools with a system cannot be detected. An example of the passive tool is Tripwire (identify a modification to a file on the basis of hash value).

Wireless Scanner and Cracker

A unique security tool. These tools can do following:

- Wireless Monitoring
- Wireless attack
- Cracking

Command Line Security Tools

Ping:

- Command to test if another device is available on the network.
- Used to calculate round trip time between the user device and another device on the internet.
- It uses ICMP (Internet Control messaging protocol).
- Ping is also sometimes used for troubleshooting or security.

Netstat:

- It is abbreviated as Network Statistics.
- netstat –a: Shows all active connections.
- netstat –b: Show binaries.
- netstat –n: Do not resolve names.

Traceroute:

- Determines the route to destination a packet takes.
- Uses function of ICMP to traceroute.
- In Windows, the command used to traceroute is "tracert" whereas in Linux the command used is "traceroute."

Nslookup:

- Lookup information from DNS servers like IP addresses, Cache times, canonical names, etc.

Dig:

- It stands for Domain Information Grouper.
- More advanced domain information.

Address Resolution Protocol (ARP):

- Determine MAC address based on IP address.
- arp –a: View local ARP table.

ARP is a stateless protocol that is used within a broadcast domain to ensure the communication by resolving the IP address to MAC address mapping. It is in charge of L3 to L2 address mappings. ARP protocol ensures the binding of IP addresses and MAC addresses. By broadcasting the ARP request with IP address, the switch can learn the associated MAC address information from the reply of the specific host. In case of an untraceable map, or if the map is unknown, the source will send a broadcast to all nodes. Node with matching IP address responds with its MAC address. The switch will learn the MAC address and associated port information into its fixed length CAM table.

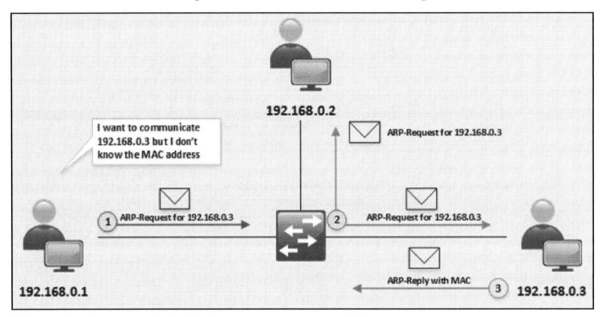

Figure 2-07: ARP Operation

As shown in the figure, the source generates the ARP query by broadcasting the ARP packet. A node having the MAC address, the query is destined for, will reply only to the packet. The frame is flooded with all ports (other than the port on which the frame was received), if CAM table entries are full. This also happens when the destination MAC address in the frame is the broadcast address. MAC flooding technique is used to turn a switch into a hub in which switch starts broadcasting each and every packet. In this scenario, each user may catch an unwanted packet along with the wanted ones.

Ipconfig:

Determines TCP/IP and network adapter information and some additional IP details. In Windows, the command used is "ipconfig" whereas, in Linux and Mac, the command used is "ifconfig."

Tcpdump:

Captures packets from the command line.

Nmap:

Nmap, in a nutshell, offers Host discovery, Port discovery, Service discovery. Operating system version information. Hardware (MAC) address information, Service version detection, Vulnerability & exploit detection using Nmap scripts (NSE).

Using Windows or Linux command prompt, enter the following command: nmap –sP –v <target IP address>

Upon successful response from the targeted host, if the command successfully finds a live host, it returns a message indicating that the IP address of the targeted host is up along with the media access control (MAC) address and the network card vendor.

Apart from ICMP Echo Request packets and using ping sweep, nmap also offers a quick scan. Enter the following command for quick scan: -

> nmap –sP –PE –PA<port numbers> <starting IP/ending IP>

For example:

> **nmap** –sP –PE –PA 21,23,80,3389 <192.168.0.1-50>

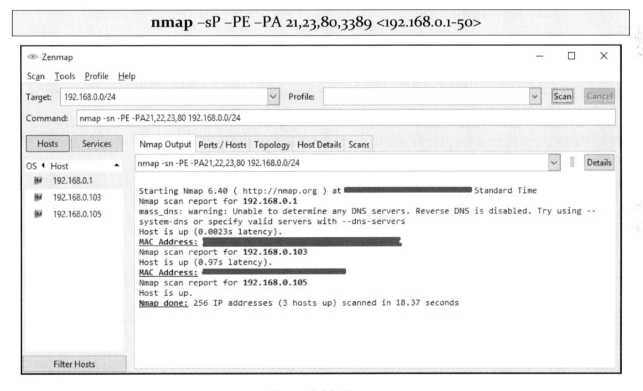

Figure 2-08: Nmap

Netcat:

- Used to read or write information to or from the network (open a port and send or receive some traffic).

Multiple functions

- Listens to a port number.
- Scans ports and sends data to the port.
- Transfers data.

Common Security Issues

Unencrypted Credentials

All data must be encrypted in order to have the best security when the internet is accessed with unencrypted credentials, it is not authenticated over the internet world, and clear texts and passwords can easily be violated in this way. Some applications and protocols send information in clear text from which we need to protect the network.

Logs and Events Anomalies

The attacker can also gather as much information as possible about what is happening within the network and unfortunately, many different resources are there to provide such anomalies of your confidential data, like firewalls, intrusion detection system, switches, routers, IPS, servers, etc. Every network should use information and event management systems, so it can examine the analysis and logs of the activities taking place inside the network.

Permission Issues

Another most common mistake over the internet is observed to be the permission issue; it happens when a file is shared over the internet, and it is not protected with the righteous permissions and anyone can access that file and use it in a way it is not supported. Therefore, permission and permission logs should be audited actively for such behavior in order to keep the network secure.

Access Violations

An access violation occurs when an application or an applicant tries to access the part of memory or information which is restricted. Operating systems also provide checks and logs about restricted data so that no one can access the network more than it is allowed to. Otherwise, some major steps are taken like the denial of service and blocking the applicant in order to protect the network.

Certificate Issues

Another most important credential in the security world is Trust. Some sort of certificates should be signed by someone whom you and your computer trust to eliminate the possibility of violation inside the network. These certificates should also be taken care of the time duration like performance check, so that validity of the certificate is authenticated.

Data Exfiltration

It is the process when data from a network is taken in an unauthorized way and used against the law. It is something of a security threat when someone can easily copy or retrieve data from inside of a network and take it outside as their own.

Misconfigured Devices

A threat is associated with configurations, while the devices on the network are configured. It happens when installation is set to default while configuring the device and no proper secure access is allotted to the device. It is always good to set up active usernames and passwords for devices. Outdated software can also be a reason for such threat.

Firewall

Some devices are also likely to provide vulnerability to the network. Firewalls can be questionable when it comes to having monitored the complete traffic for a very large network. It becomes difficult to perform rules and regulations, to allow or block traffic for accessing the networks.

Content Filter:

Content across the network needs to be protected. Everything that is used to access the network is vulnerable like the URLs provided and some protocols. These things may become vulnerable to the network.

Access Points:

Access points are used to access the network, so it is obvious for the network to authenticate the access points with proper encrypted credentials so that no configurations can be violated easily.

Weak Security Configurations

The security configuration becomes weaker by the time, For example, the security mechanism your network is using today may not be used in the next 20 years, so the upgrades are mandatory. Weak security configurations are found vulnerable as for

example, a security key of small key size was secure 40 years ago, but today it is not. The chances of threat and vulnerability with weak configurations increase with wireless networks.

Personnel Issues

Personnel issues are related to people or human beings that are most likely to make mistakes. They can be of two types, intentional or by mistake, but both are harmful to the network.

Policy Violation

Proper policies or security documentation should be taken care of in order to survive in network world.

Insider Threat

It is guaranteed that someone inside the network can destroy the network more easily than anyone outside the network. The security related to rights and access permission must be granted correctly in order to secure the network.

Social Engineering

Social Engineering can destroy tiny network like cakewalking. Even if you are doing your job by making your network socially active, it is so much easier for anyone to steal and copy your data, if they have enough information about your network.

Social media

Social media is indeed a blessing, but when it comes to security, it easily applies some question to the system. Valuable information must be kept secure from the public sphere as much as possible. Every company should have some secure boundaries for the marketing strategies they follow.

Personal Email

Personal emails are more of a security threat nowadays, as the organization that provides email access to their employees are, in a way, giving them access to the resources of the company. The resources can also be used against the company itself, or anyone can attach information that is vulnerable to the organization and can share it anywhere he/she wants.

Unauthorized software:

Unauthorized softwares are most likely to put your network in danger. Almost every organization blocks individual access to download any software on the internet. There might be a malicious software hiding with the download package with a legitimate

software. Licensed and trusted softwares are appreciated for the security of the network. Software updates and upgrades should also be kept active. Trusted softwares also have their hash value with are the proof of their integrity. User can calculate and compare the hash value to detect modification in the package.

Baseline Deviation:

While the installation and configuration of the network is taking place, evidence and proper documentation must be maintained in order to verify the security of the network. Technical evidence has much worth in dealing with the network. Proper alerts and activity logs must be configured for the access, and there must be strong verification for the applications that give remote access to the network.

License Compliance Violation

The license is always required for the authorized access to the network, every system has a unique format for that license, Varies by categories like software and hardware. The documentation of license agreement should also be properly maintained.

Availability: Availability of data is authorized according to the license. When the license is renewed or valid, all data is available but when the expiry date arrives some sort of data access can be denied.

Integrity: A bad license can also be vulnerable to the network. The accuracy of the license agreement should be properly maintained.

Asset Management

Data is asset and asset needs management. When it comes to network, it needs to be managed properly for the sake of security. There must be a complete tracking data of computing assets. The proper and timely response should be given to the vulnerabilities. Keep a good eye on everything that's going on in your network.

Authentication Issues

Authentication issues are most likely to happen to the network. For taking care of these factors, the solution is to gather as many facts and figures you can provide to make sure the person trying to access is authorized or not. Fingerprint, access codes, and other ways are the solution to this problem. Authentication failed alerts must also be active on the network.

Analysing Security Output

Host-based IDS/IPS

- IDS and IPS are the soft wares that we run on our operating system these days.

- These soft-wares were separate applications, but now they are integrated into many endpoint products like antiviruses or anti-malware.
- It is often called endpoint security agent.
- Protect our system based on signatures.
- Look for specific kind of traffic pattern, and if it sees those patterns, it is able to allow or block traffic.
- It protects based on activity.

Host-based IPS/IDS is normally deployed for the protection of specific host machine, and it works closely with the Operating System Kernel of the host machine. It creates a filtering layer and filters out any malicious application call to the OS.

There are four major types of Host-based IDS/IPS:

- **File System Monitoring:** In this configuration, IDS/IPS works by closely comparing the versions of files within some directory with the previous versions of same file and checks for any unauthorized tampering and changing within a file. Hashing algorithms are often used to verify the integrity of files and directories which gives an indication of possible changes which are not supposed to be there.

- **Log Files Analysis:** In this configuration, IDS/IPS works by analyzing the log files of the host machine and generates warning for system administrators who are responsible for machine security. Several tools and applications are available which works by analyzing the patterns of behavior and further correlate it with actual events.

- **Connection Analysis:** IDS/IPS works by monitoring the overall network connections being made with the secure machine and tries to figure out which of them are legitimate and how many of them are unauthorized. Examples of techniques used are open ports scanning, half open and rogue TCP connections and so forth.

- **Kernel Level Detection:** In this configuration, the kernel of OS itself detects the changing within the system binaries, and an anomaly in system calls to detect the intrusion attempts on that machine.

Anti-Virus:

- A kind of log that commonly scans in the operating system.
- The software is running on our operating system and looking for viruses to be downloaded or executed in our system.
- It alerts when identifies malicious activities and stops downloading or executing the software and prevent the user to visit known bad URL.

File Integrity Check:

- If the malware has modified any file or any part of the operating system, it is identified and repair by this file integrity check.
- In Windows, this software is called SFC.

Host-based Firewall:

- It prevents someone from accessing the user's computer from the outside or prevent the application running on the computer from accessing the exterior network.
- The restriction is based on application and port numbers.
- The firewall includes centralized logs to allow the user to see exactly what traffic is allowed or blocked.

Advance Malware Tool:

- Specifically designed to identify malware and remove it.
- When malware infects the system, it captures the system from its core and consequently spreads into all parts of the operating system and become difficult to remove.

The best recovery is to delete everything and restore the operating system from good backup.

Securing Mobile Devices

Mobile Device connection methods

The following are some ways that one can use to connect portable technology:

Cellular Network

- Through this, our cell phones are able to communicate over a wide network that is separated into sectors called cells.
- There is an antenna in mobile phones can communicate to the antenna that may be in the local areas.
- There are various security concerns with this, i.e., Traffic monitoring, Location tracking, Wide access to mobile devices.

Wi-Fi

- Another common way to connect devices is through Wi-Fi.
- This is 802.11 wireless network.
- We have to make sure that every data that is being sent or received is encrypted.

- If the data is not encrypted, then a man in the middle and denial of service attack risk will increase.

Standard	Frequency	Modulation	Speed
802.11a	5 GHz	OFDM	54 Mbps
802.11b	2.4 GHz	DSSs	11 Mbps
802.11g	2.4 GHz	OFDM , DSSS	54 Mbps
802.11n	2.4 . 5 GHz	OFDM	54 Mbps
802.16 (WiMAX)	10 - 66 GHz	OFDM	70-1000 Mbps
Bluetooth	2.4 GHz		1 – 3 Mbps

Table 2-04: Wireless network speed comparison

Satellite Communication (SATCOM)

- This is perfect for a place where there is no wireless or cellular network (remote areas).
- There are many technologies that use satellite communication. Some connect to a satellite in lower earth orbit or some to the geostationary satellite.
- As it uses digital communication, therefore both the voice and data can be sent over it.
- SATCOM has many security concerns to the mobile device like remote code execution, operating system vulnerabilities, etc.
- It is suggested to keep all the soft-wares on the device to be updated.

Near Field Communication (NFC)

- It is commonly used when the communication is between the mobile device and a device that is nearby.
- Commonly used in the payment system.
- Also used to help with other wireless technologies like, it is used to help the pairing process for Bluetooth, also used as identity system where one can identify their selves using the phone.

Some of the security concerns with NFC are as follows:

- It is a wireless network (although short range), but someone with an antenna can capture and listen to the conversation.
- Someone could jam the frequency and attack through denial of service.
- There is also a concern about replay attack.
- If NFC device is lost, it could be a major security issue because the person who stole the device will be able to use that NFC instead of the legitimate user.

ANT/ANT+

- A relatively new type of mobile device network communication is ANT/ANT+.
- It is a wireless sensor network protocol.
- It uses 2.4 GHz ISM band.
- Use mostly in IOT (Internet of Things) like Fitness device, heart rate monitors, etc.
- It is not 802.11, not Bluetooth; it is a separate wireless service.
- Specifically designed for low power devices.
- Some of the security concerns are as follows:
- Denial of service (Spectrum Jamming).
- Encryption is optional. Therefore, it is possible for someone to gain access or capture the data and see information inside of that data stream.

IR (Infrared)

- In modern times, it is used in phones, tablets, smart-watches to be able to control IR devices.
- It could also be used for file transfer.

USB (Universal Serial Bus)

- Most common mobile device connection.
- It uses the physical wired connection.
- It is more secure than wireless protocol.

Mobile Device Management:

- Centralized management of the mobile devices.
- Set policies on application, data, camera, etc.
- Manage access control like force screen locks, PINs on a single user device.

Content Management

- In content management, the security administrator has to make sure that only the legitimate user has access to the data but no unauthorized user is gaining access to this data.
- Data could be in the cloud or on the on-site server.
- Many mobile devices include DLP (Data Loss Prevention) option, which prevents someone from copying data from inside server and passing it into the information that might be going outside the organization.
- Make sure that the data is encrypted.
- DLP function can be managed by Mobile Device Manager, and policies can be set for every user.

Application Management

Application management is a challenge. Not all applications are secure and some are malicious, which is a rapidly growing security concern is.

Whitelist Application Management: The organization generates a list of applications added to the whitelist through which the user can only be able to install the applications recorded or – we can say - approved in the whitelist. A management challenge is to constantly check and update the whitelist.

Geolocation

- On the basis of GPS or signals triangulation or other techniques, geo-locate the device.
- In case a mobile device is lost, you can easily track where it is.
- However, this can also be used for a bad purpose like someone could know exactly where you are or be able to track. where you happen to be, based on the location of the mobile device.
- Mobile device allows you to enable or disable this feature.
- It is usually managed through Mobile Device Manager.

Remote Wipe

- Remote wipe is the security requirement of the security administrator. It removes all the data from the mobile device often managed by Mobile Device Management.
- It secures the data from unauthorized access if the device is lost, so it is important to have a backup of some private data.
- Needs to be configured ahead of time.

Figure 2-09: Remote wiping

Screen Lock

- An important security feature of any mobile device is to have that device lock its access.
- Allows access to the device if the passcode or password is known.
- The password can either be Numeric or Alphanumeric. This is an option that you can set through the mobile device manager and set it as requirement to access any data in the device.
- You can also decide what to do with the device on which password is entered wrong too many times.
- You get to choose what that lockout policy might be. Like;

Erase the data on the device.

- Slow down the process to prevent brute force attack.

Biometrics

- A very popular way to set security control on the mobile device.
- The user can use face or fingerprint to gain access, but this is not the most secure option.
- It is much more secure to use password or passcode rather than biometric security.
- It is turned on and off through MDM (Mobile Device Management).

Context-Aware Authentication

Context-aware authentication is a little beyond two-factor authentication. There, the user can check another type of access to the device that can help to determine if the device is in the hands of the right person. This certainly may not qualify to be the only type of authentication, but it could be another security check.

The decisions are made upon following factors:

- Where the user normally logs in.
- Where the user normally frequent (GPS).
- Another device that may be paired (Bluetooth).

Containerization

- Containerization is implemented where it is difficult for the user to maintain both personal and business data.
- Security management is difficult for someone who uses a mobile phone for corporate use at work and after work; it is used as a personal phone.
- Containerization helps to separate organization's data and application from user's personal data and application.

- It creates a virtual container for company data that can also help to wipe all the organization's data, if someone leaves the organization instead of wiping all the mobile device data, keeping personal data secure.

Full Device Encryption

- Full device encryption is a popular method used by people these days.
- No one could gain access to the encrypted data, in case the device is lost.
- It is handled in different ways by different devices and different operating systems. *For example:* In Android, the encryption is configured from strong to strongest level to the mobile device.
- It is therefore suggested and advised not to forget the passcode, keep a backup of all the data and passcode because if the passcode is lost, the user will not be able to gain access to the mobile data.

Mobile Device Deployment Models:

BYOD

- BYOD stands for Bring Your Own Device or Bring Your Own Technology.
- One of the most common ways for Mobile Device Deployment.
- Employees own the device and bringing their own personal phone into the workplace and using them for corporate use and personal use simultaneously.
- The device needs to meet the requirement of the company.

The challenge with respect to the security is that it is difficult to manage these devices because it contains both corporative and personal information/data.

The basic purpose of implementing mobile device management (MDM) is deployment, maintenance, and monitoring of mobile devices that make up BYOD solution. Devices may include the laptops, smartphones, tablets, notebooks or any other electronic device that can be moved outside the corporate office to home or some public place and then gets connected to corporate office by some means.

Some of the functions provided by MDM are:

- Enforcing a device to be locked after certain login failure attempts.
- Enforcement of strong password policy for all BYOD devices.
- MDM can detect any attempt at hacking BYOD devices and then limit the network access of these affected devices.
- Enforcing confidentiality by using encryption as per organization's policy.
- Administration and implementation of *Data Loss Prevention (DLP)* for BYOD devices. It helps to prevent any kind of data loss due to end user's carelessness.

COPE

- It stands for Corporate Own, Personally Enabled.
- The device is purchased by the company, and it is used as both the personal and corporate use.
- The organization keeps control of the device usually through a centralized mobile device, and it is managed in a similar way as the company manages laptop and desktop computer.
- Everything stored is under the preview of the company.

Centralized Owned Model

- In the corporate-owned model, the device is purchased and owned by the company and also controlled by the company.
- It is not for personal use at all.
- It is used where security is most important, as they do not want the personal data to be mixed with company's data or information.

VDI/VMI

- It is the most popular mobile deployment model.
- It stands for Virtual Desktop Infrastructure/Virtual Mobile Infrastructure.
- Applications are separated from the mobile devices that the employees use.
- Data and applications are running on the remote server, and the employees are simply using their mobile device as a window into that application.
- Data is securely stored in the centralized area and not on the mobile device.
- No data will be lost if the device is lost.
- The application is written once for the VMI platform, and everyone can access through that platform.
- The application is managed centrally and no need to update all device.

Secure Protocols

SRTP

- It stands for Secure Real-Time Transport Protocol (Secure RTP).
- It is the secure version of RTP.
- It is the secure version of RTP that is seen with other VOIP, but it adds encryption, using AES to make sure that all the videos and audios are confidential.
- It includes 'authentication integrity' and 'replay protection' by including HMAC-SHA1 (Hash-based message authentication code using SHA1) as a hashing function.

- With this in place, the user knows that he is receiving the original audio and video and there is nobody sitting in the middle of the path listening to the conversation.

NTP

NTP is Network Time Protocol used in a network to synchronize the clocks across the hosts and network devices. The NTP is an important protocol, as directory services, network devices and host rely on clock settings for login purposes and logging to keep a record of events. NTP helps in correlating events by the time system logs are received by Syslog servers. NTP uses UDP port number 123, and its whole communication is according to coordinated universal time (UTC).

NTP uses a term known as *stratum* to describe the distance between NTP server and device. It is just like TTL number that decreases every hop a packet passes by. Stratum value, starting from one, increases by every hop. For example, if we see stratum number 10 on local router, it means that NTP server is nine hops away. Securing NTP is also an important aspect as the attacker may change time at first place to mislead the forensic teams who investigate and correlate the events to find the root cause of the attack.

- It is used to synchronize all the devices that are connected to the network.

- It is around since 1985but do not have any security feature, and it is seen that the threat actor has found a way to use it in denial of service attack.

- NTPsec is a new protocol that is created to make NTP more secure.

- This more secure version of NTP protocol started around June 2015.

- In NTPsec, the code base of NTP is updated, and all the vulnerabilities are patched.

S/MIME

- Secure/Multipurpose Internet mail Extension.

- This protocol allows the user to digitally sign and encrypt the information that is being used.

- It has to be initially configured as the PKI is required or at least a way to manage key so that the user will be able to provide public and private key to be used in S/MIME communication.

SSL/TLS

- SSL stands for Secure Socket Layer, and TLS stands for Transport Layer Security.

- TLS is an updated version of SSL.

- SSL uses a combination of Symmetric and Asymmetric encryption to provide confidentiality.

FTPS

- It stands for File Transfer Protocol Secure, i.e., FTP over SSL.

- This is not SFTP (SSH FTP), where SSH is used instead of SSL.

LDAP

- It stands for Lightweight Directory Access Protocol.

- Protocol for reading and writing directories over an IP network.

- It uses an ITU standard that is X.500 and uses TCP/IP.

- By enabling LDAPS, it can be made more secure.

- Another way is to implement SASL (Simple Authentication and Security Layer).

SSH

- It stands for Secure Shell.

- This is an encrypted terminal communication.

DHCP

- It stands for Dynamic Host Control Protocol.

- It does not include any built-in security.

- There is no secure version of DHCP.

Practice Question

1. Software-based Firewalls installed usually on the endpoints are known as?
2. When a firewall does not find a match in the list, the traffic is dropped. This is known as?
3. For blocking the suspicious traffic, what is location of NIPS deployment in a network?
4. Type of antenna which radiates equally in all direction is called?
5. Which type of antenna is best for long distance communication?
6. Which of the following is not a SIEM option?

   A. Micro Focus ArcSight

   B. McAfee ESM (Enterprise Security Manager)

   C. IBM Security QRadar

   D. Splunk Enterprise Security

   E. Nessus

7. For encryption keys, the temper protection can be provided by which of the following device?

   A. HSM

   B. DLP

   C. NIDS/NIPS

   D. NAC

8. ANT is correctly described by which of the following?

   A. It is similar to Bluetooth enhanced mode.

   B. It operates in the 5-GHz spectrum.

   C. It encrypts HTTP traffic.

   D. It functions well in the crowded 2.4-GHz spectrum.

Chapter 03: Architecture and Design

Frameworks and Configuration Guide

Industry Standard Frameworks and Reference Architecture

Industry standard framework and reference architecture can be referred to as conceptual model that describes the operation and structure of the IT system in any organization.

Regulatory

The business processes and procedures that are compliance related are known as Regulatory bodies. There are some rules and regulations that are required to be followed for performing specific functions. For example, public companies deal with a lot of Sarbanes Oxley (SOX) regulation.

Non-Regulatory

Some processes in an organization are not compliance concern which means that there is no rule of law required to perform a particular function. Example: NIOSH (National Institute for Occupational Safety and Health) is a non-regulatory body.

National vs International

There are a lot of national and international frameworks that provide proper instructions and practices for information security. Example: FISMA (Federal Information Security Management Act) is the United States' law developed for the protection of government data and resources against dreadful threats.

Industry-specific Framework

The industry-specific framework has been formed by bodies within a specific industry for addressing regulatory requirements or because of industry-specific risks or concerns. Examples of Industry Specific Framework are HITRUST Common Security Framework (CSF) and COBIT (Control Objectives for Information and Related Technologies).

Benchmarks/Secure Configuration Guides

When the operating systems, database servers, web servers, or other technologies are installed, they are far away from the secure configuration. Systems with default configuration, are not secure. Some guidelines are needed to keep everything safe and secure.

Platform-specific Guide

The platform-specific guide is the finest guide that comes from the manufacturer. This guide includes all the essential principles regarding installation, configuration and sometimes operations as well.

Web Server

Web servers provide a link between clients and web pages. They are susceptible to attacks as they are open to the internet. Therefore, proper setting of external facing applications is the key to avoid unnecessary risk. For web servers, several reliable and prescriptive sources of instruction are available to support administrators to properly protect and secure the application.

Operating System

Operating system serves as the interface between the physical hardware and the application. Configuration guide, from all the significant operating systems' manufacturers, is available on CIS platform.

Application Server

Application server resides between the back-end database and the web server. It is sometimes called as Middleware. A proper configuration guide for application servers is available at CIS and STIGs.

Network Infrastructure Device

Routers, switches, firewalls, concentrators and all the devices that are essential for the network to work properly, are called network infrastructure devices. It is challenging but necessary to configure these devices properly because any failure can negatively influence the security of the data being handled.

General Purpose Guide

CIS controls is a first-rate general purpose guide that comprises of 20 common security control sets. The framework maintained by the Center for Internet Security can be found on this link: https://www.cisecurity.org/controls/

Defense in depth/ Layered Security

IT security strategy for any organization that involves multiple security technologies and devices are commonly referred to as Defense in depth. Defense in depth is an assortment of multiple devices and security technologies in order to strengthen security.

Vendor Diversity

When you have multiple suppliers, it creates vendor diversity and reduces the risk from a particular supplier. Relying on a single vendor increases risk factor. For example, if you have two firewalls from two different vendors it reduces risk and adds diversity because you can turn to the other firewall in case something happens to one firewall or if the firewall contains flaws.

Control Diversity

Control diversity is also important because it provides layered security that helps in generating the desired result.

Administrative Control

Administrative control is by all means necessary. Administrative control includes all the policies and procedures that are required to be followed by everyone in order to maintain security.

Technical Control

Technical control is also essential to ensure that the hardware and software we use are hardened or not. The active directory authentication, firewall, and disk encryption are all parts of technical control.

User Training

Users are fundamental elements in the security defense of an organization. Users also serve as a significant reason behind vulnerabilities, therefore, it is necessary to have strong security defense that can be achieved by enforcing user training program for guiding the users to recognize between safe and unsafe computing behavior.

Secure Network Architecture Concept

The overall IT system's security is maintained through Secure Network Topology. The following are some network topologies that are commonly implemented to secure network.

Zone / Topology

DMZ

DMZ stands for Demilitarized Zone. It is the region between trusted internal network and untrusted network.

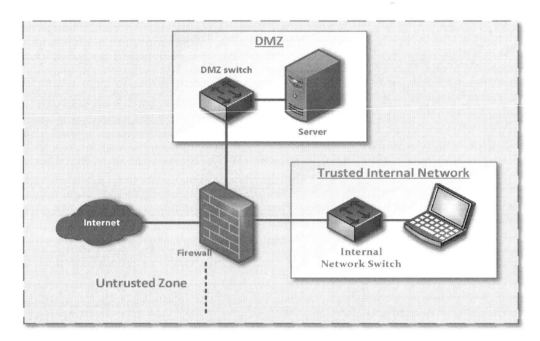

Figure 3-01: DMZ (Demilitarized Zone)

It functions as a buffer region between the internet and the internal network. The idea is to secure internal network and not to allow direct access from the internet to the trusted internal network, by directly forcing the user to make at least one hop in the DMZ before accessing internal network information.

The servers which are directly accessed from the outside (untrusted zone) should be placed in DMZ like Remote access server, Web server, External email server, etc. Similarly, all the other standard servers like a Database server, DNS, File server, Print server, application server etc. should be placed in the internal network for security purpose.

Extranet

There are some trusted third parties to whom we want to lend access to the resources inside the internal network. A *private DMZ*, that is called 'Extranet', is created to lend access to trusted third parties.

The extranet is separate from the internal network and provides access to the outside of the company. The authentication credentials are required from the user in order to gain access to the resources. This additional authentication helps to allow only authorized user to access the resources.

Intranet

A private network that is only accessible from within the network and not outside it.. In an intranet, the important resources or important internal documents are placed, and the access is given only to the organizational users (employees of the company) and no other users are allowed/permitted to gain access to those resources.

Ad Hoc

Using Ad hoc wireless networking, devices can connect directly without an access point. It is commonly used in mobile devices with the application (like Contact sharing application, AirDrop) for file transfer.

As people are connecting directly with each other, therefore it is difficult to manage. Ad Hoc functionality can be allowed or disallowed using Mobile Device Manager, or some types of parameters can also be set through the Mobile Device Manager for the usage of Ad Hoc. For instance, one can set authentication credentials to log in to the use of Ad Hoc functionality or may limit application use of Ad Hoc.

Honeynets

A honeynet is a virtual system which is basically designed to attract threat actors or attackers and trap them. It is a group or collection of honeypots designed to look like a real corporate network which, in reality, is fake.

NAT (Network Address Translation)

It has been calculated that over 20 billion devices want to get internet access, but IPv4 can only uphold 4.2 billion IP addresses. The complication grows about how to allocate 4.2 billion IP addresses to almost 20 billion devices. Network Address Translation is the technique through which we can make 20 billion devices to communicate. When the traffic is passing through the network, it simply maps one IP address onto another. Private IP addresses are translated into Public IP addresses when accessing the internet.

NAT is not a reliable source for protection. Mostly, the threat actors know how to get around NAT, in case if there are no other security parameters set to protect network. For maintaining security, NAT is generally associated with Stateful firewall, and this firewall ensures protection over NAT.

Segmentation of a Network

Reasons for segmentation are as follows:

Security: User should not communicate directly to the database server.

Performance: High bandwidth application.

<u>Compliance</u>: Mandated segmentation (PCI compliance).

Physical Segmentation

In physical segmentation, the devices are physically divided.

Logical Segmentation

In logical segmentation, the devices are logically divided into different segments such as configuring VLANs.

VPN Technologies

VPN abbreviates as Virtual Private Network. There are many diverse paths to connect VPN together.

- Site-to-Site VPN

In site to site VPN, the traffic is encrypted between sites.

- Host to Site VPN

It is a type of VPN that is remotely accessible, and it requires software on the user device.

- Host to Host VPN

In host to host VPN, there is user-to-user encryption. It is software based, and no hardware is demanded.

Security Technology Placement

Sensors and Collectors

The critical spots in a network contain sensors and collectors. These sensors and collectors gather information from the network devices. These may be integrated into the router, firewall, and switches, etc. or might be built-in within the network.

The information that the sensor gathers, varies from system to system. For instance, authentication logs information is going to be different from database transaction logs or web server access logs etc.

Difference between Sensor and Collector

When the raw data is provided by the sensor, the collector converts this raw data into logical information or the information that makes sense.

Filters and Firewalls

Firewalls and filters (packet filter) are used in the network for blocking or allowing a certain type of traffic, flowing through the network. Packet filter simply filters traffic on the basis of port information and addresses of the packets against the set of rules (different for different direction) and does not track any network state.

State-based filtering is an advanced filtering method of the firewall. It is same as packet filtering but the difference it maintains "state table" in the memory. Firewall filters traffic on the basis of IP addresses, Port numbers, Applications, etc. Firewall is usually placed at the ingress and egress point of the network, but sometimes it is placed inside the network.

Proxy Server

Proxy servers are the intermediate point between users and the services accessed by them. This process explains the traffic flow between devices:

1. The request is made to the target server by the client.
2. Proxy server request the target server on behalf of client.
3. The service then responds to the proxy server.
4. The proxy server then sends the response to the request initiator after examining the response.

Useful features like URL filtering, Access control, content filtering, etc. can also be defined in the proxy for the purpose of security control.

SSL (Secure Socket Layer) Accelerator

It needs to be placed between the client and the web server. Its work is to provide secure delivery of web application using SSL/TLS encryption and decryption and decrease the web server's load. The traffic between client and web server is authenticated and protected through SSL Accelerators.

Load Balancer

The load balancer distributes the load among different servers. A load balancer must be placed in a traffic pathway between a server and a requestor. The basic purpose of traffic pathway is to manage the workload on various systems by distributing traffic. The following diagram will help you to understand the function of Load Balancer.

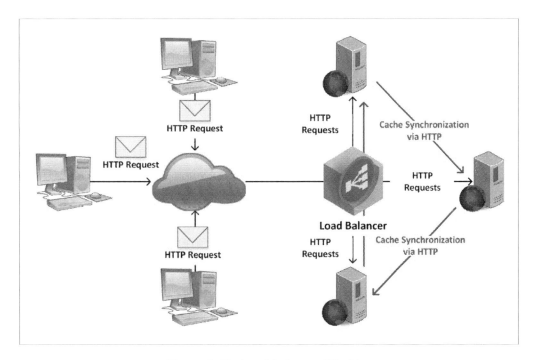

Figure 3-02: Load Balancer Working

DDoS Mitigator

The DDoS mitigators shield against unwanted DDoS packets. It must be located outside the area it is protecting. As it is protecting the DDoS attacks, so it must be placed before other devices that are at the very edge of the network.

TAP & Port Mirror

TAP stands for Test Access Point. It is a mechanism of passive splitting. It is located between the network and the device of interest.

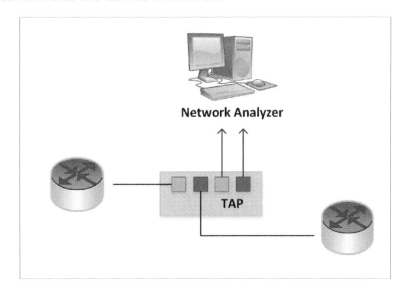

Figure 3-03: TAP

Port mirror is also known as SPAN which stands for Switch Port Analyzer. Typically, a switch is configured with Source and destination SPAN ports. Activities running on source SPAN ports are duplicated on destination SPAN port. Monitoring Station attached through destination SPAN port can view the traffic passing through source ports.

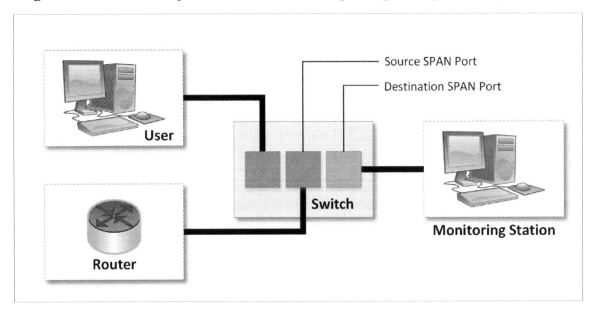

Figure 3-04: SPAN

TAP	SPAN
Test Access Point	Switches Port Analyzer
Cannot monitor intra-switch traffic; costly.	Cannot handle full duplex links without dropping packets. Filters out physical layer errors.
Eliminates the risk of dropped packet, all packets are received by monitoring device including physical error. Provides full visibility in full duplex network.	SPAN is a low cost monitoring solution operating on datalink layer capable of capturing intra-switch traffic. Remote-SPAN can also be configure to send duplicate traffic to remote monitoring station.

Table 3-01: Difference between TAP and SPAN

Introduction to Security System Design

Hardware / Firmware Security

Full Disk Encryption (FDE)

Everything on the storage drive is encrypted through full disk encryption. Full disk encryption protects all of the files and operating system automatically. Every information stored on the disk will be encrypted. Once a disk is fully encrypted, access to the drive (encrypted) is password protected. It is mostly built-in within systems, For example, Linux has Unified Key Setup, Microsoft uses BitLocker, and Apple has FileVault. There are

some drives that do not need any OS software for encryption and decryption, instead they have built-in capabilities for data encryption/decryption. These drives are known as Self – Encrypting Drives (SED).

Trusted Platform Module (TPM)

Replacing and formatting the existing hard drive will not be enough to provide security to it, it's better to take advantage of the built-in Trusted Platform Module (TPM), that is an embedded security chip that stores encrypted keys, passwords, and digital certificates. Different services can use the TPM chip even without a cost of this service, when you use the TPM with a BIOS-level Administrator password and a User password required at power-on, the system becomes virtually useless to a thief.

A piece of hardware that is in charge of handling all the cryptographic functions. TPM contains persistent memory that comes with unique keys. It also contains versatile memory that store configuration information, storage keys or other different types of data. TPM is password protected (requires authentication for gaining access) and there is no chance of dictionary attack on TPM.

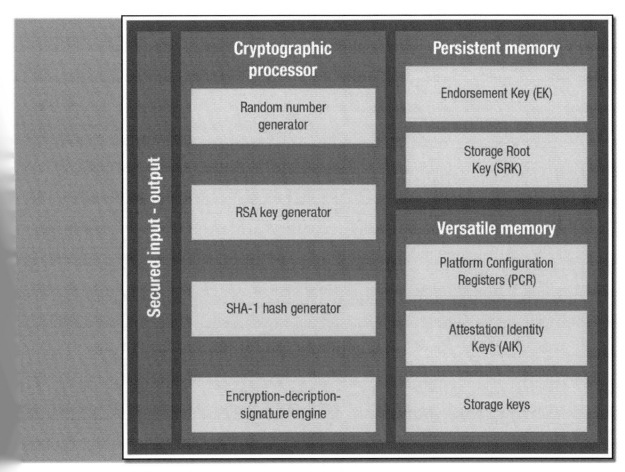

Figure 3-05: Internal components of TPM

Hardware Security Module (HSM):

It manages and stores keys in a secure location by keeping the backup of the key. HSM provides facilities to the Cryptographic functions like hashing, encryption, etc. In order to restrict access to the key that HSM secures, it has a technique called tamper protection technique.

It is a peripheral device that is usually "attached through USB or a network connection."

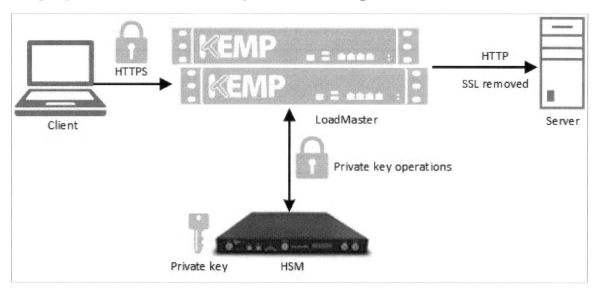

Figure 3-06: Hardware Security Module

UEFI/BIOS:

BIOS stands for Basic Input/ Output System. It is stored on the chip that is fixed to the motherboard of the PC. It is the very first software that runs when you start the Computer. It ensures that all the hardware components are working properly and runs the bootloader. Before the Operating system boots, the BIOS goes through Power on Self-Test (POST). In BIOS you can configure multiple settings like system time, hardware configuration, boot order etc.

UEFI abbreviates as Unified Extensible Firmware Interface and is a replacement for BIOS. It has significant changes over BIOS like compatibility with modern peripherals, platform independency and enhanced boot time and speed. BIOS uses the Master Boot Record (MBR) to save information about the hard drive data while UEFI uses the GUID partition table (GPT). It is more secure (provides secure booting by allowing only authentic drivers and services to load at boot time). All modern(new) systems are based on UEFI.

Secure Boot:

Operating system's security is a challenge as it possesses multiple drivers and add-ons. These pathways can enable a medium through which malicious softwares can attack a machine, in case if these programs are not properly vetted before installation. The viruses become difficult to detect and defeat if the attack occurs at booting time.

Secure boot is a solution to this problem that is offered by UEFI. By enabling secure boot mode, only signed drivers and OS loader can invoke. Linux's major version and Microsoft Windows support "Secure Boot."

Hardware Root of Trust:

Trust is the base of security. Hardware root of trust refers to the hardware on which security relies upon. HSM and TPM, discussed above (See pg. 11-12) are the hardware examples that are used on the basis of trust. This hardware's are trusted because they are designed in a way that is difficult to circumvent. It means that they are secure by design.

Supply Chain:

In September 2015, the researchers found that many Cisco routers are infected by a malicious firmware called "SYNful Knock." This malicious firmware allows the threat actor to gain backdoor access to the infrastructure devices which creates trust issues. End users realized that they need vendors in the supply chain that they can trust, so they know exactly where this hardware is coming from. They also need to check and make sure that these very critical devices are not connected to the Internet before security is in place. It is always useful to verify in some way that the hardware and the firmware inside of that hardware are secure.

EMI/EMP:

EMI stands for "Electromagnetic interference" and EMP stands for "Electromagnetic Pulse." The researchers are finding ways to take advantages of EMP and EMI created by the hardware. One security aspect on which security researchers focus upon is EMI leakage. Researchers are able to detect and identify the electromagnetic interference occurring by the devices such as keyboards, hard drives and other computer peripherals. By retrieving the interference, researcher successfully recreate what people are typing on their keyboard and watching on their screen.

Another aspect of security in this area is not just listening to the Electromagnetic interference, but injecting their own signals into the EMI. By doing this, they can change data that may be captured on sensors, or input information into the keyboard input by using their own electromagnetic signals. These are the few reasons why organizations set special precautions in place to protect or shield against EMI and EMP. These are certainly

found in a military installation, places that deal with national security, or networks that are highly secure.

Operating System (OS) Security

An Operating System is an interface (system software) to make a hardware functional. It is an intermediary between applications and computer hardware. Windows, macOS, ChromeOS, BlackBerry, Linux are the common and popular operating system.

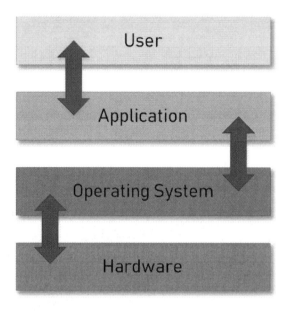

Figure 3-07: Working of an Operating System

Types of Operating System

Some types of Operating system are discussed below:

- Network Operating System:

Network Operating System is used by the network components to provide computation and configuration portion for networking. Every networking equipment vendor has their own operating system like Cisco has IOS, Juniper has Junos, etc.

- Server Operating System:

The gap between a running application on the server and server hardware is bridged by the *"Server Operating System."* Windows Operating system and Linux Operating System are two examples of Server operating system. Windows Operating System has a commanding lead in the market due to its Active Directory Technology and built-in Hyper-V capability.

- Workstation Operating System:

Functional working space and the graphical interface are provided by the *Workstation Operating System*, for a user to interact with the system and its different applications. Windows is commonly seen in the role of Workstation Operating System due to the reason of a high level of user interaction with the workstations.

- Appliance Operating System:

Special-purpose appliances typically have their own operating systems. These are the special purpose operating systems for usually vendor specific appliances design to perform specific functions only considering economics portability and functionality.

- Kiosk:

Kiosks are machines that are usually set up with auto-login in a browser. The OS in Kiosk is locked down to minimal functionality to prevent users from making any configuration changes.

- Mobile Operating System:

A type of Operating system that is optimized for the mobile hardware. The Mobile Operating System is categorized into two main types; Google's Android OS and Apple's iOS. These Operating Systems are optimized to both Device capability and Desired functionality.

Patch Management

Patch management is the process of software and application patch upgradation including installing patches, acquiring and testing. All Operating Systems require an update and have different methods for the users to keep their systems up to date.

There is a hierarchy that is followed by the vendor for software update:

- **Hotfix**: A small software update that is usually designed to discover problems that are produced and released quickly. For example: buffer overflow.

- **Patch**: Refers to larger updates as compared to Hotfix. This can address several problems. Patches not only include enhancement or additional capabilities but it can also fix bugs.

- **Service Pack**: A large collection of Hotfixes and Patches, rolled in one single package that makes the system up to date at once, is called Service Pack. It saves users from downloading different updates.

Patch Management Life-Cycle

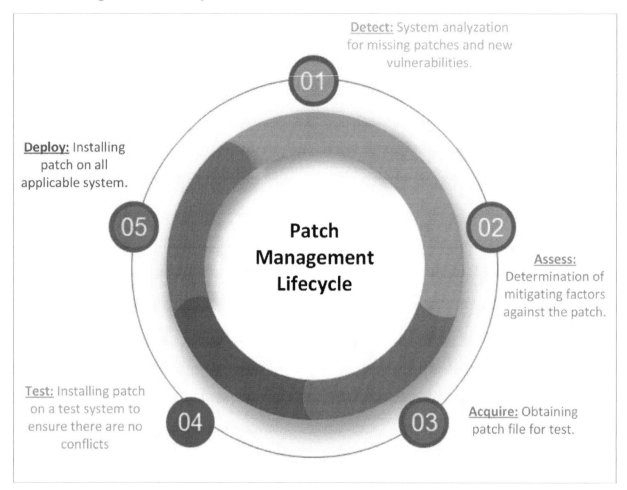

Figure 3-08: The Life Cycle of Patch Management

Disabling Unnecessary Ports and Services

To identify the system's specific need for proper operation and enabling items that are necessary for those functions, is a management issue in running a secure system. System's ports and connections that are not in use, need to be disabled. Disabling Unnecessary Ports and Services increase system's throughput and security by restricting their use from the unauthorized users.

Least Functionality

Least Functionality is the principle that allows a system to do *ONLY* what it is supposed to do. Additional functions serve as an added surface for the enemy to attack and provide no additional benefits to the organization.

Trusted Operating System

A type of operating system that permits "multi-level security." The maintenance and creation of Trusted OS is an expensive approach because recertification process is required after any kind of changes in existing OS. Government agencies and contractors used Trusted Operating System for the system that requires high-level security that is sensitive systems.

Application Whitelisting/Blacklisting

Blacklisting and Whitelisting are the methods for controlling/managing the applications of the Operating System.

- **Application Blacklisting**: It is a method that determines which application(s) should not be allowed to run on the machine.
- **Application Whitelisting**: the opposite of blacklisting is whitelisting that determines which application(s) should be allowed to run on the machine.

Microsoft uses two methods that are part of OS, to control the use of applications to their specified users. These methods are:

- **Software Restrictive Policies**: This is a primary mode that is used by the machine and not by the users. It allows significant control over application, executable files, and scripts and employed through group policies.
- **User Account Level Control**: Used by the enterprise to control over who can access and use installed software. It is enforced through AppLocker and allows which user can use which application and programs.

Disable Default Accounts and Passwords

User accounts are necessary for any system. Operating system includes a number of different users' accounts. These users are assigned with different privileges. System administrator may have to enable or disable default user account such as guest accounts and modify the credentials of root accounts.

If you disable guest account, it means you have created a limit on people, accessing your system. By disabling interactive login for the account that is used as service, the only actual user is able to log in interactively to the operating system.

Peripheral Security

Wireless Keyboard and Mouse

As far as security is concerned, we do not think about mice and keyboard, yet wireless mice and keyboard create a security concern because they communicate in clear. Wireless mouse and keyboard use 2.4 GHz frequency and proprietary wireless communication

protocol. Though these devices use the proprietary protocol as there is no encryption method is used, it is easy for anyone to interfere and capture data.

Someone could act as a keylogger and capture every bit of data that you are typing into your keyboard, or maybe they are able to reverse the process and inject keystrokes into your system as if they were sitting in front of your keyboard. There is a known vulnerability called KeySniffer that allows somebody to perform these types of functions over insecure mice and keyboard configuration.

Therefore, for security purposes, the manufacturers of wireless keyboard and mouse have implemented AES encryption between mouse and keyboard. It means the communication between wireless keyboard and mouse that supports AES encryption is secure, and nobody would be able to put their keystrokes, neither they would be able to interfere the communication nor can see what is being typed.

Displays

By interfering in the electromagnetic radiations that come from different components of the system, the researchers could reconstruct what the user operates on the screen. Another security issue is that many display systems do not have any security associated with the firmware upgrade. The display system has an operating system and requires a firmware upgrade, but there is no check or authentication that ensures that the firmware being installed is really the proper firmware for the system.

Wi-Fi-enabled microSD card

Wi-Fi microSD card has the ability to transfer the files wirelessly, without removing the SD card from the device and plugging it into the laptop or computer and then eject it to slot back to the device after the transfer of file is completed. In short, with Wi-Fi enabled micro SD card, one can simply transfer files from SD card to computer wirelessly without moving it from device to device. These Wi-Fi enabled micro SD cards also include authentication vulnerabilities; the hacker can access the SD card and easily read files over the Wi-Fi.

The Application Programming Interface (API) that allows the third party to use the capabilities of the wireless card by just writing up an application, could result in data leakage and loss of data. Therefore, it is important for the manufacturer of the SD card to implement strong security controls to the API that nobody could be able to gain access to the SD card by circumventing the security.

Printer/Multi-Function Devices (MFDs)

Many modern printers are multi-functional because they not only print documents but are able to scan, fax and copy the documents. The multi-functional devices contain a lot

of information that can be used for exploration (like activity log files or address book, etc.). Some of the devices store information in the local spooling file so that one could possibly gain access to the device and retrieve a copy of what the user printed on the MFD. If someone is able to bypass the security, then he may be able to access the last stored data without authentication.

External Storage Device

The external storage device often does not require authentication. Someone could easily connect and read or transfer files that are on the external device. Therefore, it is important to enable encryption to the files in the external device to make sure that if you lose the device, nobody can access and read or transfer the files.

Digital Cameras

Another security concern is Digital Cameras. It captures images and videos and store them in a digital storage device. It is an important measure of security to have secure deployment of cameras and the secure internal and external storage. Intruder may attempt to access the storage media or sniff the connection to monitor what is going on.

The firmware inside the device is also compromised and allows the third party to access into the security camera. This is why security cameras are also vulnerable.

Secure Deployments

Sandboxing

To execute code in an environment that isolates target system and the code from direct contact is called Sandboxing. Sandbox is used for the execution of unverified and untrusted code. Sandbox works just like a *virtual machine* and can mediate a number of system interactions like accessing memory, network access, and accessing another program, device, and file system. Sandbox offers protection, and its level of protection depends upon isolation level.

Working Environment

Development environment

There are many secure environments available for development purposes like code writing. The developers take the code and move it to the sandbox for the additional testing purpose.

Testing Environment

The testing environment looks similar to the production environment. The purpose of the test environment is to investigate a system well prior to deploying it into production to assure that it is error free and will not breach the production environment.

Staging Environment

Stage deployment is another method of deployment in which software or program is deployed to a part of the enterprise, and then unseen problems are watched. It basically serves as a sandbox for testing, and it is an optional environment.

Production environment

In a production environment, the system deals with the real data and do what it is intended to do.

Embedded System

SCADA

SCADA abbreviates as "Supervisory Control and Data Acquisition System." It is a process used to control the system that is automated in a cyber-physical environment like a traffic light, energy networks, water plants, refineries, environmental controls, building automation manufacturing plants, etc. SCADA contains its own smart components, each of which is an example of embedded system.

SCADA is also known by different other names like Industrial Control System (ICS) and Distributed Control System (DCS), and this variation depends on the configuration and industry.

Smart Devices/ IOT (Internet of Things)

The devices that are comprised of the Internet of Things or the Smart devices have taken the world's market by storm. Anything that contains microcontroller seems to be connected to the web so that it can be controlled remotely.

Wearable Technology: The use of smart devices, that are wearable, have majorly increased. These wearable technologies include everything from smart watches, to step counters, to health monitors and more. As these devices are connected to the person, they are able to track the location of the person. The security concern that arises from the usage of these wearable gadgets is the data/information stored and who can access that data/information.

Home Automation: The driving factor behind the IoT movement is Home Automation.

Home automation or smart home is a system in which every device is connected to the internet and is controlled through the internet like doorbells, lights, fans, AC, TV, Door Locks, etc.

These IOT devices are smart devices, and they know when we are home and when we are not. In case if someone is able to gain access to this home automation system, it means they have potentially gained access to the entire house.

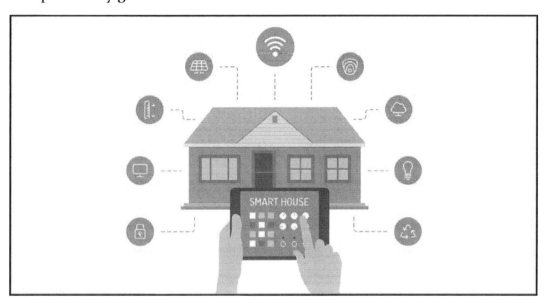

Figure 3-09: Home Automation

HVAC

It is an acronym for Heating, Ventilating, and Air Conditioning. A complex system that is designed by the HVAC system expert and is installed in large building or enterprises. It is not a standalone unit; it is usually integrated with other components within the infrastructure. A centralized PC is responsible for managing all these HVAC units that include making heating and cooling decisions for data centers and workspace.

HVAC systems are usually not built keeping security in mind, and this leads to difficulty in recovering from the infrastructure's DOS (Denial of Service).

SOC

It is an acronym for "System on a Chip". It is one of the most popular embedded system these days. Multiple activities take place on a single piece of a silicon chip that is multiple components run on a single chip. The whole process mainly relies on the chip including functioning of peripheral devices.

For Example: In Raspberry Pi 2, the Broadcom chip is the "System on a Chip" and everything else then this chip is an interface that gets you to the network USB interfaces or HDMI video interface.

Low power consumption and efficient designs are the reasons due to which the SOCs are very common in the markets. As far as the implication of security on the SOC-based system is concerned, all the security issues are handled by the system and not by the specifics of SOC aspects.

RTOS

It is abbreviated as "Real Time Operating System." The system in which the processing must occur in real time and where the data cannot be queued for significant time-length. The 'Real Time Operating System' is designed for such types of system

RTOS is designed and programmed for a specific purpose. The scheduling algorithm in RTOS deals with the time collision. However, generally, RTOS processes each input as it is received or within a specific time, defined as 'response time.' Mostly, multi-tasking system lacks in real-time processing, therefore, the RTOS, instead of handling multiple tasks, emphasize the thread in processing.

Special Purpose Systems

As the name implies, these systems are for a special purpose. Some of the special purpose devices targeted by the CompTIA are Aircraft/UAV, Medical Devices, and Vehicles.

Aircraft/UAV (Unmanned Ariel Vehicle)

The embedded systems are also inside the Aircraft or Unmanned Ariel Vehicles (UAV). Flight Control System (FCS) and Air Traffic Control (ATC) are two primary control systems of an airplane consisting of different components and embedded systems. Some of the security issue arises when somebody performs denial of service (DoS) and create some interference to disturb the communication. Not only it would damage the aircraft but would also be dangerous for the people on the ground.

Medical Devices

Embedded systems are also used for Medical purposes like heart monitor or insulin pump. The security concern related to these medical devices is that how the kernel is patched, in case the vulnerabilities are found because the medical devices are designed and manufactured for a static system that does not require updating and patching. In case if the changes are made, then it will force towards a lengthy, time consuming, expensive, requalification process. Therefore, it is recommended by most of the manufacturers not to connect the medical devices to the outside network (isolate the device) which in reality is not possible.

Note: In 2017, nearly half a million pacemaker were recalled for software vulnerability that allows the hacker to gain access to the device and make changes to the performance characteristics of these devices. The good news related to this security issue is that without removing the device, it can be patched, but it requires a doctor visit to install the new firmware.

Secure Application Development and Deployment

Development of Life Cycle Models

Software production is the result of processes that involve tasks like requirement gathering, planning, designing, coding, testing and supporting. These tasks are performed according to the process model enabled by the team members.

Two of them are discussed below:

Waterfall Model

One of the frameworks of application development is waterfall model which is a "sequential design process". In this process each step is taken sequentially, that is, the second step is followed by the completion of the first and then third step is followed by the second and so forth. Waterfall model can be implemented in multiple ways, but they almost follow the similar steps or path.

Some of the most common advantages and disadvantages of Waterfall model are as follows:

Pros	Cons
It is a sequential approach.	The developers cannot go back to the previous step to make changes i.e. every step is final.
Emphasizes methodical record keeping and documentation.	Fault in instruction can result in havoc as the project depends upon the initial input and instruction.
Clients know the expectation at every step.	Only at the end of the sequence, the test is performed.
Strong documentation results in less hassle.	Change implementation can be a nightmare for developers.

Table 3-02: Pros and Cons of Waterfall Model

A common framework for application development:

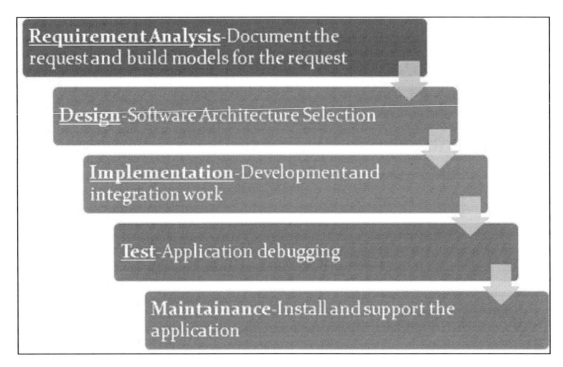

Figure 3-10: Waterfall Model

Agile Model

In the agile model, there is no sequential path that is followed, instead, multiple tasks are being performed simultaneously in the development. An advantage of the agile model is that making changes to the model is easy i.e. the development process in the agile model is continuous.

The two major forms of agile development are as follows:

- Scrum
- Extreme Programming (XP)

Some of the most common advantages and disadvantages of the Agile Model are as follows:

Pros	Cons
It is a team-based approach.	Mismanagement could lead towards code sprints with no ends.
Allows us to make changes.	The final project could completely be different from a planned project that is lack of a definite plan.
At every step, testing can be performed.	Impossible for an outsider to tell who is working on what.
Simultaneous testing helps in	Lack of emphasis on documentation.

launching project soon.	

Table 3-03: Pros and Cons of the Agile Model

Secure DevOps

Security Automation

Automation is the key element of the DevOps and it relies on it for most of its efficiencies. Security automation as the name refers, automatically handles the security related tasks.

Continuous Integration

Continuous integration in the DevOps refers to the continuous upgradation and improvement of the production code base. Through high-level automation and safety nets, this CI (Continuous Integration) permits the DevOps team members to update and test minor changes without much overhead.

Baselining

Standardizing the performance and functionality at certain level is known as Baselining. It provides a reference point when changes are made. This is the reason why it is important to DevOps and Security. Reference point are used to represent the improvements with changes. At the time of major changes or development, it is important for the development team to baseline the system.

Immutable System

A system that is never patched or upgraded once it is deployed is known as an Immutable system, and if upgradation is needed, then it is simply replaced with a new patched or upgraded system. In a typical system (Changeable system), it is difficult to perform authorized software and system update and lock down directories at the same time because when the system is updated, it creates temporary files in the directories and these directories contain some files that should never be modified. This problem is resolved by the immutable system.

Infrastructure as Code

The infrastructure as code or programmable infrastructure refers to the usage of code to build system, despite using normal configuration mechanism to manually configure them.

Infrastructure as code, a way of using automation to build out a system that is reproducible and efficient and it is also considered as a key attribute of enabling best practices in DevOps.

Version Control and Change Management

Changes like bug fixes, security patches, the addition of new features, etc. in an application are guaranteed. During the application development process, multiple changes need to be implemented, and that requires version control.

Version Control

Version control tracks changes and can also revert back to see what changes have been made. This version control feature is used in multiple softwares, also used in the operating system, cloud-based files, and wiki software. It is also important from a security perspective because it identifies required modification with respect to time.

Provisioning and De-Provisioning

Provisioning refers to "making something available" like deploying an application. The provisioning of the web server, database server, certificate updates, user workstation configuration, etc. are necessary.

De-provisioning is the process of removing an application. An important factor related to the de-provisioning of application is that every instance of the application should be removed and made sure that there are no open holes left.

Secure Coding Technique

The basic concept of Secure Coding

The security of an application starts with a code that is secure and free from all the vulnerabilities. However, all the codes have vulnerabilities and weaknesses, thus the goal is to make a code that can maintain desired security level and possesses effective defense against vulnerability exploitation.

A secure application can be created if the configuration, errors, and exceptions are handled properly. The security risk profile of the system can be determined if the application is tested throughout the Software Development Life Cycle (SDLC).

Software Development Life Cycle Methodology (SDLM) possesses elements that can assist in secure code development. Some of the SDLM processes that can improve code security are as follows:

- Cross-site Scripting
- Cross-site Request Forgery
- Input Validation
- Error and Exceptional Handling

Proper Error Handling

Error and Exception encounter in an application is common, and it needs to be handled in a secure manner. One of the attack methodologies forces an error to move applications from normal to exceptional handling. If the exception handling is improper, it can lead towards a wide range of disclosure. For example, SQL errors disclose data element and data structure, Sensitive information like server, filename, and path can be disclosed by RPC (Remote Procedure Call) error, and programmatic error can disclose information like stack element or line number on which exception occurred.

Proper Input Validation

As we have moved towards web-based application, the errors also have shifted towards input handling issues from buffer overflow. In order to prevent malicious attacks, it is the duty of a developer to handle the input properly. A buffer overflow may be considered as improper input, but recent attacks include arithmetic and canonicalization attacks. The most important mechanism that can be employed for defense is "Input Validation."

Many attacks that are based on common vulnerabilities can be mitigated if all the inputs are hostile before validation. The following are vulnerabilities that require input validation as a defense mechanism:

- Cross-site Scripting
- Cross-site Forgey Attack
- Buffer Overflow
- Incorrect Calculation of Buffer Size
- Path Traversal
- In Security Decision, Reliance on Untrusted Inputs

Stored Procedure

A pre-compiled method that is implemented within a database engine is known as "Stored Procedure." It is a secure coding mechanism that offers user input the isolation from actual SQL statement being executed. In other words, it is a primary mechanism for defense against SQL injection attack. The stored procedure has better performance than other data access forms, and that is why many major database engines support it.

Code Signing

A mechanism performed by the end user to verify the code integrity is "Code Signing." It applies a digital signature to the code for code integrity verification. In addition, it also provides evidence as to the source of the software. It relies on established PKI, and the developer needs a pair of the key to decrypt that data. For which the public key is to be recognized by the end user and needs to be signed by the certification authority.

Encryption

To have secure and usable encryption in an application, proven algorithm and code bases are needed to adopt and utilize.

Obfuscation

Obfuscation is also known as Camouflage means *"to hide the obvious meaning of observation."* Obfuscation is added to the system so that it becomes hard to be exploited and understood by any attacker.

The Obfuscation works well for data names or other such exposed elements, but it does not work well for code construction. Obfuscated code is not just hard to read but nearly impossible to read, and an example of such code is ticking time bomb. The basic question that arises is that how it functions if someone needs the code to figure out how it works or in case if any modification is needed if it stops working. These are some of the reasons which are not considered good for the construction of code.

Original Source Code Before Rename Obfuscation	Reverse-Engineered Source Code After Rename Obfuscation
<pre>private void CalculatePayroll(SpecialList employeeGroup) { while(employeeGroup.HasMore()) { employee = employeeGroup.GetNext(true); employee.UpdateSalary(); DistributeCheck(employee); } }</pre>	<pre>private void a(a b) { while (b.a()) { a = b.a(true); a.a(); a(a); } }</pre>

Figure 3-11: Code Obfuscation Example

Code Re-Use/ Dead Code

1. Code Re-Use

Code re-use or use of old code or components like libraries or common functions etc. reduces development costs and time. However, massive re-use of code also results in a ripple effect across the application. Therefore, it is necessary for the development team to make a decision about the appropriate level of code re-use. Code re-use is preferred for a complex function like cryptography.

The challenge with the re-use of code is that if the old code contains vulnerabilities then reusing the code will transfer those vulnerabilities to other application. Another challenge with this code reusing is the symptoms of dead code.

2. Dead Code

The result produced by the dead code is never used anywhere in an application while it may be executed which simply means that the machine is running the executables (code is executed). It generates results, but these results are never used anywhere else in the application, thereby making it a dead code. Almost every code has security problems therefore by removing the dead code; the application can be made more secure.

Validation

1. Server-Side Validation

When there is a need for validation of data, it can be validated at multiple places like 'on the server'. This validation is known as server-side validation. In server-side validation, all the check occurs on the server itself.

2. Client-Side Validation

As the name implies, this validation process occurs at the front end of the application, that is, the client-side. It helps in filtering legitimate input from a genuine user and also benefits the user by providing the additional speed.

<u>*Note:*</u> Validation on the Server-side is always needed, but it will be best if both the validation, i.e., Server-Side Validation and Client-Side Validation are used.

Memory Management

Memory management refers to those actions that are needed to coordinate and control computer memory, assigning memory to variables, and reclaiming it when no longer needed. Memory management errors lead to the memory leak problem. The cleaning process of memory that is no longer in use is called garbage collection. The programming languages like Java, Python, C#, and Ruby provides automatic management of memory with garbage collection, but where there is no automatic garbage collector like in C programming, the programmer has to allocate free memory.

Use of Third-Party Libraries and SDKs

To extend the functionality of the programming language, third-party libraries, and software development kit (SDK) are used.

Data Exposure

During operation, the loss of data control is known as "Data Exposure." Protection of data is really important, it must be protected every time and at every step of a process like during communication or transmission, during use and also when at rest that is during storage.

It is the responsibility of the programming team to chart the data flow and to ensure the protection of data exposure (ensures that data is protected from exposure). Exposed data can result in confidentiality failure (data can be lost to an unauthorized person) and integrity failure (data can be changed by the unauthorized person).

Code Quality and Testing

Application developers use tools and techniques to assist them in testing and checking the security level of the code. The code analyzation is performed to find weaknesses and vulnerabilities in the code. This analyzation can be performed either dynamically or statically.

Code Analysis

Code analysis is the process of inspecting vulnerabilities and weaknesses in the code. It is divided into two types, i.e., Static and Dynamic. The static analysis examines the code without execution whereas dynamic code examines the code with execution.

Code Testing

Code testing is the process to verify that the code meets the functional requirement as laid out in the business requirements process.

Static Code Analyzer

Static code analysis can be performed on both source and object code. It is used when the code is examined without execution. It can be performed both by tools and by human. However, this is performed mostly through tools because tools can be used against any form of the code base. Various names are given to these tools like static code analyzer or source code analyzer or sometimes binary code scanner or bytecode scanner.

Dynamic Analysis

Dynamic analysis is performed on the emulated system or target system while execution of software. Specialized automation is required by the dynamic analysis to perform specific testing. A brute force method that addresses vulnerabilities and input validation issues is known as Fuzzing (Fuzz testing).

Stress Testing

Finding bugs is not the only objective of the performance testing, but also it includes finding performance factor and tailbacks. Stress testing basically increases the load of the application to see what happens. This can lead towards unintended results like error messages, kernel or memory dumps, and application details that are not intended to show to the users are displayed to the users, etc. There are many options to perform stress testing that are as follows:

- Automate individual workstation.
- Simulate Large Workstation loads.

And in both the cases, extensive report, response time and results are generated that describe how the application is affected by the stress test.

Sandboxing

To execute code in an environment that isolates target system and the code from direct contact is called Sandboxing. Sandbox is used for the execution of unverified and untrusted code. Sandbox works just like a *virtual machine* and can mediate a number of system interaction like accessing memory, network access, and accessing another program, device, and file system. Sandbox offers protection, and the protection level it offers depends upon the mediation offered and isolation level.

Model Verification

To ensure that the code is doing what it is supposed to do. In model verification, the program results are needed to match with the desired design model for verification. This testing process consists of two steps that are validation and verification.

Verification

A process that checks whether the software is working properly, if there are any bugs there to address, or if the product meets the model specification.

Validation

Validation refers to the process of determination of an application to meet certain requirements including high level requirements, secure software building requirements, security requirements, compatibility. It also investigates if the product it right for an organization or not.

Compiled vs Runtime Code

When the source code is compiled into an executable, it is called Compiled code. Once the code is compiled, the source code becomes hidden (you don't see it). During the process of compilation, the bugs and errors are also identified by the compiler that can be resolved by recompiling the code. After fixing the bugs, an error-free application can be developed.

Some softwares or applications that we use are runtime code. For example, the PHP code of PHP based application is a runtime code. In runtime code, the source code is viewable, and it executes at the time application initially runs. It means there is no compiler to check for bugs and these bugs are only found when the code is executing. It is different from compiled code because in a compiled code. the errors and bugs are identified before the application is provided to the end user.

Cloud and Virtualization

Hypervisor

Hypervisor which is also referred to as virtual machine monitor is a software that manages virtual machines. It keeps all the operating systems separated from each other and also allocate memory, CPU and other required resources to the VM. The hypervisor is of two types: Type I and Type II.

Type I

Type one hypervisors do not require a host-based OS. It is also known as an embedded hypervisor. You are just required to install the type I hypervisor and then load the virtual machine on it, no additional OS is needed.

Type II

Type II hypervisor runs on an existing host-based OS. The hypervisor that runs on Window, Linux, and MAC OS is a type II hypervisor.

Application Cells/Containers

A container is a form of lightweight virtualization that possesses the same essence as the host system. The application container is designed to run a sole service. Commonly used for packaging applications and services without a launch of VM for every application.

VM Sprawl Avoidance

When virtual machines are running and you are not sure about which application is related to which virtual machine, the scenario is called VM sprawl. This makes de-provisioning very difficult. Therefore, in order to avoid this situation, a formal process and detailed documentation is required (all the virtual object should contain detailed information).

VM Escape Protection

VM escape is a type of vulnerability through which the threat actors can break out of the VM and directly interact with the host OS, hardware, or hypervisor. Therefore, in order to avoid such situation, keeping virtual environment up to date with recent security patches, is essential.

Cloud Storage

Cloud storage is a popular cloud service that allows us to store our data into it and it is accessible to us anywhere, anytime, on any device we use, after proper authentication process if we have a network connection.

Cloud Deployment Models

To deploy the Cloud, there are several deployment models, each of which has specific way for agencies. Due to the different characteristics and trade-offs of the various cloud computing deployment models, the most important thing to consider is that the agencies of IT professionals should have a clear understanding of their agency's specific needs as well as how the different systems can help them to meet these needs.

Let us have a look at some of the key differences:

SaaS

SaaS is an acronym for Software as a Service. It offers a complete product as a web service that is run and maintained by the service provider along with the management of the underlying infrastructure.

PaaS

PaaS is an acronym for Platform as a Service. It manages its own underlying infrastructure, usually hardware and OS, and provides application development program.

IaaS

IaaS is an acronym for Infrastructure as a Service which is also known as HaaS (Hardware as a Service). It provides basic building blocks for cloud IT by offering access to networking features, computers, and data storage space.

Private

Cloud-based applications can be worked with respect to low-level infrastructure pieces or can utilize a larger amount of benefits that give abstraction from the administration, architecting, and scaling prerequisites of core infrastructure. In private clouds, the application is totally deployed in the cloud, therefore, all the components of that application run on that cloud. We can use private clouds by either creating applications on the cloud or migrate the cloud from an existing framework to another for taking more benefits or for other purpose.

Public

A public cloud deployment model is something that is made available on the internet to everyone. For example, when we go to Amazon or Microsoft and take benefit of their cloud-based offers, we use a public cloud.

Hybrid

A hybrid deployment is a procedure to combine any framework and applications between cloud-based resources and existing resources that are not situated to the cloud. The most

well-known strategy for deploying hybrid method between the cloud and existing on-premises infrastructure to broaden, and grow an organization's foundation into the cloud while interfacing cloud resources to the interior framework.

Community

Community deployment model is a recent innovation on the private cloud model and it presents a complete cloud solution for business communities. It allows multiple business corporations to share the same resources.

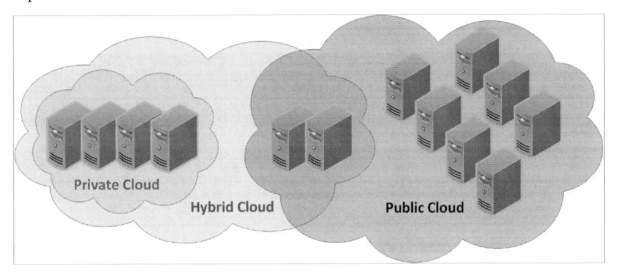

Figure 3-12: Different models of Cloud

On-Premise vs. Hosed vs. Cloud

__On-Premise__: A type of model that uses the same legacy IT infrastructure and run cloud resources within its own data center. It is also called private cloud for its ability to provide dedicated resources while maintaining total control and ownership of the environment.

__Hybrid__: A type of model that includes a mix of on-premises private cloud and third-party public cloud. Hybrid deployment is between the cloud and existing on-premises infrastructure to achieve a unified scalable environment.

__Cloud__: A type of model in which third-party makes computing resources for the public over the internet. Cloud-based applications are fully deployed and run on the cloud. There is no need to setup and maintain own cloud servers in-house.

VDI/VDE

VDI is an acronym for Virtual Desktop Infrastructure. It virtualizes the user's desktop and runs it in the cloud or data center which means that the application we use, runs in the

data cloud. It is also known as VDE (virtual Desktop Environment). In VDI, all the computing power is in the cloud. Two major advantages of VDI are as follows:

- Client's work station has small computing requirements.
- High security (centralized and can be managed easily).

Cloud Access Security Broker (CASB)

By integrating CASB, you can make security policies to work in the cloud. It can be implemented as client software, local security appliances or cloud-based security solution. CASB provides Visibility, Compliance, threat prevention, and Data security.

Security as a Service (SECaaS)

Security as a Service (SECaaS) is a type of business model in which the security services of the service provider are integrated into an organization's infrastructure. Therefore, instead of managing your own security solution, you just have to move it to the cloud and only have to pay for what you use.

Resiliency and Automation Strategies

Automation/Scripting

For the administrators and clients, automation and scripting is a powerful tool that provides protection along with the efficiency to execute tasks. Automation provides accuracy and reduces risks as it is a use of tools and procedures to perform tasks, otherwise these tasks are manually performed by humans using command line execution or GUI operations. Whereas, scripts can be connected to reduce the complexity of actions that require a sequence of commands to be performed.

Automated courses of actions

Scripting system can be assumed as a best friend for all the professionals who believe in effective technical work as it provides *automated course of actions* to save time. The importance of Scripts and Automation can be seen by the fact that it is specified by the National Institute of Standard and Technology Special publication in 800-53 series.

Continuous Monitoring

Continuous monitoring is a term that defines the procedure followed to keep a check on the functioning and to reduce risk. It can simply be called a risk assessment procedure. It follows NIST Risk Management Framework (RMF) methodology that is used for security controls.

Configuration Validation

As the time changes, the system becomes outdated. We first design and configure the system in a way that it should perform for what it has been designed for along with the validation of configuration against security standards. For the timely upgradation of configuration, a method called automated testing can be used to resolve issues that may include multiple configuration management.

Templates

Templates can be defined as a key element for the making of servers, programs or for the entire system too. It can be said that the templates enable an infrastructure into a real service. Templates enable the setting of business standards and technology stacks used by the clients.

Master Image

An organization can be fully patched into a master image that would consider the backup of all the applications, operating systems and the most important thing i.e. the data. By using master image, many of the administrative tasks can be made easier and free of errors. The master image can also be used for enterprises with multiple desktops because if any error found, it can be removed by fixing a single and deploying it on any of the single pc.

Non-Persistence

A system is said to be non-persistence when the changes made in it are not permanent. Making the system non-persistence secures it from certain malware as the files, applications or programs installed in it are not permanent because the changes made in its configuration are not saved.

Snapshots

A snapshot can be a prompt point in any machine which allows the virtual machine to restore the previous points. Snapshot has a great importance because they are like a memory-point for the entire system.

Snapshot helps get back to the previous point as if you want to make any change in your system, take a snapshot and make changes and if you do not like the change get back to the previous point by the help of the taken snapshot.

Revert to Known State

The capability of an operating system to snapshot any virtual machine is understood as reverting to a known state. Most of the operating systems has this capability as a built-in

program. This option is mainly found in Microsoft office where the system creates a restore point by default before the update processes.

Rollback to known Configuration

Rollback to a known configuration can be also defined as getting back to a known state. For example, you can use this option if you make any incorrect configuration to your system and you want to get back to the older state.

Live Boot Media

A bootable system known as live boot media is concluded to an optical disc or USB which is specially designed to be bootable from the media. This is used to boot the system from an external operating system.

Elasticity

Increasing the capacity of a system to handle the workload by using an additional hardware to scale out space. This can also be set to an automatic mode in some environments such as cloud environment, where the resources are only based on the payment for the resources used.

Scalability

A design that makes a system to accommodate more load by using additional hardware or sources is known as scalability. This term is commonly used in server farms and database clusters because these two mostly face scaling issues due to workload.

Distributive Allocation

When a request is made to a range of resources for transparent allocation, is called Distributive Allocation. When a number of servers are trained to respond a load, it is the point where distribution allocation handles the task.

Redundancy

Redundancy in computer networks means making additional or alternate resources available for use usually as a back-up or fail-over plan. Typically, instances of network devices, network links, and other equipments are setup redundantly in an architecture. Commonly, datacentre and ISPs have redundant links to ensure high availability.

Fault Tolerance

Fault tolerance is defined as an uninterrupted functioning of the system, which means the data and services has no disruption despite the occurrence of fault. This can be done by mirroring the data and services. This can be a useful tool in servers because they are more critical to operations.

High Availability

High availability is the ability of a system to maintain a space for data and operational services regardless of any disrupting events (faults). High availability has the same goal as fault tolerance along with the availability of data and services.

RAID

RAID stands for Redundant Array Independent Disks. It is used to increase the reliability of the storage disk. It takes data that is commonly stored on the disk and sends it to many others so that the data can be stored in many places. RAID is also used to increase the speed of data recovery because different disks would be busy to recover data instead of waiting for a single disk to recover the data.

Physical Security Controls

Lighting

An essential part of physical security is proper lighting. Areas that are dimly lit or unlit makes it easy for the intruder to perform unauthorized activities without fear of being noticed or observed. Both internal and external lighting is important to keep aware of any unauthorized activities and other security purposes.

Signs

For both security and safety purposes, signs are important. There are multiple kinds of sign that provides information like "the area is dangerous," "fire exit," "keep doors locked," etc. A sign is commonly used in high-security facilities to signal where the visitor is allowed or where protection/escort is required (secured areas).

Fence/Cage

Fencing is referred to as a physical barrier around any secure area. It basically prevents free movement of unauthorized visitors around secure areas. Multiple types of the fence like perimeter fence, chain link fence, the Anti-scale fence is used outside of the building. Chain link fence can also be used inside of the building to prevent networking gear, server, & sensitive items from unauthorized access.

Security Guard

Security guards are a visible presence to direct security responsibility. Security guards are responsible for monitoring entrance and exit and maintaining access log. These guards are eyes and ears of the company for any suspicious activity, so they need to be more educated and trained in the network and physical security because most of the security guards are not security experts or trained.

Alarms

The function of an alarm is to alert the operator about any abnormal condition or activity. If a company has too many alarm conditions, then the operator will not react to the condition as desired. Tuning an alarm will provide accurate, useful, and desired information.

Safes

Safes are physical storage devices that prevent unauthorized access to the content it contains. Safes are of various shapes, sizes, and cost. They are not considered perfect. They are rated on the basis of how long they can protect or secure content from fire or theft, and the cost of the safe is directly proportional to the rating, i.e., better rating-high cost.

Protected Cabling

During cable installation, the Protected Distribution or Protected Cabling is needed to protect the cable from physical damage and avoid communication failure. It safeguards the cable between system physically, from physical hazards like tapping & interception.

Airgap

The logical or physical separation of a network from all other networks is referred to as Airgap which is designed to prevent unauthorized transfer of data to or from the network. However, the flaw behind this airgap logic is that the data can be moved by other means like USB drive, and this unauthorized bypassing of the air gap is called "Sneakernet."

Mantrap

The implementation of a mantrap is an approach to oppose tailgating. A mantrap contains two doors closely spaced together. Opening and closing of these doors are setup in a way that only one door is open at a time. These doors usually secure with card/pin authentication. It eliminates the risk of tailgating and piggybacking.

Screen Filters

Screen Filters are optical filters that reduce the angle of view-ability to an extremely limited range, making it tough for others to visually eavesdrop. Screen filters have a broad range of uses, from road warrior laptops to kiosks, to receptionists' computers, or places where sensitive data is presented (medical data in medical environments).

Key Management

Key management is the process of maintaining a record of the keys and users who have approach to it. A physical security environment that does not have a system of key

management is not verifiably secure. Key management will be essential when, say, a server in a locked area goes missing, and management needs to identify who owns the keys that can provide them to approach that area.

Practice Question

1. Which of the following is the purpose of using Tunneling?

   A. Eliminate an air gap
   B. Connect users to a honeynet
   C. Remote access from users outside the building
   D. Intranet connections to the DMZ

2. Which one of the following does not support the Defense in Depth??

   A. Vendor diversity
   B. User diversity
   C. Control diversity
   D. Redundancy

3. Which of the following can result in the highest risk if configured improperly?

   A. The operating system on a server
   B. Web server
   C. Application server
   D. Network infrastructure device

4. Why is UEFI preferred over BIOS?

   A. UEFI resides in the hardware, making it faster than BIOS.
   B. UEFI is stored in volatile hardware storage.
   C. UEFI has limited ability to deal with high-capacity storage and high-bandwidth
    communications and thus is more optimized.
   D. UEFI has more security designed into it, including provisions for secure booting.

5. Which of the following is not performed by a Secure Boot?

   A. It provides all approved drivers needed.
   B. It enables attestation that drivers haven't changed since they were approved.
   C. It only allows signed drivers and OS loaders to be invoked.
   D. It blocks malware that attempts to alter the boot process.

6. What is not true about hardware roots of trust?

   A. They are secure by design.
   B. They have very specific functionality.

C. They are typically implemented in hardware that is isolated from the operating system.

D. They provide security only at their level, not to higher layers of a system.

7. What is a simple way of improving the security of a system?

   A. Enabling all ports and services
   B. Maintaining comprehensive access control rules
   C. Disabling unnecessary ports and services
   D. Optimizing system throughput

8. Which statement is not true regarding systems on a chip?

   A. They provide the full functionality of a computing platform on a single chip.
   B. They typically have low power consumption and efficient design.
   C. Programming of SoC systems can occur at several different levels and thus potential risks are easily mitigated.
   D. Because these devices represent computing platforms with billions of devices worldwide, they have become a significant force in the marketplace

9. Which aspect is important to remember while dealing with the medical device's security?

   A. They are still relatively new in their usage.
   B. They can directly affect human life.
   C. Security is not related to safety.
   D. They are almost exclusively stand-alone devices, without Internet connectivity.

10. Which term describes the loss of control over data during operations?

   A. Sandboxing
   B. Data exposure
   C. Data Breach
   D. Runtime release

Chapter 04: Identity and Access Management

Introduction to Identity and Access Management

AAA (Authentication, Authorization, and Accounting) Framework

The AAA (Authentication, Authorization, and Accounting) framework is the base of network security. The process of identifying ourselves by providing ID and password when we log into some account goes through this AAA framework.

Authentication

The part of the framework that deals with the authentication of any person who claims to be authorized. For that, the person generally provides ID and password and usually other additional authentication data.

Authorization

Once the identification process is completed now the authorization part will figure out what the person can access or what access to the person has to the sources.

Accounting

Accounting keeps the record of the following things:

- Person who logs in
- Login time
- What data is delivered and received
- Log out time

Multifactor Authentication

In an AAA authentication mechanism, a user is asked for multi factor authentication like *who you are, what you have, what do you know, what do you do,* and etc. These additional items may have a cost combined with them.

Who you are

Biometric Authentication: Biometric authentication like fingerprint does not actually keep your real fingerprint, instead it keeps a mathematical representation of your biometrics. The mathematical values used for biometric representation are complex to modify because these biometric values are unique.

What you have

Smart Card: These cards are inserted into the computer, and usually these cards are combined with Personal Identification Number or PIN so that, if some unauthorized

person may get access to your card he may have to provide that additional information or PIN.

USBToken: USB Token is another way for authentication. A specialized certificate is stored on the USB and used for authentication when required.

Hardware and Software Token: Synchronized pseudo-random codes are generated by this token for the purpose of authentication.

Your Phone: Messages or codes are sent to the phone, and then those messages or codes are used for the authentication purpose.

What do you know

Password: The most common way of authentication is password. The password is a secret word, code or characters that are known to the only person who created that password.

PIN: PIN is abbreviated as Personal Identification Number. These PINs are usually asked us when we use ATM that is generally 4-digit code and used for authentication.

Pattern: A pattern is also a type of authentication. These types of pattern are seen on the mobile phone lock screen nowadays commonly.

Figure 4-01: Password and Pattern Authentication

Where you are

Your Location: A useful method of authentication that is based on your geographical location. In this type of authentication when a person logs in to a system, he has to provide the details of where he is, and the process of the transaction only completes if that person is in a particular location.

IP Address: Another way to authenticate where the person is, is through IP address. It does not provide accurate geography but can help to some extent.

Mobile Device Location: Mobile devices provide accurate geographical location as compared to others through GPS (Global Positioning System).

What do you do

Handwriting Analysis: Handwriting and signatures are another way to authenticate who the person is.

Typing Technique: Typing technique is also used to determine the person because every person has some kinds of typing pattern.

Single Sign-on (SSO)

It is a feature that allows one-time authentication, that is, users do not have to type ID and Password every time they want to access device or account or connect to a service. This saves a lot of time of the users. In Windows, there is Kerberos to accomplish Single sign-on.

Transitive Trust

Trust is the factor on which authentication relies on. Types of trust are as follows:

- **One-way trust**: A type of trust in which 'B' trusts 'A' but 'A' does not trust 'B'.
- **Two-way trust**: It means the trust is mutual between both parties, that is, 'A' trusts 'B' and 'B' also trusts 'A'. Hence it is Two-way trust.
- **Non-transitive Trust**: When the trust is created only for a single domain or entity and applied specifically to that domain is called Non-transitive trust.
  Transitive Trust: A trust that can be extended is called transitive trust. For example; if 'A' trusts 'B' and 'B' trusts 'C' then it allows 'A' to trust 'C'.

Identity and Access Services

Gaining Access:

To gain access to network resources, credentials are needed that are first investigated by the AAA server. For example, consider a client wants to get access to the resources of a network and he is authenticating through a VPN concentrator. The client first requests the VPN concentrator for getting access. This request contains authentication credentials such as username/password. VPN Concentrator authenticates the connection request through AAA server. If the credentials are matched, AAA approves the authentication. After validating the authentication credentials, the connection is established.

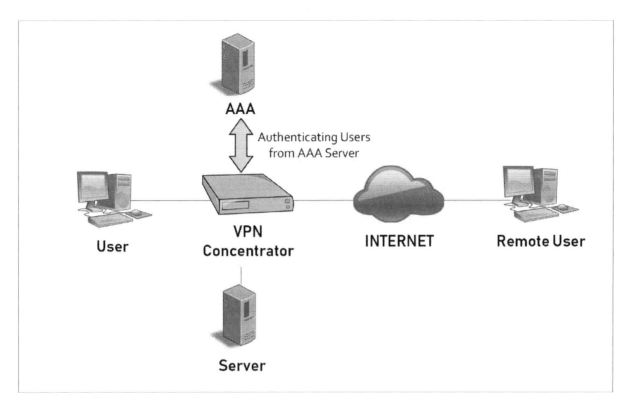

Figure 4-02: Access Gaining Process

There are many protocols that are used by the AAA server for this authentication process:

RADIUS (Remote Authentication Dial-in User Service)

RADIUS is a popular protocol for authentication. It supports numerous devices or networks, other than dial-in networks. The services of RADIUS can be used to centralize for a single authentication for various systems like Routers, Switches, Firewall, etc. The services of RADIUS are almost available for every Operating System.

TACACS (Terminal Access Controller Access Control System)

It is a remote protocol for authentication that is typically needed to control access to dial-up lines.

- **XTACACS**: It is abbreviated as Extended TACACS. It is created with new features induced by Cisco. It is only for Cisco devices as it is Cisco proprietary and supports accounting and auditing too.
- **TACACS+**: It is an authentication protocol developed by Cisco and released as an open standard beginning in 1993. TACACS+ is an entirely new protocol and is not compatible with its predecessors. TACACS+ encrypts all the information mentioned above and therefore does not have the vulnerabilities present in the RADIUS protocol.

This table summarizes and compares the unique features of RADIUS and TACACS+.

	TACACS+	RADIUS
L4 Protocol	TCP port 49.	UDP ports. 1812/1645 for authentication 1813/1646 for accounting.
Encryption	Encrypts full payload of each packet	Encrypts only passwords.
Observations	Proprietary to Cisco, very granular control of authorization, separate implementation of AAA.	Open Standard, robust, great accounting features, less granular authorization control. Another protocol named DIAMETER may replace RADIUS in the near future with enhanced capabilities.

Table 4-01: Comparison of RADIUS and TACACS+

LDAP (Lightweight Directory Access Protocol)

The original standard referred to as X.500. This version was DAP (Directory Access Protocol) that runs on the OSI protocol stack whose specification was created by the ITU. A lightweight version that is LDAP was designed for TCP/IP. This LDAP is for a vast directory of services and for reading and writing directory over an Internet Protocol (IP) network. It is generally needed to deal with user authentication and authorization and access control. LDAP is now ordinarily ran in Apple Open directory, Windows Active Directory, Open LDAP, etc.

LDAP Database

In LDAP, information is stored as fields.

Fields-Attributes	Description
Common Name-CN	Person or Object Identification.
Organizational Unit-OU	Organization's department.
Locality-L	Area or City.
State-ST	Province or State.
Country-C	Two-character ISO Code of Country (like PK for Pakistan)
Domain Component-DC	Object's Domain Component

Table 4-02: LDAP Database

The attributes are represented by the value using an equal sign like "CN=IPSpecialist, OU=Marketing" and so on. This helps in building an information tree.

Microsoft NTLM

The only method of challenge and response of Windows is Microsoft NTLM for authentication in window domain. The NTLM is a type of authentication method that is a combination of NT operating system and LAN manager operating the system. The NTLMv2 (version 2) is common these days. For authentication, it uses a hash challenge, but the method it uses is insecure that is MD4 (as hash type). Vulnerabilities that are found in NTLM hash are removed by the Kerberos which is a standard method nowadays for authentication in Windows.

Kerberos

The latest and the most trusted method of authentication is Kerberos. In Kerberos, you only need to authenticate once that means it is an SSO (no need to re-authenticate every time for access gaining) method. It also prevents man in the middle attack or replays attack by allowing mutual authentication between the server and the client. Kerberos were first introduced in 1980 by MIT. Microsoft started using this in Windows 2000, and now it has been made compatible with all Windows System.

For providing protection against Kerberos, use extensive cryptography.

How Kerberos Works

The Client provides a Ticket Granting Ticket to a Ticket Granting Service. The Ticket Granting Service then provides Service Ticket to the client. All the services on the network are, then, authenticated through the Service Ticket. This means the user gains access by simply showing the ticket behind the scene, and he does not have to be re-authenticated by putting ID and password again and again.

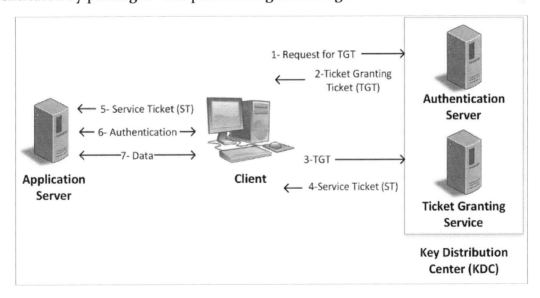

Figure 4-03: Kerberos Working Mechanism

Only the devices that are compatible with the Kerberos can use Kerberos authentication. Other types of system that are not Kerberos friendly, can use LDAP, RADIUS or TACACS for authentication purposes.

Introduction to PAP, CHAP, & MS-CHAP

For authentication in Point-to-Point network like ISDN, point-to-point protocol is required. The derivatives of PPP are PPTP and PPPoE.

- **PPTP** stands for Point to point tunneling Protocol-Used for authentication in Windows operating system
- **PPPoE** stands for Point to point protocol over Ethernet. Generally used for DSL authentication.

The protocols that are used for *authentication through non-Ethernet networks* are as follows:

1. PAP
2. CHAP
3. MS-CHAP

PAP

PAP is abbreviated as Password Authentication Protocol. Used in old systems (mostly legacy systems) and not popular these days. PAP is a weak authentication method because no encryption method is used which means all the information that is being delivered is in clear text. Analog dial-up lines do not need encryption because it is not imaginable for someone to sit somewhere between the communication path to seize data.

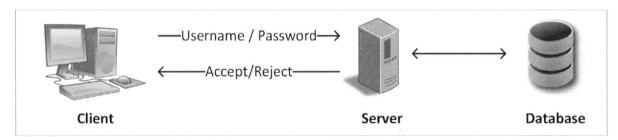

Figure 4-04: PAP Authentication Process

Basic Commands for PAP authentication	
Configuring Hostname	Router(config)#hostname R1
Configuring remote router hostname for incoming request	R1(config)# username <remote_username> password <password>
PPP Encapsulation Command	Router(config-if)#encapsulation PPP
PPP Authentication with PAP	Router(config-if)#ppp authentication pap
PPP Debugging Command	Router#debug PPP authentication

Table 4-03: PAP Authentication Commands

CHAP

CHAP is abbreviated as Challenge Authentication Protocol. For delivering credentials over the network, it uses an encrypted challenge. A three-way arrangement is used by CHAP for authentication that is:

1. The client sends credentials to the server, and in response, the server sends an encrypted challenge to the client.
2. The client responds to the challenge with a hash, by combining the password and the challenge together.
3. The server compares its database information (that is its hash) with the hash it has received. If both matches, then the user's authentication is correct and is authorized to communicate over the network.

Figure 4-05: CHAP Authentication Process

The challenge and response mechanism happens multiple times during the connection without the user being aware of it.

CHAP Authentication Commands	
Configuring Hostname	Router(config)#hostname R1
Configuring remote router hostname for incoming requests	R1(config)# username <remote_username> password <password>
PPP Encapsulation Command	R1(config if)#encapsulation ppp
PPP Authentication with PAP	R1(config-if)#ppp authentication chap
PPP Debugging Command	R1#debug PPP authentication

Table 4-04: CHAP Authentication Commands

MS-CHAP

MS-CHAP is abbreviated as Microsoft-CHAP. The CHAP is personalized by the Microsoft and then named as MS-CHAP that is ordinarily used in PPTP. MS-CHAP has two versions that are MS-CHAP v1 and MS-CHAP v2. Because of using DES protocol both the version suffers vulnerabilities and that cause people to shift to other secure VPN communication like IPSec or L2TP, etc.

LAB 04-1: Configuring PPP PAP and CHAP authentication and verification

Main Objective: The basic objective of this lab is to fully guide you how to configure PPP encapsulation with PAP and CHAP authentication protocol in multi area OSPF network.

The following topology shows four routers R1, R2, R3, and R4 that are connected through serial cable. CHAP authentication is needed between R1 andR2 whereas between R2 and R3 PAP is needed to be configured and both PAP and CHAP are required between R3 and R4.

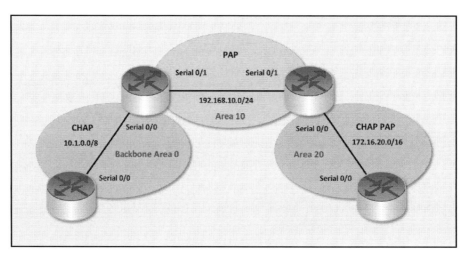

Figure 4-06: Topology for configuring PAP and CHAP Authentication

Let's start the lab.

Step 1: Configure all the devices in the topology

The following are screenshots in which basic router configuration commands and steps are shown.

Perform all the basic configuration on all the routers: Assign hostname and disable DNS lookup. Also, configure all the interfaces on R1, R2, R3, and R4with IP address as shown in the topology.

Configuring R1 Interfaces
Go to Router 1 and configure the following commands:

```
Router(config)# Hostname R1

R1(config)# no ip domain-lookup

R1(config)# interface serial 0/0

R1(config-if)# ip address 10.1.0.1 255.0.0.0

R1(config-if)# no shutdown

R1(config-if)# ex
```
```
*Jun 15 10:58:49.052: %LINK-3-UPDOWN: Interface Serial0/0, changed state to up

*Jun 15 10:58:50.053: %LINEPROTO-5-UPDOWN: Line protocol on Interface Serial0/0,
changed state to up
```

Configuring R2 Interfaces
Go to Router 2 and configure the following commands:

```
Router(config)# hostname R2

R2(config)# no ip domain-lookup

R2(config)# interface serial 0/0

R2(config-if)# ip address 10.1.0.2 255.0.0.0

R2(config-if)# no shutdown

R2(config-if)# exit
```

```
*Jun 15 11:11:12.973: %LINK-3-UPDOWN: Interface Serial0/0, changed state to up

*Jun 15 11:11:13.977: %LINEPROTO-5-UPDOWN: Line protocol on Interface Serial0/0,
changed state to up


R2(config)# interface serial 0/1

R2(config-if)# ip address 192.168.10.1 255.255.255.0

R2(config-if)# no shut

R2(config-if)# ex

R2(config)#

*Jun 15 11:12:08.086: %LINK-3-UPDOWN: Interface Serial0/1, changed state to up

*Jun 15 11:12:09.094: %LINEPROTO-5-UPDOWN: Line protocol on Interface Serial0/1,
changed state to up
```

Configuring R3 Interfaces

Go to Router 3 and configure the following commands:

```
Router(config)# hostname R3

R3(config)# interface serial 0/1

R3(config-if)# ip address 192.168.10.2 255.255.255.0

R3(config-if)# no shut

R3(config-if)# exit

*Jun 15 11:19:18.100: %LINK-3-UPDOWN: Interface Serial0/1, changed state to up

*Jun 15 11:19:19.106: %LINEPROTO-5-UPDOWN: Line protocol on Interface Serial0/1,
changed state to up


R3(config)# interface serial 0/0

R3(config-if)# ip address 172.16.20.1 255.255.0.0

R3(config-if)# no sh

R3(config-if)# ex

*Jun 15 11:19:47.996: %LINK-3-UPDOWN: Interface Serial0/0, changed state to up

*Jun 15 11:19:49.000: %LINEPROTO-5-UPDOWN: Line protocol on Interface Serial0/0,
changed state to up
```

Configuring R4 Interface

Go to Router 4 and configure the following commands:

```
Router> en
Router# config t
Enter configuration commands, one per line.  End with CNTL/Z.

Router(config)# hostname R4
R4(config)# no ip domain-lookup
R4(config)# interface serial 0/0
R4(config-if)# ip address 172.16.20.2 255.255.0.0
R4(config-if)# no shut
R4(config-if)# ex
*Jun 15 11:29:08.216: %LINK-3-UPDOWN: Interface Serial0/0, changed state to up
*Jun 15 11:29:09.222: %LINEPROTO-5-UPDOWN: Line protocol on Interface Serial0/0,
changed state to up
```

Step 2: Now configure OSPF on the devices according to the topology.

Configuring OSPF on Router 1, Router 2, Router 3, Router 4.

Configuring OSPF on Router 1

Go to Router 1 and configure OSPF commands:

```
R1(config)# router ospf 1
R1(config-router)# router-id 1.1.1.1
R1(config-router)# net 10.1.0.0 0.255.255.255 area 0
R1(config-router)# ex
```

Configuring OSPF on Router 2

Go to Router 2 and configure OSPF commands:

```
R2(config)# router ospf 2
```

```
R2(config-router)# router-id 2.2.2.2

R2(config-router)# network 192.168.10.0 0.0.0.255 area 10

R2(config-router)# network 10.1.0.0 0.255.255.255 area 0

R2(config-router)# ex

*Jun 15 11:43:15.949: %OSPF-5-ADJCHG: Process 2, Nbr 1.1.1.1 on Serial0/0 from
LOADING to FULL, Loading Done
```

Configuring OSPF on Router 3

Go to Router 3 and configure OSPF commands:

```
R3(config)# router ospf 3

R3(config-router)# router-id 3.3.3.3

R3(config-router)# net 192.168.10.0 0.0.0.255 area 10

*Jun 15 11:47:14.748: %OSPF-5-ADJCHG: Process 3, Nbr 2.2.2.2 on Serial0/1 from
LOADING to FULL, Loading Done

R3(config-router)# network 172.16.20.0 0.0.255.255 area 20

R3(config-router)#ex
```

Configuring OSPF on Router 4

Go to Router 4 and configure OSPF commands:

```
R4(config)# router ospf 4

R4(config-router)# router-id 4.4.4.4

R4(config-router)# net 172.16.20.0 0.0.255.255 area 20

R4(config-router)# ex

*Jun 15 11:52:38.218: %OSPF-5-ADJCHG: Process 4, Nbr 3.3.3.3 on Serial0/0 from
LOADING to FULL, Loading Done
```

Step 3: Check routing tables of the routers.

Use 'show ip route' command to check the routers routing table

```
R1# show ip route
```

```
R1                                                    —    □    ×

R1>
R1>en
R1#show ip route
Codes: L - local, C - connected, S - static, R - RIP, M - mobile, B - BGP
       D - EIGRP, EX - EIGRP external, O - OSPF, IA - OSPF inter area
       N1 - OSPF NSSA external type 1, N2 - OSPF NSSA external type 2
       E1 - OSPF external type 1, E2 - OSPF external type 2
       i - IS-IS, su - IS-IS summary, L1 - IS-IS level-1, L2 - IS-IS level-2
       ia - IS-IS inter area, * - candidate default, U - per-user static route
       o - ODR, P - periodic downloaded static route, H - NHRP, l - LISP
       a - application route
       + - replicated route, % - next hop override

Gateway of last resort is not set

      10.0.0.0/8 is variably subnetted, 2 subnets, 2 masks
C        10.0.0.0/8 is directly connected, Serial0/0
L        10.1.0.1/32 is directly connected, Serial0/0
O IA  192.168.10.0/24 [110/128] via 10.1.0.2, 00:12:04, Serial0/0
R1#
```

R2# **show ip route**

```
R2                                                    —    □    ×

R2#show ip route
Codes: L - local, C - connected, S - static, R - RIP, M - mobile, B - BGP
       D - EIGRP, EX - EIGRP external, O - OSPF, IA - OSPF inter area
       N1 - OSPF NSSA external type 1, N2 - OSPF NSSA external type 2
       E1 - OSPF external type 1, E2 - OSPF external type 2
       i - IS-IS, su - IS-IS summary, L1 - IS-IS level-1, L2 - IS-IS level-2
       ia - IS-IS inter area, * - candidate default, U - per-user static route
       o - ODR, P - periodic downloaded static route, H - NHRP, l - LISP
       a - application route
       + - replicated route, % - next hop override

Gateway of last resort is not set

      10.0.0.0/8 is variably subnetted, 2 subnets, 2 masks
C        10.0.0.0/8 is directly connected, Serial0/0
L        10.1.0.2/32 is directly connected, Serial0/0
      192.168.10.0/24 is variably subnetted, 2 subnets, 2 masks
C        192.168.10.0/24 is directly connected, Serial0/1
L        192.168.10.1/32 is directly connected, Serial0/1
R2#
```

R3# `show ip route`

```
R3                                                          —   □   ✕

R3#show ip route
Codes: L - local, C - connected, S - static, R - RIP, M - mobile, B - BGP
       D - EIGRP, EX - EIGRP external, O - OSPF, IA - OSPF inter area
       N1 - OSPF NSSA external type 1, N2 - OSPF NSSA external type 2
       E1 - OSPF external type 1, E2 - OSPF external type 2
       i - IS-IS, su - IS-IS summary, L1 - IS-IS level-1, L2 - IS-IS level-2
       ia - IS-IS inter area, * - candidate default, U - per-user static route
       o - ODR, P - periodic downloaded static route, H - NHRP, l - LISP
       a - application route
       + - replicated route, % - next hop override

Gateway of last resort is not set

O IA  10.0.0.0/8 [110/128] via 192.168.10.1, 00:14:46, Serial0/1
      172.16.0.0/16 is variably subnetted, 2 subnets, 2 masks
C        172.16.0.0/16 is directly connected, Serial0/0
L        172.16.20.1/32 is directly connected, Serial0/0
      192.168.10.0/24 is variably subnetted, 2 subnets, 2 masks
C        192.168.10.0/24 is directly connected, Serial0/1
L        192.168.10.2/32 is directly connected, Serial0/1
R3#
```

R4# `show ip route`

```
R4                                                          —   □   ✕

R4#show ip route
Codes: L - local, C - connected, S - static, R - RIP, M - mobile, B - BGP
       D - EIGRP, EX - EIGRP external, O - OSPF, IA - OSPF inter area
       N1 - OSPF NSSA external type 1, N2 - OSPF NSSA external type 2
       E1 - OSPF external type 1, E2 - OSPF external type 2
       i - IS-IS, su - IS-IS summary, L1 - IS-IS level-1, L2 - IS-IS level-2
       ia - IS-IS inter area, * - candidate default, U - per-user static route
       o - ODR, P - periodic downloaded static route, H - NHRP, l - LISP
       a - application route
       + - replicated route, % - next hop override

Gateway of last resort is not set

      172.16.0.0/16 is variably subnetted, 2 subnets, 2 masks
C        172.16.0.0/16 is directly connected, Serial0/0
L        172.16.20.2/32 is directly connected, Serial0/0
R4#
```

We can see that R4 (area 20) is disconnected to the area 10 and backbone area 0. Therefore, in task 03, we are going to use OSPF virtual link in order to mitigate the issue.

Step 4: Configure PPP encapsulation with PAP and CHAP authentication on all the serial connection.
Configuring PPP encapsulation with CHAP between R1 and R2

R1(config)# **username R2 Password IPS**

R1(config)# **interface serial 0/0**

R1(config-if)# **encapsulation ppp**

*Jun 15 12:07:59.469: %OSPF-5-ADJCHG: Process 1, Nbr 2.2.2.2 on Serial0/0 from FULL to DOWN, Neighbor Down: Interface down or detached

*Jun 15 12:08:01.469: %LINEPROTO-5-UPDOWN: Line protocol on Interface Serial0/0, changed state to down

R1(config-if)# **ppp authentication chap**

R1(config-if)# **ex**

```
🖳 R1                                                              —    □    ✕

R1(config)#username R2 Password IPS
R1(config)#interface serial 0/0
R1(config-if)#enca
R1(config-if)#encapsulation ppp
R1(config-if)#
*Jun 15 12:07:59.469: %OSPF-5-ADJCHG: Process 1, Nbr 2.2.2.2 on Serial0/0 from FULL
to DOWN, Neighbor Down: Interface down or detached
R1(config-if)#
*Jun 15 12:08:01.469: %LINEPROTO-5-UPDOWN: Line protocol on Interface Serial0/0,
changed state to down
R1(config-if)#ppp authentication chap
R1(config-if)#ex
R1(config)#
```

R2> **en**

R2# **config t**

Enter configuration commands, one per line. End with CNTL/Z.

R2(config)# **username R1 password IPS**

R2(config)# **interface serial 0/0**

R2(config-if)# **encapsulation ppp**

```
*Jun 15 12:12:33.404: %LINEPROTO-5-UPDOWN: Line protocol on Interface Serial0/0,
changed state to up

*Jun 15 12:12:33.444: %OSPF-5-ADJCHG: Process 2, Nbr 1.1.1.1 on Serial0/0 from
LOADING to FULL, Loading Done
```

R2(config-if)# **ppp authentication chap**

```
*Jun 15 12:12:48.240: %LINEPROTO-5-UPDOWN: Line protocol on Interface Serial0/0,
changed state to down

*Jun 15 12:12:48.241: %OSPF-5-ADJCHG: Process 2, Nbr 1.1.1.1 on Serial0/0 from FULL
to DOWN, Neighbor Down: Interface down or detached

*Jun 15 12:12:48.299: %LINEPROTO-5-UPDOWN: Line protocol on Interface Serial0/0,
changed state to up

*Jun 15 12:12:48.359: %OSPF-5-ADJCHG: Process 2, Nbr 1.1.1.1 on Serial0/0 from
LOADING to FULL, Loading Done
```

R2(config-if)# **ex**

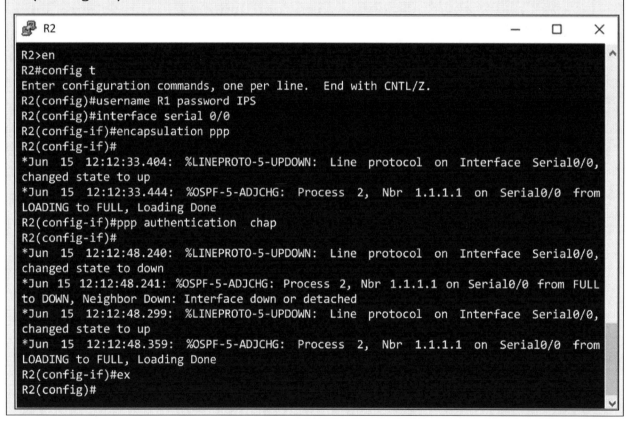

Configuring PPP encapsulation with PAP between R2 and R3

R2# **config t**

Enter configuration commands, one per line. End with CNTL/Z.

R2(config)# **username R3 password IPS1**

R2(config)# **interface serial 0/1**

R2(config-if)# **encapsulation ppp**

R2(config-if)#

*Jun 15 12:18:44.904: %OSPF-5-ADJCHG: Process 2, Nbr 3.3.3.3 on Serial0/1 from FULL to DOWN, Neighbor Down: Interface down or detached

*Jun 15 12:18:46.903: %LINEPROTO-5-UPDOWN: Line protocol on Interface Serial0/1, changed state to down

R2(config-if)# **ppp authentication pap**

R2(config-if)# **ppp pap sent-username R2 Password IPS1**

R2(config-if)# **ex**

```
R2                                                        —    □    ✕

R2#config t
Enter configuration commands, one per line.  End with CNTL/Z.
R2(config)#username R3 password IPS1
R2(config)#interface serial 0/1
R2(config-if)#encapsulation ppp
*Jun 15 12:18:44.904: %OSPF-5-ADJCHG: Process 2, Nbr 3.3.3.3 on Serial0/1 from FULL
to DOWN, Neighbor Down: Interface down or detached
*Jun 15 12:18:46.903: %LINEPROTO-5-UPDOWN: Line protocol on Interface Serial0/1,
changed state to down
R2(config-if)#ppp authentication pap
R2(config-if)#ppp pap sent-username R2 Password IPS1
R2(config-if)#ex
```

R3(config)# **username R2 password IPS1**

R3(config)# **interface serial 0/1**

R3(config-if)# **encapsulation ppp**

R3(config-if)# **ppp authentication pap**

R3(config-if)# **ppp pap sent-username R3 password IPS1**

R3(config-if)# **ex**

```
*Jun 15 12:24:28.021: %LINEPROTO-5-UPDOWN: Line protocol on Interface Serial0/1,
changed state to up

*Jun 15 12:24:28.079: %OSPF-5-ADJCHG: Process 3, Nbr 2.2.2.2 on Serial0/1 from
LOADING to FULL, Loading Done
```

```
R3                                                              —    □    ✕

R3(config)#username R2 password IPS1
R3(config)#interface serial 0/1
R3(config-if)#encapsulation ppp
R3(config-if)#ppp authentication pap
R3(config-if)#ppp pap sent-username R3 password IPS1
R3(config-if)#ex
*Jun 15 12:24:28.021: %LINEPROTO-5-UPDOWN: Line protocol on Interface Serial0/1,
changed state to up
*Jun 15 12:24:28.079: %OSPF-5-ADJCHG: Process 3, Nbr 2.2.2.2 on Serial0/1 from
LOADING to FULL, Loading Done
```

Configuring PPP encapsulation with CHAP-PAP between R3 and R4

R3(config)# **username R4 password IPS2**

R3(config)# **interface serial 0/0**

R3(config-if)# **encapsulation ppp**

*Jun 15 12:28:54.683: %OSPF-5-ADJCHG: Process 3, Nbr 4.4.4.4 on Serial0/0 from FULL
to DOWN, Neighbor Down: Interface down or detached

*Jun 15 12:28:56.679: %LINEPROTO-5-UPDOWN: Line protocol on Interface Serial0/0,
changed state to down

R3(config-if)# **ppp authentication chap pap**

R3(config-if)# **ppp pap sent-username R3 password IPS2**

R3(config-if)# **ex**

```
R3                                                    —    □    X

R3(config)#username R4 password IPS2
R3(config)#interface serial 0/0
R3(config-if)#encapsulation ppp
*Jun 15 12:28:54.683: %OSPF-5-ADJCHG: Process 3, Nbr 4.4.4.4 on Serial0/0 from FULL
to DOWN, Neighbor Down: Interface down or detached
*Jun 15 12:28:56.679: %LINEPROTO-5-UPDOWN: Line protocol on Interface Serial0/0,
changed state to down

R3(config-if)#ppp authentication chap pap
R3(config-if)#ppp pap sent-username R3 password IPS2
R3(config-if)#ex
R3(config)#
```

R4(config)# **username R3 password IPS2**

R4(config)# **interface serial 0/0**

R4(config-if)# **encapsulation ppp**

*Jun 15 12:33:12.563: %LINEPROTO-5-UPDOWN: Line protocol on Interface Serial0/0, changed state to up

*Jun 15 12:33:12.612: %OSPF-5-ADJCHG: Process 4, Nbr 3.3.3.3 on Serial0/0 from LOADING to FULL, Loading Done

R4(config-if)# **ppp authentication chap pap**

*Jun 15 12:33:27.975: %LINEPROTO-5-UPDOWN: Line protocol on Interface Serial0/0, changed state to down

*Jun 15 12:33:27.976: %OSPF-5-ADJCHG: Process 4, Nbr 3.3.3.3 on Serial0/0 from FULL to DOWN, Neighbor Down: Interface down or detached

*Jun 15 12:33:28.016: %LINEPROTO-5-UPDOWN: Line protocol on Interface Serial0/0, changed state to up

*Jun 15 12:33:28.068: %OSPF-5-ADJCHG: Process 4, Nbr 3.3.3.3 on Serial0/0 from LOADING to FULL, Loading Done

R4(config-if)# **ppp pap sent-username R4 password IPS2**

R4(config-if)# **ex**

```
R4                                                          —   □   ×

R4(config)#username R3 password IPS2
R4(config)#interface serial 0/0
R4(config-if)#encapsulation ppp
*Jun 15 12:33:12.563: %LINEPROTO-5-UPDOWN: Line protocol on Interface Serial0/0,
changed state to up
*Jun 15 12:33:12.612: %OSPF-5-ADJCHG: Process 4, Nbr 3.3.3.3 on Serial0/0 from
LOADING to FULL, Loading Done

R4(config-if)#ppp authentication chap pap
*Jun 15 12:33:27.975: %LINEPROTO-5-UPDOWN: Line protocol on Interface Serial0/0,
changed state to down
*Jun 15 12:33:27.976: %OSPF-5-ADJCHG: Process 4, Nbr 3.3.3.3 on Serial0/0 from FULL
to DOWN, Neighbor Down: Interface down or detached
*Jun 15 12:33:28.016: %LINEPROTO-5-UPDOWN: Line protocol on Interface Serial0/0,
changed state to up
*Jun 15 12:33:28.068: %OSPF-5-ADJCHG: Process 4, Nbr 3.3.3.3 on Serial0/0 from
LOADING to FULL, Loading Done

R4(config-if)#ppp pap sent-username R4 password IPS2
R4(config-if)#ex
```

Step 5: Configure OSPF Virtual link to connect area 20 to area 0
Configuring OSPF virtual link on R2 and R3
R2> **en**
R2# **config t**
Enter configuration commands, one per line. End with CNTL/Z.
R2(config)# **router ospf 2**
R2(config-router)# **area 10 virtual-link 3.3.3.3**
R2(config-router)# **ex**

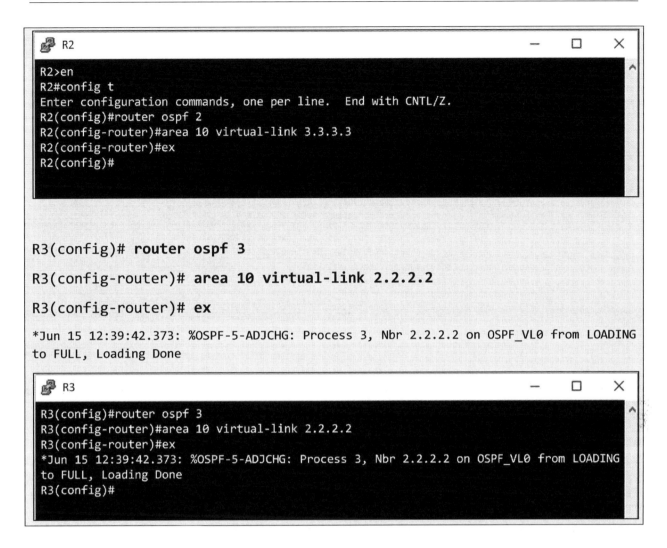

Step 6: Ping all the routers.

R4 now have a route in the routing table to ping R1 (interface so/o). And for verification, the ping test result is shown in the below figure.

Ping result of R1 from R4:

R4# **Ping 10.1.0.1**

```
R4                                                        —  □  ✕

Press RETURN to get started.


R4>en
R4#ping 10.1.0.1
Type escape sequence to abort.
Sending 5, 100-byte ICMP Echos to 10.1.0.1, timeout is 2 seconds:
!!!!!
Success rate is 100 percent (5/5), round-trip min/avg/max = 25/25/26 ms
R4#
```

Ping result of R3 from R1:

R1# **Ping 172.16.20.1**

```
R1                                                        —  □  ✕

Press RETURN to get started.


R1>en
R1#ping 172.16.20.1
Type escape sequence to abort.
Sending 5, 100-byte ICMP Echos to 172.16.20.1, timeout is 2 seconds:
!!!!!
Success rate is 100 percent (5/5), round-trip min/avg/max = 16/17/18 ms
R1#
```

Ping result of R4 from R2:

R2# **Ping 172.16.20.2**

```
R2                                                        —  □  ✕

Press RETURN to get started.


R2>en
R2#ping 172.16.20.2
Type escape sequence to abort.
Sending 5, 100-byte ICMP Echos to 172.16.20.2, timeout is 2 seconds:
!!!!!
Success rate is 100 percent (5/5), round-trip min/avg/max = 17/17/18 ms
R2#
```

Ping result of R1 from R3:

R3# **Ping 10.1.0.1**

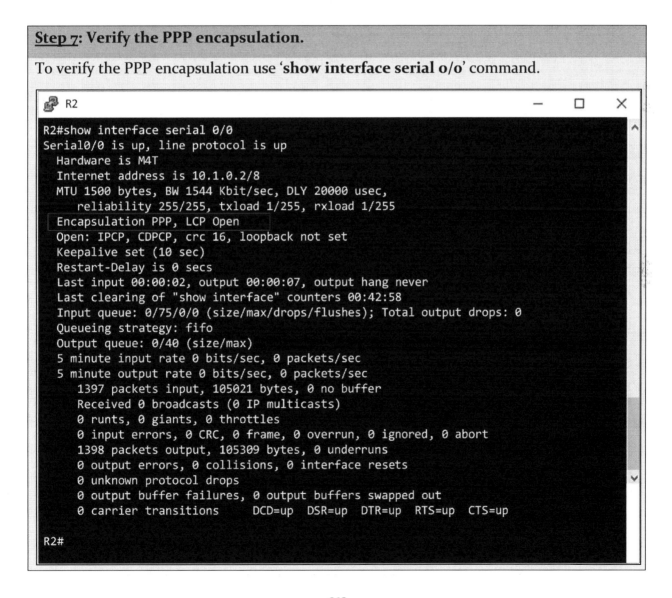

Step 7: Verify the PPP encapsulation.

To verify the PPP encapsulation use '**show interface serial 0/0**' command.

```
R2#show interface serial 0/0
Serial0/0 is up, line protocol is up
  Hardware is M4T
  Internet address is 10.1.0.2/8
  MTU 1500 bytes, BW 1544 Kbit/sec, DLY 20000 usec,
     reliability 255/255, txload 1/255, rxload 1/255
  Encapsulation PPP, LCP Open
  Open: IPCP, CDPCP, crc 16, loopback not set
  Keepalive set (10 sec)
  Restart-Delay is 0 secs
  Last input 00:00:02, output 00:00:07, output hang never
  Last clearing of "show interface" counters 00:42:58
  Input queue: 0/75/0/0 (size/max/drops/flushes); Total output drops: 0
  Queueing strategy: fifo
  Output queue: 0/40 (size/max)
  5 minute input rate 0 bits/sec, 0 packets/sec
  5 minute output rate 0 bits/sec, 0 packets/sec
     1397 packets input, 105021 bytes, 0 no buffer
     Received 0 broadcasts (0 IP multicasts)
     0 runts, 0 giants, 0 throttles
     0 input errors, 0 CRC, 0 frame, 0 overrun, 0 ignored, 0 abort
     1398 packets output, 105309 bytes, 0 underruns
     0 output errors, 0 collisions, 0 interface resets
     0 unknown protocol drops
     0 output buffer failures, 0 output buffers swapped out
     0 carrier transitions    DCD=up  DSR=up  DTR=up  RTS=up  CTS=up

R2#
```

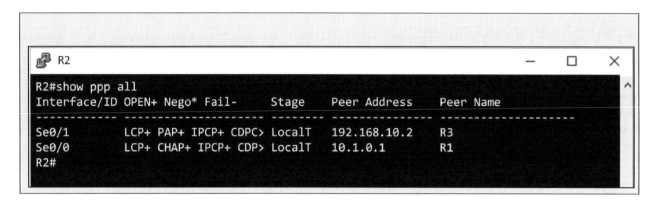

An Overview of Federated Identities

Server Based Authentication

Web communication is stateless communication because every command or request is unique that means it has no link to the preceding request or command. This is why authentication through the web is a challenge. So the question is, how we can extend that authentication of the request made previously?

Conventionally, this is achieved through Server-Based Authentication. In Server-Based Authentication, the server has a record of login. A session ID is granted to every user during login, and when the user sends a request, the server checks the session validity. This process adds overhead and ends in scalability issues to the server as the users increase.

The process of Server Based Authentication:

1. When the client logs in the session, information is received by the server.
2. The server checks the session information when the client sends an application request.
3. If the session information is authentic, then the feedback is sent to the client.

Token-based Authentication

It is also stateless based authentication like web communication (HTTP). In this authentication process session information is not saved on the server, but instead, the server sends a token to the client and the client store that token. The token is moved with the request when the client made a subsequent request. The server checks the validity of the token, and if the token is valid, then the server responds accordingly to the client. This process is secure because the token expires after a certain amount of time and also scalable because now the session information is kept by the client and not by the server.

The process of Token-based Authentication

1. The client login to the server.
2. After investigating the validity of the authentication process, a token is sent to the client.
3. The client sends that token along with the application request.
4. If the token is valid, server responds to the client.

Federation

Federation is a system that grants access to the other users also who may not have local-login. It means a single token is given to the user who is entrusted or authenticated across various systems just like in SSO (Single Sign-On). Federated network is created by third parties so that users can log in with separate credentials. For example; Facebook credentials, Twitter Credentials, etc. In establishing the federated network, the third party has to create a trust based relationship beforehand.

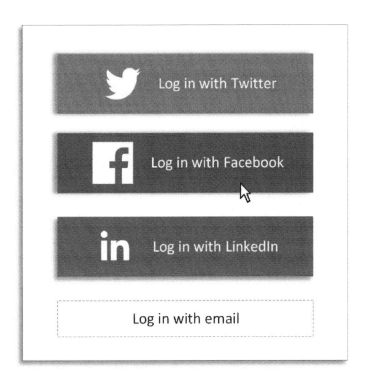

Figure 4-07: Example of Federation

Security Assertion Mark-up Language (SAML)

SAML is an authentication and authorization method that is an open standard. The user is authenticated through a third party for achieving entry to local sources. Shibboleth software is an example of SAML. Modern mobile networks do not have SAML because it was not created for mobile devices that are its major weakness.

OAuth

It is introduced by Google, Twitter, and other parties. It serves as an authorization to what resources a user can gain. OAuth is usually observed to be used by Facebook, Google, etc. It is not a protocol for authentication and just provides authorization between applications. OAuth is combined with OpenID Connect (handles SSO) and then OAuth decides what resources a user may gain.

Identity & Access Control Management

Access Control Models

The first step towards 'access' is the authorization. Authorization is a combination of two things: policy definition and policy enforcement

- **Policy Definition**: Decision making about the resources a user is given access to
- **Policy Enforcement**: Ensures that the user is accessing only the authorized resources

Through access control models, a user determines what rights he has or what resources he can access. Access control models vary from organization to organization depending upon their goals of controlling access.

Mandatory Access Control (MAC)

The operating system describes the limit on how much a user can access the resources based on clearance level of security. Each object that somebody requires to access is assigned a label (confidential label, secret label, etc.) and then users are provided with some rights that are decided by the administrator which the users cannot change. Through these rights, a user can determine what he can access. Some users may access confidential resources; some may access secret resources and so on.

Discretionary Access Control (DAC)

Commonly used in most operating systems. It is a type of model in which the owner decides who can access the object or what type of access the user can gain. The owner can also modify access at any time.

The advantage of DAC: Flexible Model. The owner can easily determine who can gain access and modify the access control whenever he wants to.

The disadvantage of DAC: Security is weak. The whole system's security depends upon the security settings made by the owner. For example, suppose you create a spreadsheet and as an owner, you decide who can access the objects of the file and what objects of the file. You can modify the settings when required.

Role-Based Access Control (RBAC)

Role-based access control model is a type of model that offers access based on the role of user in the organization like CEO, manager, director, team leader, etc. Type of access depends on the user's role.

The administrator is responsible for allowing access to the users according to their designated roles. The RBAC allows users to gain access implicitly. For example, if some type of access is provided to the team leader, then by becoming the part of team leader group, a group member can also enjoy the rights of team leader. Windows group is used in Windows Operating System for providing Role-based Access Control.

Attribute-Based Access Control (ABAC)

In ABAC model, the right of accessing the resources is allotted to the user depending upon the policies collectively with the attributes. It is also considered as *Next Generation Model* of authorization because there are many different attributes through which it can be determined that what type of access a user can have. These attributes may include *who is accessing (Role), from where is accessing (Location), what is being accessed (Resource),* and *when is it being accessed (Time).*

Rule-based Access Control (RBAC)

In rule-based access control model, the administrator creates a set of rules. These rules describe the limits and restrictions to access. Firewall is one of the rule-based access control models we are familiar with. Example of rules are: "Only the people in Pakistan can gain access to the web page," "the web form can only be accessed through explorer browser," "the web form can only be accessed between 4 to 8 pm", etc.

File System Security

File is mostly protected over time by the operating system itself or could also be maintained by the proprietor. An access control list is kept by the operating system that contains a list of users along with the rights and permission. Some file systems also allow encryption and decryption of data for higher security.

Database Security

Database server possesses their own access control. Database security is implemented through different approaches or database servers have different choices for their security purpose such as; Encryption, Data Integrity (helps to avoid data loss), etc.

Access Control Technologies

The following are some technologies through which the access to the resources can be controlled:

Proximity Cards

A passive device that is used to unlock doors. A proximity reader reads the card, compare the information with the information in the database and then grant or deny access.

Smart Card

Integrated Circuit (IC) card, is mostly used for access control. It is a physical card that the person can slide into the computer or another device to gain access and typically contain a digital certificate for the purpose of authentication.

Biometric Factors

For controlling access, numerous biometric factors are used such as fingerprint, voice recognition, retinal scanner, facial recognition, and iris scanner.

Token Generator

This is another method of access control. The token generator generates pseudorandom tokens that are used along with various authentication methods.

HOTP

It stands for HMAC-based One Time Password. The type of method in which different tokens are used every time for authentication means new token is used only once and never again. These tokens or passwords are generated through a secret-key and a counter.

TOTP

It stands for Time-based One Time Password. These tokens or passwords are generated through the time of day and a secret key. Many organizations like Facebook, Microsoft, Google, etc. use this method.

Authentication through Certificate

Popular access control method. This method of certificate-based authentication. It is used in various forms or types like PIV cards, CAC cards, and Smart cards. In these cards, the certificates are built-in for authentication or identification.

Account Management

Account Types

User Account:

This is a type of account that is most common among users and associated with a single person. It allows limited access to the operating system. Each user is assigned with a particular identification number by the user account. Multi-users can use the same computer for accessing their resources only, by using *User Account*, which also keeps

each user's data secure from another unauthorized user. This means that by using the User Account, multi-user can log in to the same computer and but they can only access their own resources.

Shared Account

As the name suggests, this account can be used by more than one person. For example, some operating systems allow the user to log in to a guest account (Guest Login). The shared account is difficult to manage because it is hard to identify the person logging in. If the password of the shared account is changed, then everyone needs to be notified that the password is changed and this brings complexity to the management of the password. It is recommended to use User account on the system rather than Shared Account.

Service Account

The operating system or services of operating system use an internal account that is referred as Service Account. It is used to run database or web server. Used only on the local computer and no user can login interactively. Different types of access permission can be set up for various services when using Service Account, which means database and web server rights may vary from each other. Some of the services accounts require username and password, and some do not.

Privileged Account

Also known as Root account or administrator. Generally, these accounts can access the complete operating system. If you have to install application or device drivers or have to manage hardware, then you need to log in to Privileged Account.

General Concepts

Least Privilege

Least privilege is considered as a significant principle in the management of the account. The principle that allows the user to have only the rights and permission that are necessary for them to perform their task or accomplish their objective and no extra rights are given to the user. By limiting the access rights of objects (user, process, or application), the administrator can also limit the cause of harms and malware.

On-Boarding

On-Boarding refers to the hiring of new personnel in the organization. For account management, it is very important for the administrator to have an agreement and AUC (Acceptable Use Policy) to be signed by the on-boarding member. After the agreement signing step, the administrator creates an account of the new member and put him to an appropriate access control group according to their requirement.

Off-Boarding

Prior to on-boarding, Off-boarding refers to the removal of personnel from the organization or group or team. When the member is off-boarded there are some proper steps that should be followed by the administrator that is, the off-boarding personnel's account should be disabled (not deleted) and he should be removed from the access group.

Perform Routine Audits

Routine Auditing allows the administrator to check or to assure that the account policies are being followed by everyone. It means that the administrator will check validation of all the accounts of the users and ensure if all members are in their respective group. The routine auditing is necessary because of timely On-Boarding and Off-Boarding of the members. Some audits are automatic that automatically generate a list of alerts.

Auditing

Auditing can be categorised into two main types; one is Permission Auditing and second is Usage Auditing.

- **Permission Auditing**-Type of auditing to ensure that every user has legit permission or only the permission they need. It also assures that all the users are in a proper group.
- **Usage Auditing**-Type of auditing to assure that all the resources are being used correctly and to review how and where the files are being stored, and if the system is secure.

Standard Naming Convention

One of an essential part of maintaining the account is Standard Naming Convention. A username is typically assigned to everyone when they set up an account. The Naming Convention should hold the following features:

- **Uniqueness** - It should be Unique and does not conflict.
- **Consistency** - It should be consistent like, if a person is asked to enter the Last name and then the First name, then everybody should be asked to enter the username in the same pattern.
- **Persistency** - It should be persistent, which means the user must use the same username every time.
- **Memorable** - It should be memorable but not recognizable.

Account Maintenance

Account maintenance includes the creation of an account, Periodic updates and De-provision of account.

- **Creation of Account** - It includes the provision of appropriate username, group, and access.
- **The Periodic Updates**-The process to update about the changes.
- **Account Deactivation**-The deactivation of the account after any member leaves the group.

Group-Based Access Control

It refers to the provision of correct rights and permission to the user that are changeable by the time. The first step is to create a group then set rules for each group according to the access rights given in particular. The user is sorted into the group according to their rights to access.

Location Based Policies

Access policy can also be set based on the location of the user like GPS (accurate), IP address (completely inaccurate sometimes), etc. By using this policy, the user can be restricted from accessing data based on the location.

Account Policy Enforcement

Credential Management

Credential management is necessary when it comes to credential security. The credential that is being used should be stored on the server instead of on the client. And the credentials must not be sent in clear (should be encrypted) over the network.

Configuring Setting

It is difficult to create individual policies for large organizations. In Windows Operating system, the administrative tools like Windows Group Policy Management help to set security rules and apply an administrative setting in the system. This Group Policy Management is different from NTFS.

Group Policy Control

Group policy control is used by the administrator to limit people access right in the network. Multiple Security policies can be implemented on the network including the password length limit, Smart card authentication requirement, security log size limit, login restriction, etc.

Password Complexity and Length

To make strong and unrecognizable password, one must use a combination of uppercase letters and lowercase letters, numbers, and symbols and must be of long length (that can easily be remembered). The organizations can set rule for password requirement like the password must be of 12-character length and must contain uppercase and lowercase letters plus at least one number and symbol.

Password Expiration and Recovery

Using the same password for a long time open paths for the hackers to hack password through brute force attack. For this reason, many organizations force users to change their password after a certain amount of time. In case of password loss, the password recovery method helps to reset the password. There is a formal procedure for recovering the password to ensure that the authentic person is recovering the password.

Account Lockout

Account lockout means that the account is temporarily blocked for the user due to incorrect entry of password too many times. Automatic Lockout is very common on most of the systems.

Access Control and Identity Management Mind Map

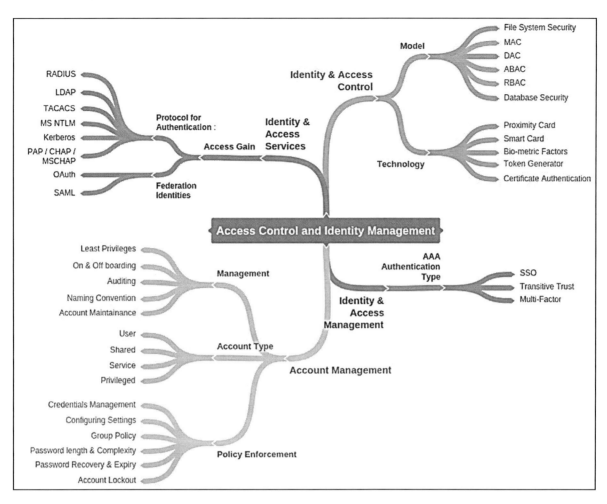

Figure 4-08: Access Control & Identity Management

Practice Question

1. Which account is used to run processes that do not involve human interference to start or stop?

   A. Guest account
   B. Process account
   C. Service account
   D. Root account

2. A person who works in the IT department of the bank informs you that the tellers are permitted to access their terminal from 9 A.M. to 5 P.M., Monday to Saturday only. This restriction is an example of which of the following?

   A. User auditing
   B. Least privilege
   C. Time-of-day restrictions

D. Account verification

3. The process of assigning a computer ID to a particular user is identified as?

   A. Authentication
   B. Validation
   C. Authorization
   D. Identification

4. Which is not a true category of authentication factors to be used if you are developing a new multifactor authentication system for your company?

   A. Something you know
   B. Something you see
   C. Something you are
   D. Something you do

5. Which one of the following passwords seems hardest to break?

   A. An eight-character password based on a common dictionary word
   B. A six-character password using only uppercase letters
   C. A seven-character password using a completely random mix of letters, symbols, and numbers
   D. An eight-character password using only lowercase letters

6. The process of ensuring that every account on a mail server is owned by a valid and active employee is known as?

   A. Recertification
   B. Privilege auditing
   C. Password cracking
   D. Payroll auditing

7. What should occur when a user is no longer authorized or no longer desires to use a system?

   A. Account recovery
   B. Account deletion
   C. Account reset
   D. Account audit

8. For managing identities across corporates and systems, the protocols, policies, and practices are defined by which of the following?

   A. Transitive trust
   B. Single sign-on

C. Identity Federation

D. Account management

9. Which of the following scenarios is suitable to use a shared account?

A. On a server maintained by different personnel

B. On a publicly accessible PC running in kiosk mode

C. If the account is used only to administer e-mail accounts

D. If the account is used by the CEO and their assistant

10. For generating a one-time password which algorithm uses the secret key with a current time stamp?

A. Hash-based Message Authentication Code

B. Date-hashed Message Authorization Password

C. Time-based One-Time Password

D. Single Sign-on

Chapter 05: Risk Management

Overview of Security Policies, Plans, and Procedures

Standard Operating Procedure

For handling IT operation, every organization has its own procedures. These procedures are known as Standard Operating Procedures. The standard operating procedure assures that all the applications and systems are secure.

Here is a simple example of a standard operating procedure when a new account needs to be made:

Agreement Types

Interoperability Agreement

To provide product and services, every organization needs to work with a third-party. It is important to make an agreement before handling sensitive data of your organization to a third party. The question that arises is why would an organization share its sensitive data to a third party. One reason might be that the organization may need a third party that provides web hosting, firewall management or payroll services to your organization.

ISA

ISA stands for Interconnection Security Agreement. A type of agreement which takes place between the organization and the interconnected IT system. The requirements of the security that are associated with the interconnection are documented in ISA agreement. The document is detailed with all the legitimate plans of action about how the connection will be established, maintained and disconnected by the two parties.

MOU/MOA

It stands for Memorandum of Understanding. It is an agreement which can be bilateral or multi-lateral, i.e., between two or more parties. It is a type of agreement between two or more parties, containing "set of intended actions" that direct towards a common goal.

SLA

SLA stands for Service Level Agreement. It is a type of agreement that takes place between the client and the service provider. SLA agreement defines the terms of services that exist between the client and the service provider.

R&S®Service Level Agreement	Warranty 1 year	Basic 1 to 4 years	Advanced 1 to 4 years	Premium 1 to 4 years
24/7 problem reporting: access to online ticketing system	●	●	●	●
Technical phone support during business hours	●	1 working day	4 hours	2 hours
24/7 emergency support technical support, even outside of business hours			4 hours	2 hours
Overview of your requests (service level agreement reporting)	●	●	●	●
Maintenance releases (software updates)	●	●	●	●
Remote error analysis	●	●	●	●
Remote system updates		●	●	●
Access to feature request system	●	●	●	●
Repair services	●		10 working days	5 working days
Hardware exchange service				shipped no later than the next working day
Managed local spare parts pool	optional	optional	optional	optional
On-site support	optional	optional	optional	optional
Regular maintenance of your Rohde & Schwarz system	optional	optional	optional	optional
Warranty extension to service level		1 year – optional	1 year – optional	1 year – optional

Figure 5-01: Service Level Agreement template

Personnel Management

Mandatory Vacations

Mandatory vacations are a part of employee ship and a requirement in some organizations. On mandatory vacations, the employees are required to take vacation for a certain period of time during the year.

In some organizations, employees are forced to take mandatory vacations and in case, if they do not want to, the organization becomes cautious of the possibility of them being involved in any illegal activity or fraud. Therefore, mandatory vacations, in some way,

helps the organization to discover illegal activities of employees. Thus, the policy may prove to be a security protection mechanism at times.

Job Rotation

Job rotation policy keeps employees rotating over different assigned responsibilities. It has multiple benefits like it gives a better understanding to the employees about the overall mechanism of an organization and how its different parts hinder or enhance the business.

It also benefits the organization in terms of security, as relying on an individual for security expertise is not good for the organization because if the person leaves the organization or harms the security system, it would become difficult for the organization to deal with the loss.

Separation of Duties

Separation of duties is also a part of the business policy. Separation of duties is divided into two types, i.e., Split Knowledge and Dual Control. Split knowledge refers to the separation of duties in which no single person has all the information needed to perform a specific task. Rather, it is split into two arsons. It means that each person has the half of a safe combination.

Another type is a Dual Control that requires both the persons to be present at the same time for performing a specific task. Both persons have their secret keys. (they do not have to disclose their secret keys with each other). Secure access will require both keys at a time.

Clean Desk

One of the very effective business security policies. Clean Desk policy enforces that when an employee leaves their desk, it should be when the person leaves the desk, it should be clean and clear i.e. PC should be shut down properly, and no paperwork should be left on the desk. In short, employees should clean their desk before leaving the office, so no one could see any of their information. It is an efficient security policy for the one who deals with sensitive data.

Background Checks

A background checks also called pre-employment screening. A background check is performed by the organization to check if the person they are hiring is trustworthy and verify if their provided information is authentic or not. This basically provides all the necessary information to the HR members so that they can make the right decision.

Exit Interview

In terms of security, an exit interview can be a powerful tool for gathering information when an employee leaves the organization. This also includes termination of all the accounts and collection of mobile devices supplied to the employee at the time of hiring.

Role-based Awareness Training

Data Owner

One of the roles for which the training is offered is "Data Owner." This designated post is of executive level and has the responsibilities of administrating data and application.

System Administrator

The system administrator is the one who administrates the operation of the system., The responsibilities of a system administrator includes modifying product access privileges for other members, changing operational roles of members and inviting/removing members to/from an organisation. An organisation can have more than one administrator.

System Owner

A system owner is the one who purchases the subscription. A system owner has all the privileges including buying, upgrading, downgrading and cancelling subscriptions. Also, modifying product access privileges and removing/inviting members from/to an organisation comes under his authority.

User

The users are those who have least privilege access to the applications. As the name implies, the users are the application users. Users can be categorized into two types which are as follows:

- **Privileged User**

A user who has a higher level of rights and permission is known as "Privilege User." This may be an area manager or the one who creates a report. Someone has permission for doing a wider range of tasks. A database administrator is also an example of a privileged user, who needs database function's access but not to all servers or operating system option.

- **Executive User**

A user who is holding the responsibility of overall application use and operation. He is responsible for making a decision related to the usage of data or application.

NDA

NDA stands for Non-Disclosure Agreement that is a standard document of a corporate that sets the boundaries of information and secret material of the company. This agreement is responsible for controlling the disclosure of any secret or confidential information to the unauthorized person or party.

On-boarding

An important element when on-boarding workforce is to assure that the workforce must understand and be aware of its responsibilities related to securing information and assets of the company.

Continuing Education

Advancement in technology and security is a continuous process, therefore proper training and education is required for retaining skilled personnel in security. To modify the skill set of the security personnel, the *"Continuing Education"* programs help a lot.

Acceptable Use Policy/ Rules of Behavior

The AUPs (Acceptable Use Policies) are those policies that describe the right usage of the organization's resources (like Computer, Internet, and Network). These policies are described by the organization, as they should be concerned about any personal use of these resources that does not serve the organization.

Adverse Actions

When employees violate the rules or policies, an adverse action is taken against them. There are two types of adverse actions that are as follows:

- **Zero Tolerance**

Zero tolerance means no flexibility will be given to the employees upon breaking the rules or not correctly following the policies. One of the advantages of this action is that the organization maintains a code of conduct which results in better performance. There is also a downside to this action, that is, the organization may lose an outstanding long-term employee due to a single mistake under strict rules.

- **Discretionary Action**

Adverse issues are examined by adopting the rule that is "violation will be punished through a variety of HR actions including termination." This is more challenging for the management of the organization to figure out the correct adverse action. This action offers flexibility to the valuable workforce member who made uncharacteristic mistakes.

General Security Policies

Social Media Network/Application

In today's world where everyone is connected to each other socially, the organization needs social media policies for security purpose which establish a balance between company's requirement and social media.

These policies represent the company's requirement and expectation (company's code of conduct). It is the part of social media policy that the confidential information of company should not be shared on social media and it the personal responsibility of each employee to put only the information on social media, that the company approves.

Personal Email

The policies that are used for a business email account by the company is known as Personal Email Policies. Some companies allow their corporate email account for both personal and business use. Typically, business email addresses are for official use only. All the policies related to the use of business email account must be documented properly.

Impact Analysis

Business Impact Analysis is the process in which the source and relative impact value of risk element is determined in a process. It also refers to the document that describes the sources of risk and the steps related to its mitigation.

RTO/RPO

RTO stands for Recovery Time Objective, and as the name implies, it is the target time that is set for recovery of operation after the occurrence of the incident. Shorter RTO requires more resources and coordination. Therefore, it results in higher cost. This term is commonly used in disaster recovery operation and business continuity.

RPO stands for Recovery Point Objective which is defined as the time period that represents the maximum period of acceptable data loss. It determines the backup frequency essential for preventing unacceptable data loss. The RPO basically gives the answer to how much data loss is affordable.

MTBF

MTBF stands for Mean Time between Failure which is a measure of system's reliability, and its expression describes the average time between system failures. Mathematically, MTBF is defined as the arithmetic means of system failures set and expressed as:

MTBF = Σ (start of downtime – start of uptime) / number of failures

MTTR

MTTR stands for Mean Time to Repair. It is the time required to repair a given failure. Mathematically, MTTR is formulated below:

$$MTBF = \Sigma \text{ (start of downtime – start of uptime) / number of failures}$$

Availability is defined as the time in which the system performs its intended function. It is expressed in percentage, and its mathematical formula is as follows:

$$Availability = MTBF / (MTBF + MTTR)$$

Mission Essential Function

Mission essential function permits the security squad to properly set up defenses for securing system and data in a way corresponding to the associated risk. It also guarantees the restoration of service.

Single Point of Failure

The Single point of failure is defined as any of the system's component whose break down, or flaw could result in the entire system's breakdown. For example:

- Fine for a small firm.
- A single connection to the internet.

Impact

When an incident or risk occurs, it creates an impact on an organization. The impact can be a financial gain or instability, reputational rise and fall and much more.

- Financial gain/loss
- Variation in reputation
- Unavailability
- Degradation

Some IT systems are engaged in healthcare. Therefore, any failure of the system can cause injury and death to the victim. This loss or injury of/in life is the issue that cannot be addressed by the substitute. It is, therefore, necessary to ensure that the system is extremely superfluous in order to prevent impact.

- Property

Unmitigated risk results in property damage. Property damage to organization's property or other's property and environmental damage caused due to the toxic release in an industrial setting are all those damages that are caused by IT security failure.

- **Safety**

Safety can be defined as "Protection against risk, danger or injury." Safety issues (cause due to failure) increase losses and can cause interruption to work Computers can impact safety as they are now becoming involved in all business aspects.

- **Finance**

The final arbiter of all work is 'Finance' that helps us to manage a score. The gain can be measured by profit and loss through unmitigated threat. When impacts overreach the predicted costs linked with the planned residual risks, it turns into an issue and impact profit.

- **Reputation**

One of the essential values in marketing is Reputation. Junky history or shoddy record ruin the company's reputation and costs the company in client base and revenue. For example, nobody wants to give up personal information or contract with a bank with a junky history

Privacy Impact Assessment

Privacy impact assessment (PIA) is an organized way of figuring out the gap between the needed privacy act and actual privacy act. PIA ensures the compliance of the process and system with the existing laws and regulation. It analyzes how the PII (Personally Identifiable Information) is gathered, secured and used. All this information is provided to the users in the written privacy statement.

Privacy Threshold Assessment

A privacy threshold assessment determines whether the system has gathered and managed the PII or not. If the PII is kept, the next step is the determination of privacy impact assessment.

Risk Management Processes and Concept

Risk management can also be called *"Decision Making Process."* All the components like threat assessment, risk assessment, and security implementation approaches arranged within the process of business management, describe the risk management

Threat Assessment

An organized interpretation of threat that encounters a firm is known as Threat assessment. Threats cannot be changed, however the way it affects can be changed. Therefore, threats are necessary to figure out.

Environment

The Environment is one of the biggest sources of threat to the system. There is a variety of sources that cause an environmental change like weather, storm, flood, lightning, etc. These environmental changes disrupt the normal operation of the system and increase risk. To overcome this situation, make the system resilient that mitigate the risk sources and reduce impacts on the enterprise.

Manmade

As the name implies, the manmade threats are those threats caused by the action of a person. These threats are the result of both the adverse action of the attacker and accidents by the users. Therefore, appropriate control against intended and unintended actions are necessary to deal with the risk of the system.

External Vs. Internal

Internal threats come from inside the organization, and these threats are more damaging. These threats may be due to the dissatisfied / angry employee or may be due to a mistake or accident by a well-meaning employee. In internal threat, the risk is directly proportional to the level of access and the value of assets being worked on.

On the contrary, the external threats are those caused by the outside of the organization, without access to the system.

Risk Assessment

The process of determining potential risk based on mathematical and statistical design is called risk assessment. For measuring the risk assessment value, any of the methods can be adopted by the user. A simple technique is to calculate ALE (Annualized Loss Expectancy) that generates the financial value of impact, and its calculation starts with the measurement of SLE (Single Loss Expectancy).

Single LE

SLE refers to the loss value that is expected from an event. The mathematical formula for calculating SLE is as follows:

SLE = asset value × exposure factor

The determination of the amount of loss of a resource is called Exposure factor, or we can say, it is a measurement of the risk level of an asset (how much it is at risk).

Asset=Resource

Annualized Loss Expectancy (ALE)

ALE is calculated after the calculation of SLE by multiplying SLE and ARO, following is the mathematical formula for it:

$$ALE = SLE * ARO$$

Where;

ARO stands for Annualized Rate of Occurrence and it refers to the period of time the event is supposed to take place in a year.

Annual Rate of Occurrence (ARO)

As explained above, the ARO is the amount of time the event takes to occur in a year or less; it can also be called as *"events frequency in a standard year."*

For example: If the event is takes place twice in 15 years then the ARO is 2/15

Asset Value

The amount of money that is required to equate the value of an asset is known as "Asset Value". The term Asset Value is commonly used with the term exposure factor for the determination of SLE.

Risk Register

The risk register is something that contains the list of all the risks linked with the system and all the information regarding those risks; for example, their Types to arrange them, Mitigation factor, Possibility of occurrence, Impact to a business, etc.

Likelihood of Occurrence

The chance of occurrence of a particular risk is known as *"Likelihood of Occurrence"* which can be Quantitative or Qualitative. The likelihood of occurrence when defined qualitatively, is ordinarily described on an annual base in order to compare it with other annualized measures. If described quantitatively, it is used to generate rank-order results.

Supply Chain Assessment

All the organizations are required to look at not only the risk linked to a system, but the risk enclosed in a system. The process of exploration and identification of these risks is known as "Supply Chain Assessment."

Impact

The impact refers to the measurement of actual loss occur when risk exploits the vulnerability. The impact level can be defined in terms of cost, schedule, performance, etc.

Quantitative

To objectively figure out the impact of an action which affects a business or program is known as "*Quantitative Risk Assessment*". In order to perform to perform this assessment, the use of models and metrics are involved commonly.

Qualitative

To subjectively figure out the impact of an action which affects a business or program is known as "*Qualitative Risk Assessment*. Experienced and expert judgments are needed to perform this assessment.

Testing

The testing is the process of determining a measure of the risk that a system possesses to the business. There are two types of testing Penetration testing and Vulnerability Testing.

- **Penetration Testing Authorization**

Penetration testing is needed to mimic an attack to determine if the controls in place meet the desired standard or in other words, used to test security control. The first step in penetration testing is '*Penetration Testing Authorization*' which is used as a communication plan, i.e., the team performing test obtains permission from the system owner and explain them the specifics of the penetration test.

- **Vulnerability Testing Authorization**

Vulnerability test is used for the determination of weaknesses or vulnerabilities (that can result in damage, if left unguarded) and their level of exposure. Vulnerability Testing Authorization is the process of taking permission for vulnerability test from the management and explaining to them the purpose and risk of the test.

Risk Response Techniques

There are four different ways to respond to the risk:

- **Transfer**

Another way is to transfer the risk which you can do by purchasing insurance that transfer risks to the third party.

- **Avoid**

Although it is hard to get rid of the threat. Best practice is to reduce the risk and threats to an exceptional level. One of the most common way is not deploying the module which extends risk.

- **Mitigate**

Another way is to mitigate the risk. Through the effort of 'Control' that weakens the impact of an attack, risk can be mitigated.

- **Accept**

One of the best response to the attack is to accept the risk after the specific risk is analyzed, and the cost to mitigate, transfer, and avoid the risk is examined against its possibility of occurrence, and its possible impact.

Incidence Response Procedure

Incident Response Plan

Incident response plan refers to those steps carried out by a corporation in response to any unusual or strange situation figured out in the work of a computer system. For managing incidents when they take place, the IT squad is required to set up an Incident Response Plan that carries a table of instructions to facilitate in determining the response level.

The following are the steps of Incident Response Plan:

Documenting Incident Types/Categories definitions

Documenting incident response types/categories involves the process of determining the most critical components of a system. Possible incidents are categorized into the manageable set to facilitate the planner and responders. For example, a category will deal the service interruption incidents, other will handle malicious communication events or phishing attacks.

All organizations can have different incident categories, as they can personalize the categories of the incident to meet the need for IT.

Roles and Responsibilities

The next step is to define the roles and responsibilities of IR team representative. Roles might include team leader (the one who manages and maintain the overall incident response process), team communicator (the one who plays the role of spokesperson to all other inside or outside company's group), Technical staff (who perform tasks), etc.

Reporting Requirements/Escalation

Reporting requirement/escalation is an important step in the incident response planning that illustrates the following parts:

- Who to contact when an incident occurs?
- What to say?
- Who is required to be involved?

Contact is made on the basis of incident type. Contact can be made with corporate persons (information security head, CIO, IR team) or with non-IT internal staff (Legal department, HR, etc.), and also with an external one (system owner, law enforcement, etc.).

Cyber-Incident Response Team (CIRT)

Cyber-incident response team is a pre-defined team of professionals who are designated to review and respond to cyber incidents. In this step of planning, it is determined what type of incident needs a CIRT response. For example, it is not necessary to involve the CIRT team for an incident like virus infection, but the incidents like denial of service may require you to involve the CIRT team. CIRT team may or may not be a part of the organization.

Exercise

Exercise is to test the IR team and the planning before the incident occurs. Owning a team and process is not sufficient, the organization needs to get the team practiced and exercised the process on the system before the incident occurs.

Incident Response Process

Incidents response process refers to the action taken by the security personnel in response to an incident. These are the steps of incident response process:

Preparation

There is a number of tasks needed to be done before the incident occurs like the determination of communication method and contact information, knowledge of handling hardware and software, assurance of all the incident analysis resources availability, assurance of having a proper incident mitigation software, etc.

Identification

There are various methods to detect the occurrence of an incident. These methods possess different perception and detail levels. The identification process is challenging because the network and system are under attack all the time.

Containment

Once the incident has occurred, the next step is to prevent it from spreading. This prompt action is also known as Containment. It basically refers to the set of actions taken to contain incident production as much as possible. For example, if a virus attacks the database, it is important to protect the server which is uninfected.

Eradication

Eradication refers to the *"removing of the problem."* A key element in eradication process is to prevent the system from re-infection.

Recovery

Recovery is the process that is followed by Eradication. It is basically a process of bringing the assets back into function and restoring normal operation of those assets.

Lessons Learned

The term lesson learned is used to illustrate the following things:

- What went wrong?
- How can it be improved?

In other words, it describes actions for improving methods and correct all the weaknesses.

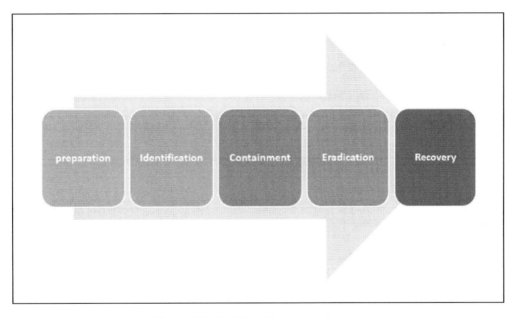

Figure 5.2. Incident Response Process

Basic Concept of Forensics

Order of Volatility

Volatility describes how long data will stick around. All rate of volatility is different for different data like, some are more volatile (stick for short time period) and some are least volatile (stick for the long time period). The following is the order of volatility from most to least:

- CPU, cache, and register content

- Routing table, process table, ARP cache, kernel statistics
- Live network connection and data flow
- Memory-RAM
- Temporary file system or swap space
- Data on hard disk
- Remotely logged data
- Data stored on archival media/backup

Chain of Custody

In the process of evidence collection, the important thing is the maintenance of integrity and control of evidence which can be done through the chain of custody.

The chain of custody records of all persons, who have ever handled or had approached the evidence. More precisely, the chain of custody shows who collected the evidence, when and where it was collected, where it was kept, and who had authority or custody of the evidence for the entire time since the evidence was collected.

These are some steps that belong to the process of Chain of Custody:

- Note each item gathered as evidence.
- Note who gathered the evidence along with the date and time it was gathered or noted.
- Create an explanation of the evidence in the documentation.
- Place the evidence in containers/catalog and tag the containers with the incident number, the name of the guy who gathered it, and the date and time it was gathered or place in the container.
- Note all message digest (hash) values in the documentation.
- Securely move the evidence to a guarded storage resource.
- Receive a signature from the person who takes the evidence at this storage resource.
- Add limits to restrict approach to and compromise the evidence while it is being kept.
- Securely move the evidence to court for actions.

Legal Hold

The IT experts may be requested to keep the evidence using legal hold. This is a legal procedure that assures that any data that may be linked with a specific legal procedure is taken and stored so that nothing is misplaced. This is commonly produced to prepare for

some approaching lawsuit, and it's generally a legal document presented to you this is normally presented as a hold notice, which notifies you specifically what kind of data and how much should be secured.

Data Acquisition

All the steps that are taken for the collection of evidence should be documented properly because these may be required in the court as evidence. Henceforth, if all the process and information is documented, then this can help in proving the authenticity of the process and information.

The points that should be kept in mind while documenting the evidence are:

- Who gathered the evidence?
- How was it gathered?
- Where was it gathered?
- Who has had custody of the evidence?
- How was it secured and kept?
- When was it disposed of from storage? Why? Who is the possessor?

Capture System Image

It is important to take a system image of the drive because the content may serve as a valuable forensic data.

Network Traffic and Logs

Many attacks take place across the network. Therefore, it is essential to retrieve all the information coming from the router, switch, firewall and every single thing linked to the network as much you can.

Capture Video

Video capturing is another way of seizing vital information at the time of data collection. Videos help you in providing high bandwidth data that shows exactly how things were planted or how the event or incident occurred.

Screenshots

At the time of evidence collection, it is necessary to take a screenshot of the state of the screen. These screenshots will help in providing proof of the authenticity of the documentation.

Witness Interviews

Another important part of data collection is "Witness" because the credibility of a witness is essential.

Preservation

It is essential to store all the forensics data because there will be a time when you are required to collect most of the data. It is necessary to have this data for present inquiry,

and you require efficient to see through all the potential evidence in order to figure out what took place during that incident. It is also necessary to preserve all the data and information for future incidents that need you to revisit the stored data and identify any correlation between incidents.

Recovery

The capability of recovering from the incident is also needed. It will be simpler to set up a plan for later use if there is more data. In security process, the ability to gather and process all the data and details and spot the solid information is really benifical. In addition, this part also helps you in carrying out policy changes and modification on the basis of the knowledge that you discovered and safeguards you in future.

Strategic Intelligence/Counter-Intelligence Gathering

Strategic intelligence collection refers to the usage of all means to carry out the decision. This also helps in determining whether an organization is ready for the threat or not. It presents information that can reduce the range of an inquiry to a manageable stage. Having the understanding of definite actions for which obvious evidence of existence and non-existence are needed, a strategic intelligence can be set up on the information.

Counter-Intelligence collection is the collection of information specifically addressing the strategic intelligence efforts. It helps you to identify what people are seeking for and what information are they receiving. It also helps in identifying the motives and possible activities of people in future.

Active Logging

One of the most important security rules is to log every information because this is the only way of recording the actions of an attacker.

Basic Concept of Disaster Recovery and Continuity of Operation

A process that the corporation needs to recover from situations that disturb regular operations is known as *"Disaster Recovery."*

Disaster Recovery Sites

It is generally very late to start the procedure of a response when a disaster takes place. Therefore, it is necessary to build disaster recovery sites. For building a disaster recovery site, there are many options available like the hot site, warm site, and cold site.

Cold Site

A cold site is a similar type of disaster recovery service that provides office space, but the customer provides and installs all the equipment needed to continue operations. You are

required to bring these things with you, and it takes weeks to get the cold site to be in operational state.

Warm Site

A warm site is a compromise between hot and cold. These sites will have hardware and connectivity already established, though on a smaller scale than the original production site or even a hot site.

Hot Site

A site that is fully configured and duplicate of your operating environment. It takes no time or few hours to operate the hot site.

Order of Restoration

During the process of application recovery, it is required to consider what applications have higher priority because all the applications do not have the same priority. Such as customer-facing application or the application dealing with billing process are of higher priority.

The priority list of application restoration should be well defined by the management of the corporation. This order of restoration list is changeable, which means the management can change the order based on its priority.

Backup Concepts

Having a backup of everything serves as the key factor in the disaster recovery of any organization. Backup can be made to tape, disk, optical drive, etc. For database backup, replication (online duplication) can be used.

Full Back up

In order to back up files in an OS, there are various strategies that can be followed. One of them is full back up. In full back up, every time the backup process is performed, every single file is copied sequentially.

Differential Back up

Differential backup only backs-up the changes and modifications that are done after last backup.

Incremental Back up

In the incremental backup, those files are copied that have been modified since the last time incremental back up is performed.

Snapshots

Using snapshots, it is common to the backup operating system. A snapshot is a replicate of virtual machines at a definite moment in time. A snapshot is a generated by replicating the files that keep the virtual machine.

Geographical Considerations

During the preparation for dealing with any type of incident, it must be kept in mind that the incident may damage everything in the building. Such as incidents like fire, flood, hurricane, etc. therefore it is necessary to plan for the worst.

Off-Site Backups

Having off-site backup is one of the best options. Off-site backup means that all the data is copied and stored on some other site (*other than your building*). It also mitigates the risk of backup lost.

Distance

Another challenge is the determination of location for backing up all the data because disasters can affect a large area. Therefore, the recovery site should be at a distance from that particular area (at a larger distance from your organization). Nonetheless, if the data is backed up at large distance, then it will also increase the time of recovery.

Location Selection

Another key element that should be kept in mind while backing up data is location selection. Backup media protection is the highest priority. Therefore, a safe and proper location is necessary. Cloud can be an ideal location.

Legal implications

The legal issues liked with the location is also a point of consideration because the business regulation varies between states. For example, if the backup is outside the country, then the recovery personnel should have a passport and must be able to clear immigration process.

Data sovereignty

Data sovereignty is relatively a recent type of rules; several states have formulated. If your data is residing in some particular state, then it will be subjected to that state's law. You can be restricted to move your data to another country.

Continuity of Operation Planning

The continuity of operation plan refers to the strategies whose goal is to figure out which subdivision of the regular operation is required to be continued during interruption

period. It involves preparing a broad plan that can be appointed during any unanticipated events. In short, it basically helps in providing trouble-free services during any disruption.

Exercises/Tabletop

Getting all the team members in a cabin around the table for discussing simulated emergency conditions is known as Tabletop exercise. All the key players examine and discuss the actions they would pick up during an incident or emergency and test their plan in order to determine if the plan is viable or not.

After-Action Reports

After testing the continuity of operation plan, it is necessary to prepare a report that describes what went right and what went wrong during the test. It also documents the objectives and standards of operation during transmission to the backup system.

Failover

Failover refers to the process of transferring from regular business operation to continuity of operation plan. The alternate processing site remains running even for months, depending on the extent of the incident.

Alternate Processing Sites

If something occurs with the primary site, there should be some alternate site to continue the normal business processes. The alternate processing sites have data synchronization and all the necessary resources for bringing the site to operation.

Alternate Business Practices

Having an alternate business practice is also a good business strategy. When a disaster or unexpected event occurs, everything can be destroyed even the technologies on which the business process relies on. Therefore, alternate practices are needed. An example is an alternate of a transaction process that is being performed on a computer is a manual transaction (provide paper receipt).

Types of Security Control

Deterrent Control

A *Deterrent Control* serves to inhibit the attacker by reducing the possibility of success from the viewpoint of the attacker.

Preventive Control

Preventive Control refers to the prevention of specific action from occurring.

For Example: Firewall

Detective Control

Detective Control helps to detect a physical security breach. It alerts the operator to specific condition and acts during an event.

Corrective Control

Corrective Control is an attempt to reduce the amount of damage and used after an event. For Example, 'Backup' that helps the rapid restoration of operation.

Compensating Control

To directly address the threat when there is no control available, one thing needed to meet the requirement is '*Compensating Control.*' For Example: 'Fire suppression System' that do not stop fire damage but can limit fire damage.

Technical Control

When some form of technology is used to address the physical security issue, it is referred to as a '*Technical Control.*' For Example: Biometrics.

Administrative Control

Limiting the security risks through policies and procedures are known as '*Administrative Control.*' For Example: Giving instructions to a security guard.

Physical Control

Physical Control refers to restricting specific physical activity from occurring. For example, Mantrap that prevents tailgating. It basically restricts the accidental operating and specific human interaction with a system.

Data Security and Privacy Practices

Data Destruction and Media Sanitization

It is important to destroy the data that is no longer in use because that data or information can be discovered and used by the criminals in malicious activities like identity theft, social engineering, etc. Dumpster diving is used by the criminals for this purpose because the value of it is well known to the criminals.

For every organization, it is vital to have effective demolition and destruction policies and associated procedures. The following are some methods of data destruction and media sanitization.

Burning

A method of destruction, which is regarded as a gold method is referred to as Burning. The data/media is carried out in a form that can be demolished by the fire and then it is

burned. This is the process which is irreversible and makes the data to be lost permanently.

Shredding

Shredding which is also referred to as physical destruction is the method of splitting things into small chunks and then mixed making the reassembling impossible or difficult. Everything that might be advantageous or useful to a criminal or dumpster diver should be shredded.

Pulping

A process of recombining a paper into new paper by suspending a paper fiber in a liquid. Once the paper is shredded, the pulping process erase the ink by bleaching, and then those shredded pieces are recombined into new paper, and in this way, the layout of the old paper is completely destroyed.

Pulverizing

Breaking things by external force into unusable pieces (that cannot be reconstructed) is known as Pulverizing which is also referred as *'Physical Process of Destruction.'* Used for hard disk driver like items. Encryption is the modern approach of pulverizing. In this method, the owner encrypts the drive's data and destroy the key. This process makes the data non-recoverable depending on the strength of encryption.

Degaussing

The files on a magnetic storage device can be destroyed magnetically, i.e., using a magnetic field; this method is known as degaussing. This is a safe technique for degaussing the data or media. In this method, the magnetic particles got realigned by discarding the organized format that displayed the data.

Purging

A process of discarding and erasing data from the storage zone permanently is known as purging. A key expression that reflects the purging is "removing data," which is planned to clear up the storage zone for re-use. For example: Circular Buffer.

Wiping

Wiping is a process of rewriting the media in storage with 1's and 0's pattern series multiple times so that every trace is eliminated of original data or media. It is ideal for the method because it is a non-destructive method. There are various data wiping protocols available with different passes like 3, 7 or 35, depending on the level of security of data.

Data Sensitivity Labelling and Handling

Confidential

A 'Confidential' labeled data on exposure to an illegitimate or unauthorized party leads to severe harm to the corporation. The data is specified by the policy that covers detail regarding who possesses the authority to issue the data. Examples are Software Codes, Trade Secrets, Product Design are all included in confidential data.

Private

A 'Private' labeled data on exposure to an illegitimate or unauthorized party leads to disruption or harm to the corporation. Private data is commonly related to the personal data that belongs to an individual or less often with the corporation. The damage level related to the private data is less as compared to the confidential data but still significant.

Public

A 'Public' labeled data can be viewed by the public and carries no protection in regards to confidentiality. Nevertheless, the protection is still required for its integrity. For example, Press Release, Public Web Pages, etc. are the examples of public data.

Proprietary

'Proprietary' is something that is owned and controlled by an individual or organization. Therefore, proprietary data is something that is confined to a business for competitive use.

Proprietary labeled data can be shared with a group of users other than a competitor, and the label of proprietary is for alerting the group not to further share that proprietary data. For protecting proprietary data, the laws of secrecy, copyright, patent are used.

PII

PII stands for Personally Identifiable Information. It indicates the information that is used to differentiate or detect an individual's identity such as individual name in combination with one or more of the following things:

- Social security number,
- Driving License number,
- Account number or credit card number or other identifying information that is linked to a specific person.

In other words, a set of a data element that leads to the identity of a specific individual. PII is mostly used in online transactions. There always exists a possibility that it can be

misused by any unauthorized person or miscreant. Therefore, it is necessary to protect that personal information.

PHI

PHI stands for Protected Health Information that refers to the health information of an individual like health care record, a payment that is made for health care, insurance information and all medical-care related information. PHI is protected by Health Insurance Portability and Accountability Act (HIPAA).

Data Roles

There is a relation between the data and the people who claim access to it. The rights and permissions to access data are given to employees on the basis of their assigned responsibilities in the organization.

Owner

One of the types of data role is the Owner or Data Owner. The data owner is usually the director or senior officer of an organization. For Example, the *sales vice president*, who holds all the customer-related data. Another example is Treasurer, who owns financial data/information.

Steward/Custodian

Steward refers to someone who manages security, privacy, and accuracy of data. They are responsible for assigning security labels and also ensures compliance with applicable standards and laws.

Privacy Officer

A person who is responsible for supervising the privacy of entire data of the organization, is the privacy officer. They set up policies and implement processes.

Data Retention

Data retention refers to the storage of data logs. Another important characteristic of data retention is to determine what data needs to be stored and for how long. Data is retained for multiple purposes like a contractual obligation, accounting, and billing, warranty history, etc. However, storing data for a long period of time may cause a risk, if not maintained properly.

Legal and compliance

Some of the data security and privacy actions are retained under legal requirements and regulatory compliance. An organization must have to follow regulations and standards to meet data security. Following are the some general-sector specific regulations:

- Federal Information Security Management Act (FISMA), U.S
- Security of Network and Information Systems (NIS Directive), Europe
- General Data Protection Regulation (GDPR), Europe

Practice Question

1. The requisite level of performance of a given contractual service is essentially set by which of the following?

   A. Inter-organizational Service Agreement (ISA)

   B. Memorandum of Agreement

   C. Memorandum of Understanding

   D. Service Level Agreement (SLA)

2. Which of the following is responsible for defining the characteristics like privacy, security, and retention policies for specific information?

   A. The data owner

   B. The privacy office

   C. The data security office

   D. An individual specifically is given this responsibility for the organization

3. Which of the following policy describes what a company considers to be the proper use of its resources (like computer policies, internet, network, and e-mail)?

   A. Resource usage policy (RUP)

   B. Acceptable use policy (AUP)

   C. Organizational use policy (OUP)

   D. Acceptable use of resources policy (AURP)

4. Which of the following is the step-by-step instruction that describes policies implementation steps in a corporation?

   A. Procedures

   B. Regulations

C. Standards

D. Guidelines

5. After an incident, the target time that is set for a continuation of operations is described by which of the following term?

    A. RPO

    B. MTTR

    C. RTO

    D. MTBF

6. The security control that is used post-event for minimizing the amount of damage is?

    A. Corrective

    B. Detective

    C. Preventative

    D. Deterrent

Chapter 06: Cryptography & PKI

The Concept of Cryptography:

Cryptography is derived from a Greek word 'Krypto' which means' hidden or secret.' Hence, it is known to be the study of secret writing i.e. encryption and decryption of a normal text to make it impenetrable. Cryptography allows us to check the integrity of data. Cryptography techniques are generally classified into Traditional and Modern Cryptography.

- **Traditional:** Conventional techniques use the simple mechanism of transportation (re-ordering of plain text) and substitution (alteration of plain text).

- **Modern:** A new technique that relies on sophisticated protocol and algorithm to retain the security of information preserved.

Cryptography is vital when communicating over an un-trusted or shared medium (like the Internet). The target is to secure static and mobile information by using cryptographic technologies. It helps us to address issues linked to Confidentiality, Integrity, and Authentication. We can examine the authenticity of any person who is linked to us. Another security factor provided by cryptography is Non-repudiation that verifies is the incoming packet is from the authentic user. You are also able to validate the information truly written by the sender. In other words, you can check if the information you have received, is any actual piece of information sent by an actual source without the modification of any impersonator. Some common terms used in Cryptography are defined below.

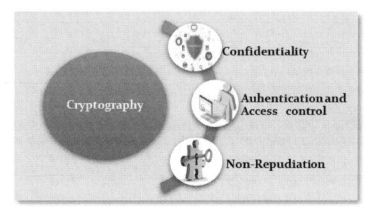

Figure 6-01: Cryptography Features

Cryptographic Terminologies:

Some common terminologies that are used in cryptographic context are:

Encryption

Transformation of plain text into a secret code by using an algorithm that uses a secret key to prevent anyone from accessing the information except the intended recipient. It provides security in terms of encryption for secure communication over an insecure medium by making the information unreadable to any impersonator or unauthorized person.

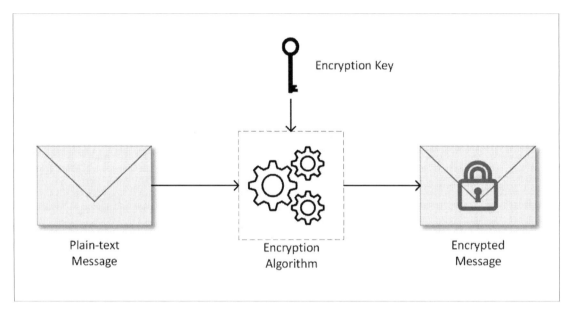

Figure 6-02: Encryption Process

Decryption:

Conversion of encrypted data back to its original form. Decryption is a reverse process of encryption which requires decryption key to achieve plain text data.

Ciphertext:

A ciphertext is an encrypted form of plain text data.

Plain Text:

The original form of data before any sort of encryption is known as 'Plain Text'.

Hash:

Hashing is a technique to validate the integrity of a message. Message digest value generated mathematically is calculated and compared to verify the integrity of a message.

Key:

To encrypt data, you require the plain text, the cipher you will apply, and then you require a key (Cryptographic key). This key is combined to the cipher to encrypt the plain text. The key size is proportional to the security, the larger the keys, the better the security will be. Therefore, to bring more, security key sizes are kept larger.

Some encryption techniques use a single key, some use multiple keys for the encryption of data, and the methodology that is employed will depend on the cipher in use.

Cryptanalysis:

The art of breaking encryption is known as cryptanalysis. There are various ways for data encryption; the investigators are working continually on identifying weaknesses and problems with the procedure through which we are encrypting and securing our data to make sure our data is harmless as possible.

Digital Signatures:

It provides integrity, so to make sure that the message that is received is originally the message sent. It also provides authentication in order to know that the message that is received is sent by the authentic sender. It's another function is non-repudiation, that is to make sure that the digital signature is not fake.

Cryptographic Algorithm:

There are generally three types of algorithms:

Symmetric Key Cryptography:

Symmetric Key Cryptography is the oldest and most widely used cryptography technique in the domain of cryptography. Symmetric ciphers use the same secret key for the encryption and decryption of data. It is also known as a secret key or pre-shared key algorithm.

Its basic purpose is to provide data confidentiality. Symmetric Key Cryptography ciphers are typically classified in two approaches:

Stream Cipher: A type of symmetric key cipher that encrypts the plain text one by one. There are various types of stream ciphers such as synchronous, asynchronous. RC4 is the most common type of stream cipher design. The transformation of encrypted output varies during the encryption cycle.

Block Cipher: A type of symmetric key cipher that encrypts the plain text on the fixed length of the group. The transformation of encrypted data does not vary in a block cipher.

It encrypts the block of data using the same key on each block. DES and AES are common types of block cipher design.

Example: A block cipher takes a 128-bit block of plain text and returns a corresponding 128-bit block of ciphertext.

Symmetric Key Cryptography Algorithm: Following are some Symmetric Key Cryptographic Algorithm:

Data encryption algorithm (DES): Most common symmetric algorithm designed by IBM in the 1970s. DES uses 56-bit key to encrypt 64-bit datagram block. It is no longer considered secure due to the reason that its keys' size is too small.

Triple-DES (3DES): It is an enhanced version of DES. It uses up to three 56 bit keys and makes three encryption and decryption passes over the same datagram block. It is mainly derived to enlarge the key length to 168 bits (Three 56-bit key). In short, it encrypts 64-bit datagram block using three 56-bit key (168-bit key).

Advanced encryption standard (AES): It is also known as 'Rijndael' and was introduced by NIST in 2001. A most important feature of AES algorithm is that it can use variable block length and key length. Any combination of key length 128, 192, 256 bits and block length 128, 192, 256 bits can be used.

Asymmetric Key Cryptography:

Unlike Symmetric Ciphers, two keys are used. One key is publically known to everyone while another key is kept secret and is used to encrypt the data by sender. Hence it is also called Public Key Cryptography. Each sender uses its secret key (also known as a private key) for encrypting its data before sending. The receiver uses the respective public key of the sender to decrypt the data. RSA, DSA and Diffie-Hellman Algorithm are popular examples of asymmetric ciphers. Asymmetric Key Cryptography delivers Confidentiality, integrity, authenticity & Non-repudiation by using Public and Private key concept. The private key is only known by the owner itself. Whereas, the Public key is issued by using Public Key Infrastructure (PKI) where a trusted Certification Authority (CA) certify the ownership of key pairs.

Asymmetric Key Cryptography is also known as Public-key algorithm and was announced publically in 1976. It uses a two-key pair; one key is for the encryption of plain text, and the other is for the decryption of ciphertext. Contrary to the symmetric algorithm, asymmetric algorithm requires no secret key sharing to securely communicate over an insecure channel. It is commonly used in digital certification and key management.

Asymmetric Key Cryptography Algorithm: Some asymmetric key algorithms are as follows:

RSA Algorithm: RSA is named after the initials of three MIT mathematicians Ron **R**ivest, Adi **S**hamir and Leonard **A**dleman, who developed this algorithm and was publically described in 1976. As it is an asymmetric algorithm, which means it uses two keys that are public and private. The public key is given to everyone, while the private key is kept secret.

Example: A user sends its public key to the server and requests for some data. The server will encrypt the data by using user's public key and sends the encrypted data to the user. The user will receive the data and decrypt it.

It is the most widely used algorithm for key exchange, digital signature, and message encryption. There are various standards of RSA algorithm, and all of them use variable size block lengths and key lengths. The standards are RC1, RC2, RC3, RC4, RC5, and RC6.

Diffie Hellman (DH): This algorithm was introduced by Stanford University professor Martin Hellman and a graduate student Whitfield Diffie in 1976. DH protocol also known as key exchange protocol is a public key distributing system that uses Asymmetric Key Cryptography method. DH permits two end users that have no previous knowledge of each other to create a shared key over an insecure communication channel, and that secret key can be used to encrypt subsequent messages using a symmetric key algorithm. DH algorithm is only used for secret key exchange and not for digital signatures and authentication.

Digital Signature Algorithm (DSA): Digital Signature Algorithm was introduced by National Institute for Standards and Technology (NIST) in 1991 for (Digital Signature Standard) DSS use, and it is also a Federal Information Processing Standards (FIPS) standard for digital signature. It is mainly used for a digital signature to assure message authentication.

Public-Key Cryptography Standard (PKCS): It is a collection of interoperable public key cryptography standards and guidelines. It is developed and published by RSA Data Security Inc.

PKCS Standards:

	NAME	DESCRIPTION
PKCS #1	RSA Cryptography Standard	Description of RSA Public and Private key's properties and format.
PKCS #2	Withdrawn	Withdrawn and merged into PKCS #1. Covered RSA Encryption

		of message digests
PKCS #3	Diffie-Hellman Key Agreement Standard	Allows two end users with no previous knowledge of each other to create a shared secret key over an insecure communication path.
PKCS #4	Withdrawn	Withdrawn and merged into PKCS #1. Covered RSA key syntax.
PKCS #5	Password-based Encryption Standard	Defined in RFC 8018 and PBKDF2.
PKCS #6	Extended Certificate Syntax Standard	Describes extensions to the old X.509 v1 certificate specification, obsolete by X.509 v3.
PKCS #7	Cryptographic Message Syntax Standard	Used to sign or encrypt messages under a PKI and also used for certificate dissemination.
PKCS #8	Private-key Information Syntax Standard	It is used to carry private certificate key pairs both encrypted and unencrypted.
PKCS #9	Selected Attribute Type	It describe selected attribute type for use in PKCS#6 (extended certificates), PKCS#7 (digitally signed messages), PKCS#8 (private key information) and PKCS #10 (certificate signing request).
PKCS #10	Certification Request Standard	Defines the pattern of messages sent to a Certification Authority to demand certification of a public key.
PKCS #11	Cryptographic Token Interface	An API is defining a generic interface to cryptographic tokens. Used in Single Sign-on, Public Key Cryptography & Disk encryption.
PKCS #12	Personal Information Exchange Syntax Standard	Defines a file format typically used to keep private keys with leading public-key certificates, protected with a password-based symmetric key.
PKCS #13	Elliptic Curve Cryptography Standard	*Apparently abandoned*
PKCS #14	Pseudo-random Number Generation	PRNG is an algorithm that generates a sequence of numbers that are not truly random.
PKCS #15	Cryptographic Token Information Format Standard	It defines a standard allowing users of cryptographic tokens to identify themselves to applications, independent of the application's cryptoki implementation (PKCS #11) or other API.

Table 6-01: PKCS standards

> **Note:** A cryptographic key is called ephemeral if it is generated for each execution of a key establishment process. In some cases, ephemeral keys are used more than once, within a single session (e.g., in broadcast applications) where the sender generates only one ephemeral key pair per message and the private key is combined separately with each recipient's public key.

Hashing

A cryptographic hash function takes the Plain text as an input and returns a fixed-size string. This string is called hash value, message digest, digital fingerprint, digest or checksum. One-way Hashing condenses a message into an irreversible fixed-length value or hash.

Hash Algorithm:

It has various names for one-way encryption, message digest, and hash function. It is used to compute a fixed-length hash value based on the original plain text. Using hash value, the original cannot be changed even with the knowledge of hash function. A hash value is a unique number that is created from a sequence of text using a mathematical formula. It is usually faster than encryption techniques.

The main purpose of the hash algorithm is to provide a digital fingerprint to any type of data in order to assure that information has not been changed during the transmission and provide a measure of information integrity. The hash algorithm is typically used for two purposes:

- Digital certificate
- Data integrity check

Some of the hash algorithms that are commonly used are as follows:

Message Digest (MD)

- MD2
- MD4
- Md5

Secure Hash Algorithm (SHA)

- SHA1

Message Digest (MD): MD Algorithm is a sequence of byte-oriented cryptographic hash function that generates 128 bits (fixed length) hash value from a random length input.

Message Digest 2 (MD2): It was developed in 1989 by Ronald Rivest. It was produced and enhanced for an 8-bit system having insufficient memory, for example, Smart Card. The message is augmented initially to assure that its length is divisible by 16 and then a 16-byte checksum is affixed to the message. The rising value is proceeded to figure out a hash value.

Message Digest 4 (MD4): It was also developed by Ronald Rivest in 1989 for 32-bit system or machine. It was identical to MD2 but specially designed for faster processing in programs. In MD4, the message is first augmented to assure that its length in bits plus 64 is divisible by 512 and then 64 bit of the original message length is linked in series to the message.

Message Digest 5 (MD5): It was developed in 1991 by Ronald Rivest. It was an improved version of the MD4 algorithm and was specially designed to overcome the weaknesses in the MD4 algorithm and ensure stronger security. MD5 continuous to survive in spite of several weaknesses but algorithmically it is not highly secure due to analytical attack and possible collision that can be found in less than 1 hour.

Secure Hash Algorithm (SHA): SHA is a type of Hash algorithm that produces 160-bit output. It was developed by National Security Agency (NSA) and declared as U.S govt. standard. SHA is more secure than MD5, but processing is slower than MD5. This algorithm also known as SHA0 was published in 1993 and after 2 years SHA1 was introduced.

Secure Hash Algorithm 1 (SHA1): Most generally used algorithm that gives 160-bit hash value as an output. It is recognized to be the replacement to the MD5 algorithm and employed broadly in multiple application and protocols such as TLS, SSL, PGP, SSH, S/MIME and IPsec. Four modifications SHA224, SHA256, SHA384 and SHA512 which is jointly called SHA2, have now been introduced. These modifications are illustrated in RFC4634 and can produce 224, 256, 384 or 512-bit length hash value. Attacks on both SHA1 and SHA0 have been noted by the cryptographer. However, no attacks have been noted on SHA 2 yet.

Cryptography Uses

For creating a balance between security provision and enough battery provision that will remain available throughout the day, we use cryptography to use less power. For that smaller symmetric key sizes or elliptic curve, cryptography is used which needs fewer resources than asymmetric encryption. Symmetric encryption or smaller key sizes are

used if you have an application that demands low latency so to encrypt and decrypt information quickly and to keep the process as active as possible.

Moreover, if you are concerned about the integrity of data, then a strong encryption technique is required that uses larger key sizes and include hashing.

Confidentiality

The biggest reason to employ encryption is confidentiality. It is a private & secret way of conveying information that only the desired recipient could see. To preserve this confidentiality, these encryptions are used; drive-level encryption, file level encryption and encryption over email.

Integrity

To ensure that the information that is received by the recipient is originally the information that was sent. It prevents the impersonator to modify or re-mold data . Therefore, hashes are used to sustain integrity. For this sender takes a hash of the data while sending the information and then the end user or the recipient performs the same hashing function and make a comparison of the two hashes. This process ensures that the transmission of information is free from any changes.

- Typically used with the transfer of the file to authenticate a successful file transfer.
- Also used to store password, to save it in a way that hides the original password yet keeps a check that everybody is authenticating properly.

Obfuscation

Obfuscation is the encryption of payload of a packet destined to a target in a manner that target host can reverse it but the can be decrypted by any other. It will exploit the end user without alerting the security devices such as IDS. It uses different techniques such as encoding, encryption, polymorphism.

Authentication

Commonly used with authentication as written before about getting the password and hashing them for comparison later. Usually, the password is merged with a random salt, and a hash of both the salt and password is produced. In this way, if somebody accesses the hash password list, all the passwords look quite unique even if the same password was shared by someone else.

Non-Repudiation

Cryptography also provides non-repudiation. Through this, it can be confirmed that if the information received by the recipient is originally sent by the third party. It can be ensured by using digital signatures that also provide integrity.

Wireless Security

The use of wireless networks has greatly increased and, therefore, the security of the protocols used in a wireless network has become a vital determinant to observe security. Its security can be ensured through the implementation of encryption.

Cryptographic Protocols

Cryptographic protocols refer to the cryptographic methods and their implementation to assure various vendors equipment interoperability.

All can have a secure wireless communication channel by configuring WPA and WPA 2 encryption that permits only people with a password to communicate.

WPA

- It stands for Wireless Protected Access
- Used for encryption on wireless networks
- It uses RC4 cipher with TKPI (Temporal Key Integrity Protocol)
- Capable of accepting much larger Initialization Vector
- In WPA, every packet has a unique 128-bit encryption key.

WPA2

- Wi-Fi protected access version 2.
- It is a modern wireless encryption and was introduced in 2004.
- Uses AES (Advanced Encryption Standard) for encryption that replaced RC4.
- Also, involves CCMP (Counter Mode with Cipher Block Chaining Message Authentication Code Protocol) that replaced TKIP.

CCMP: Block cipher mode

- Uses 128-bit keys and encrypts in 128-bit block size.
- Its services include Data confidentiality, Access control, and Authentication.
- For data confidentiality it uses AES

TKIP: Temporary key integrity protocol

- It merges the secret root key with initialization vector and prevents replay attack by adding sequence counter.
- It also defends against tempering by adding 64-bit message integrity check.
- There were some integration vulnerabilities found with TKIP that is why it was agreed to not use it further.

Authentication Protocols

EAP

- It stands for Extensible Authentication Protocol.
- It also serves as a framework for creating various types of authentication.
- WPA and WPA2 also use five various EAP types for authentication on wireless networks.

PEAP

- It stands for Protected Extensible Authentication Protocol.
- It was developed by Microsoft, Cisco, and RSA for the purpose of secure authentication.
- In PEAP, EAP is encapsulated into a tunnel (TLS tunnel). The encryption certificate is on the server side, and all the EAP communication are sent over this TLS tunnel.

EAP-FAST

- One of the EAP types is EAP-FAST. It stands for EAP Flexible Authentication via Secure Tunneling.
- It was proposed by Cisco as a replacement of LEAP (Lightweight EAP) protocol that was used with WEP.
- It is more secure protocol.

EAP-TLS

- It stands for EAP-Transport Layer Security or EAP over Transport Layer Security.
- EAP-TLS is a common way for encrypting web server traffic and authentication methods, and it is used widely.
- Common advantages include:
- Strong Security
- Support for various wireless network types.

EAP-TTLS

- It stands for EAP-Tunnelled Transport Layer Security.
- It functions almost the same as EAP-TLS like the server authenticates to the client with a certificate, but the client side authentication is tunnelled in this protocol that permits the use of legacy protocols of authentication such as PAP, CHAP, MS-CHAP, etc.

IEEE 802.1x

- A standard of authentication commonly referred to as "Port-based NAC (Network Access Control)."
- Access is not granted until the authentication process is completed.
- Over wireless, IEEE 802.1x uses either EAP based protocol or IEEE 802.11i.

RADIUS Federation

- As the name implies, RADIUS Federation simply means using RADIUS with the federation.
- Federation permits a member of one company to authenticate to another company's network using normal credentials; no separate credentials are needed for visiting separate network.

Methods

For configuring wireless access point, there are various authentication methods available.

PSK vs. Enterprise vs. Open System

An open system is the one without any set security, which means no password is needed for authentication in an open system. PSK is commonly named as *WPA-PSK* because it uses WPA2 encryption with a secret key. It stands for Pre-Shared Key. It needs to be securely shared among users.

In organizations, there are various security problems associated with using a shared key and WPA Enterprise helps reducing those problems. It authenticates all the users individually with an authentication server.

WPS

It stands for Wi-Fi /Protected setup that was originally called 'Wi-Fi simple config'. Using WPS, there are various ways of authentication such as; Using 8-digit PIN that is configured on the access point (simply add that PIN to the mobile device), Pushing a button on the access point, NFC-Near Field Communication (bring mobile near the access point).

Captive Portal

Another authentication method for wireless networks is a captive portal. A pop up that you see when you open a browser, and it asks you for credentials. This is known as a captive portal.

Public Key Infrastructure PKI

One of the challenges in cryptography is the key management. Conventional cryptography techniques based on symmetric key cryptography that use the same key for both encryption and decryption. The secure transmission of the key from one user to another is difficult because if the unauthorized user accesses the key, he can read, decrypt and modify all the information using that key.

In 1976, PKI was introduced by Whitfield Diffie and Martin Hellman to solve key management issues. In Public key cryptography, every user receives two keys i.e.

- Public – Can be published to see or use by the user
- Private – Always kept secret

In public key cryptography, no secret or private key is shared or transmitted, and all the communication involves is only through the public key. Hence, the sharing of the secret key problem in Symmetric Key Cryptography was solved using Public Key cryptography.

In Public Key Cryptography, the initial message is encrypted by the sender using receiver's public key, and then he decrypts that message using his own private key.

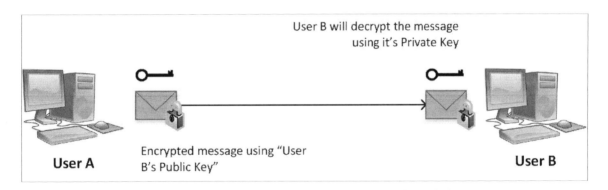

Figure 6-03: Public Key Cryptography

The following are the features of Public Key Cryptography:

- It is efficient.
- It is secure.
- It is scalable for a large number of users.

PKI Components

It describes all the procedures, policies, & people that are required to manage Digital certificate. It encapsulates the process to create, manage to revoke and distribute these certificates.

A public key infrastructure (PKI) is a set of hardware, software, people, policies, and procedures needed to create, manage, distribute, use, store, and revoke digital certificates and manage public-key encryption. It permits users of an unsecured network to securely money and exchange data over the use of a private and a public cryptographic key pair that has obtained through a trusted authority. The public key infrastructure delivers for a digital certificate that can detect an individual or an enterprises and directory services that can store and, when necessary, revoke the certificates.

PKI ties public keys with the characters of individuals, applications, and associations. This "binding" is kept up by the issuance and administration of digital certificates by a certificate authority (CA).

- **PKI certificate authority (CA):** The CA is a secure third party that issues PKI certificates to substances and individuals after checking their identity. It signs these certificates are utilizing its private key.
- **Certificate database:** The certificate database stores all certificates endorsed by the CA.
- **PKI certificate:** Certificates contain a substance's or individual's public key, its motivation, the CA that approved and issued the certificate, the date extends amid which the certificate can view as valid, and the algorithm utilized to create the signature.
- **Certificate store:** The certificate store resides on a local PC and stores issued certificates and private keys.

Use of PKI

The use of PKI is server identification certificates. SSL requires a PKI certificate on the server to prove its identity confidentially to the client. Every HTTPS web server connection uses SSL and as such uses PKI. This outreach Web concentrates on client-side applications of PKI using end user PKI certificates instead of server certificates. Client-side applications of PKI consist of categories are:

- Authentication
- Digital signatures
- Encryption

Operations of PKI:

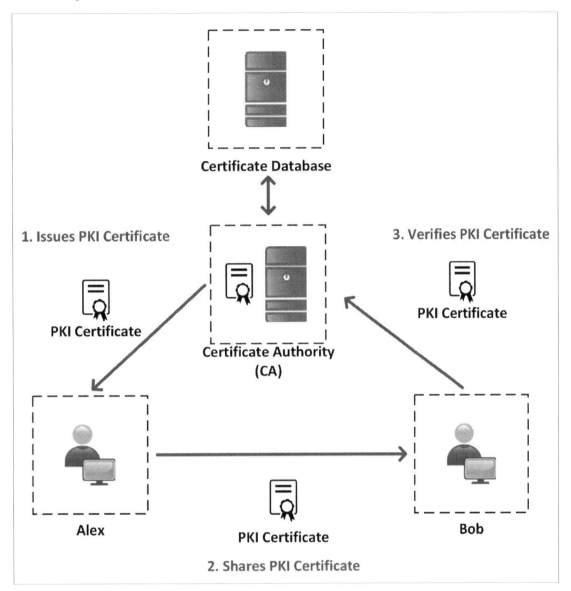

Figure 6-04: PKI Operation

- Alex initially requests a certificate from the CA. The CA authenticates Alex and stores Alex's PKI certificate in the certificate database.
- Alex communicates with Bob using his PKI certificate.
- Bob communicates with the trusted CA using the CA's public key. The CA refers to the certificate database to validate Alex's PKI certificate.

Key Management

The management of Key starts with the generation of a key. Using proper cipher, keys with the requested strength are generated. After that, the certificate is generated where a

public key is allocated to a user or device. Sequentially, it is distributed to the particular user and stored in order to prevent it from any unauthorized access. In case unauthorized gain access to the certificate then these certificates are revoked or replaced. If the certificates are not revoked, then there is an expiry date so when the certificate expires, the key management process begins again.

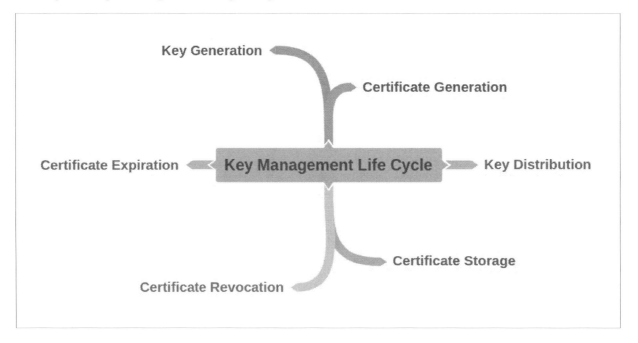

Figure 6-05: Key Management Lifecycle

Digital Certificates

A digital certificate also known as the Public key certificate is a combination of digital signature and Public key. It also contains other important details of the key holder. Digital signatures are used for the purpose of adding trust especially if it comes from a third party. For additional trust, Certification Authority (CA) is used by the PKI, and also Web of trust is used.

Digital Certificate can be created with Windows, which is a part of Windows Domain Services. In Linux, digital certificates are created by using various third-party options.

What does a Digital Certificate contain?

Digital Certificate contains various items and these items are listed below:

- **Subject** – Certificate holder's name.
- **Serial Number** - Unique number for certificate identification.
- **Public Key** – A copy of public of the certificate holder.
- **Issuer** – Certificate issuing authority's digital signature to verify that the certificate is real.

- **Signature Algorithm** – Algorithm used to digitally sign the certificate by the Certification Authority (CA).
- **Validity** – Validity of a certificate or we can say expiry date and time of the certificate.

The Digital certificate has X.509 version supported format, and it is a standard format.

Certificate Extensions

Another item such as 'certificate extension' can also be added to a digital certificate to increase functionality. There are various standard extensions added to a digital certificate. Some of them are:

Standard Extension

Extensions	Purpose
digitalSignature (0)	To sign documents digitally.
nonRepudiation (1)	For non-repudiation service use.
keyAgreement (4)	For DH (Diffie-Hellman) key agreement use.
keyEncipherment (2)	For exchange of key.
keycertsign (5)	Used for the signing of certificates by a Certification Authority (CA).
dataEncipherment (3)	Used for data confidentiality.
encipherOnly (7)	Used with the key agreement of Diffie-Hellman (DH).
decipherOnly (8)	Used with the key agreement of Diffie-Hellman (DH).
cRLSign (6)	For signing Certification Revocation List.

Table 6-02: Extensions and their Purposes

Commercial Certificate Authorities

There are hundreds of certificate authorities listed in the web browser details. These listed certificate authorities can be used to digitally sign the certificate from web servers, as they are the trusted certificate authorities.

If someone manages a website, he would get digitally signed a certificate or trusted website certificate by the certification authority (CA) to place on the website so that everyone's browser will trust him/her.

It is easy to have a digital signature by the certification authority. The process starts with the pair of key creation. One is a private key that is kept on the website, and the other is a public key that is sent to the certification authority to be digitally signed. This process is

called Certificate signing request (CSR). To verify that requested party is the real owner of that website, the certification authority performs some checks, and after that sign, the certificate and sometimes provides additional features.

Private Certificate Authority

The private certificate authority refers to the authority that is built by someone privately. The person can perform all the certification authority functions by himself at home. All the devices that are inside of a network must trust the certificate that is signed by the internal certificate authority.

For example, in a medium or large organization that have many web servers and devices that are required to be encrypted for privacy, they can have their own certificate authority that can be created simply at home, instead of going to the third party and pay to them for each signed certificate. There is a good deal of software available for building your own certificate authority. Windows Certificate Services (in windows) and some other use openCA.

PKI Trust Relationship

To build certificate authority, there are many ways:

Single Certificate Authority - Everyone or every device receives their digitally signed certificate from the same Certificate Authority.

Hierarchical - It owns a Root Certificate Authority and some other Intermediate Certification Authority underneath that Root CA.

Advantages of having multiple certificate authorities are as follows:

- Helps to balance the load of certificate creation.
- Every department in the organization can easily build and manage their own certificate.
- Revocation of an Intermediate Certificate Authority is easier to deal.

Example

Imagine if somebody has gained the access to the private key of the Intermediate certification authority. Only the certificates underneath that CA are needed to be revoked, instead of revoking the certificates of the whole organization.

Key Revocation

Through a Certification Revocation List (CRL), the certificate revocation process occurs on the certificate authority.

Reasons of Certificate revocation

- Certificate association with the server that is not in use.
- Some unauthorized person gains access to the certificate.
- Originally issued certificate has some error.

Browser-based Revocation updates

OCSP (Online certificate status protocol) – Using this protocol, the browser can check certificate revocation or the status of the certificate. The message is usually sent to the OCSP Responder through HTTP (Hyper Text Markup Language). Not all applications or browsers support the OCSP protocol.

PKI Concept

Online and Offline CA

The infrastructure of a public key relies on trust, and typically this trust is provided by the Certification Authority (CA), However, a compromised CA is a bad thing, and this also creates trust issues with the Certificate Authority.

The Intermediate Certificate is the signer/issuer of the SSL Certificate. The Root CA Certificate is the signer/issuer of the Intermediate Certificate. Once the Intermediate CA runs, and the load is distributed, the Root certificate gets offline for protection.

OCSP Stapling

As discussed above, the OCSP depends upon CA. It is the responsibility of CA to respond to all the OCSP requests of the clients. In addition, if the numbers of devices that the CA has to check are large, then this creates the issue of scalability. In this case, OCSP Stapling is implemented. In OCSP Stapling, the device that holds certificate can verify their status and provide revocation status. This information is received from the device directly rather than CA, and the information of the status is stored on the server of the certificate holder.

The OCSP status or the revocation is stapled into the TSL or SSL handshake, and digitally signed note by the certification authority is present with the OCSP stapled information.

Pinning

The purpose of the Certificate pinning is to prevent the *man-in-the-middle attack*. Certificate pinning is used when the server's certificate has been hard-coded into the application by the application itself. In this case, the application communicates to the server and receive a copy of the certificate to compare them. If both of them matches, then it means that the person is directly communicating to the server and if the certificate does not match, then a decision is made by the application accordingly. It shows an error message that the certificate does not match or it may shut it down.

PKI Trust Relationships

Certificate authority initiates with a single CA, and from that single authority, all the certificates are generated. In some organisations, the Hierarchical structure is used that consists of Root CA and Intermediate CA.

- **Mesh CA**

Some organizations employ Mesh Certificate Authority Structure. In Mesh CA structure, each certificate authority is directly connected to all other certification authorities. One of the problems with this type of topology is that it is difficult to scale large numbers of CA in a mesh topology.

- **Web of Trust**

It is an alternate to PKI. Web of Trust makes everyone an authority as an alternative to the certification authority.

- **Mutual Authentication**

In this mutual authentication scenario, both the client and the server authenticate each other's certificates. For instance, a certificate from you is trusted by the server and similarly, a certificate from the server is trusted by you.

- **Key Escrow**

Key escrow means a third party may have access to your private key or the decryption key along with the backup of that key. This can be employed by some organizations or businesses where the employee's information or partner's data needs to be accessed or decrypted.

What is it all about?

As private keys or decryption keys are very important. Subsequently, when these keys are in the hands of a third party, they need to be properly managed. For that, a clear and well-defined procedure or process is required. You should be able to trust the third party that holds your keys, and you also need assurance that the third party is able to keep your keys securely.

- **Certificate Chaining**

As mentioned above, a single certificate authority is not a good idea. However, hierarchical structures, having multiple levels within it, are preferable. All the connections between different certificate authorities is known as Chain of Trust. The list

of the certificates between Root CA and other Intermediate CA are listed in Chain of Trust.

The chain of trust initiates with SSL certificate (part of the web server) and ends with the Root certificate. In between, there is a certification authority that assigns the certificate. The certificates between SSL certificate and Root CA are called "Intermediate Certificate or Chain Certificate."

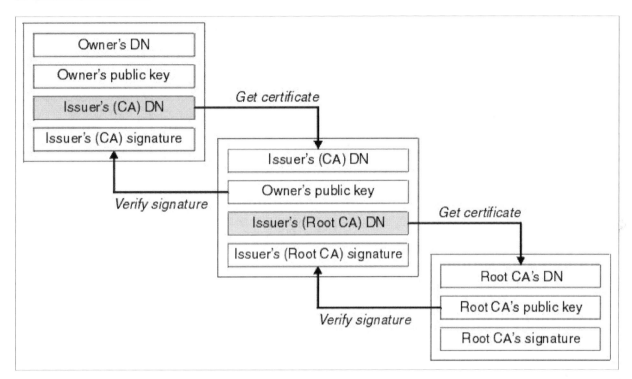

Figure 6-06: Certificate Chaining

The configuration with an appropriate chain is required by the web server, and it is common to not only configure SSL certificate, but also add Intermediate certificate between Root CA and SSL certificate.

Types of Certificates

There are various kinds of certificates that are used for different purposes. Some of them are as follows:

Root Certificate

A certificate that is public and is assigned to the Root CA and its purpose is to identify the Root CA. Everything initiates with Root certificate in PKI infrastructure. It is Root certificate that issues an intermediate certificate or another certificate.

In public key infrastructure, the root certificate is the most important certificate. In case if somebody gains access to this root certificate private key, then they would be able to generate their own certificate for any purpose of their interest.

Web Server SSL Certificate

For SSL encryption, there are a number of certificates that can be assigned to a web server. Some of them are as follows:

Domain Validation (DV) Certificate - The person having DV certificate has some control over the DNS domain associated with the SSL.

Extended Validation (EV) Certificate – The certificate receiving person is passed through some additional checks by the certificate authority. If a person passes all the checks, then that person receives EV certificate. The web owner's organization name appears in green color on the address bar of the web, that is certified with EV certificate.

Figure 6-07: Extended Validation Certificate

Subject Alternative Name (SAN) Certificate

A certificate that supports various domains in the same certificate. It is an X.509 standard extension and permits you to put a subject alternative name extension and list out all the DNS names (additional identification information) linked with the certificate.

Wildcard Domain Certificate

A Wildcard Domain Certificate can be applied to any domain and all the names associated with-it. So, the name of the server is not a piece of matter, the main aim is the replacement of the asterisk (*).

 Example: There are an asterisk and a period that a wildcard notation contains the domain name.

*.domainname.com

* replacement – ftp.domainname.com, vpn.domainname.com, IPS.domainname.com.

Self-Signed Certificate

The certificate is not required to be signed by the Certificate Authority (Public). This internal certificate is signed by the same person bearing the certificate. For this, the person creates his/her own certificate authority that issues digitally signed certificate.

This certificate is used for the web server that is only for an internal network of the company. In this way, the person does not have to pay for any external certification authority. These certificates are then installed on every device or web server within a network. Every person who, then, connects to the web server will see the Internal Certification Authority signature certificate.

Machine and Computer Certificate

The certificate that is used to allow and manage devices for communication on the network. The purpose of this certificate is the authentication of devices. It means that only authenticated devices can communicate over the network.

For that, certificates signed by the certification authority are placed on the devices so if any unauthorized person tries to connect to the network using VPN, will not be allowed to communicate over the network because that particular person will not be certified.

User Certificate

It is a type of certificate usually assigned to a single user or an individual. Generally integrated into a smart card or digital access card.

Example: ID card

Email Certificate

The type of certificate that is usually attached with email. The email certificate permits us to send the email securely by encrypting the information to the other user. To encrypt the information, it uses a recipient's key (public), and allows only the receiver to decrypt the information in the email.

This certificate can also be used as a Digital signature. In case if you do not want to encrypt the information, then you can just digitally sign it through Email Certificate.

Code Signing Certificate

Code Signing Certificates are used by software developers to digitally sign apps, drivers, and software programs as a way for end-users to verify that the code they receive has not been altered or compromised by a third party. They include your signature, your company's name, and if desired, a timestamp.

Practice Question

1. Which of the following form of cryptography makes key management less of a concern?

   A. Digital Signature
   B. Hashing
   C. Asymmetric
   D. Symmetric

2. What does Diffie-Hellman permit us to do?

   A. Exchange keys out-of-band
   B. Exchange keys in-band
   C. Neither A nor B
   D. Both A and B

3. A hash collision is bad for malware prevention. Why?

   A. The hashes are encrypted and cannot be changed.
   B. Two different programs with the same hash could allow malware to be undetected.
   C. The hashed passwords would be exposed.
   D. Malware could corrupt the hash algorithm.

4. Why ephemeral key is important for key exchange protocol?

   A. It increases security due to the usage of a different key for each connection.
   B. It adds entropy to the algorithm.
   C. It allows the key exchange to be completed faster.
   D. It is longer than a normal key.

5. What enables RADIUS to scale to a global authentication network?

   A. CCMP-delegated authentication
   B. Two-factor authentication
   C. Strong encryption
   D. Certificate-based tunneling and EAP

Additional Practice Question

1. Which of the following is an example of Embedded System?
    A. Network-enabled thermostat
    B. Web server
    C. User workstation
    D. Database server

2. During the examination of the infected laptop, it is noticed that the malware loads on start-up and also loads a file called netutilities.dll every time MS Word is opened. This is an example represents which of the following attack?
    A. Zero-day exploit
    B. DLL injection
    C. System infection
    D. Memory overflow

3. While testing a new application your group noted that when 3 or more of you click 'submit' at the same time on a particular form, the application crashes every time. This is an example of which error?
    A. A race condition
    B. A nondeterministic error
    C. Undocumented feature
    D. DLL injection

4. Which one is a Passive Tool?
    A. Nessus
    B. Nmap
    C. Tripwire
    D. Zenmap

5. From the following choose the example of Initial Exploitation?
    A. Scanning a network using Nmap
    B. Using a SQL injection attack to successfully bypass a login prompt
    C. Using cracked credentials to delete customer data
    D. Installing a backdoor to provide future access if needed

6. In which type of testing, the testers are not provided with any type of information for performing assessment?
    A. White box testing
    B. Passive testing

C. Black box testing

D. Active testing

7. From the following which is not correct regarding insider threat?

   A. Insiders have the access and knowledge necessary to cause immediate damage to an organization.

   B. Insiders may actually already have all the access they need to perpetrate criminal activity such as fraud.

   C. Insiders generally do not have knowledge of the security systems in place, so system monitoring will allow for any inappropriate activity to be detected.

   D. Attacks by insiders are often the result of employees who have become disgruntled with their organization and are looking for ways to disrupt operations.

8. Which of the following can be included in criminal activity on the internet? (Select all that apply.)

   A. Fraud

   B. Extortion

   C. Theft

   D. Embezzlement

   E. Forgery

9. Which of the following have the ability to write scripts that exploit vulnerabilities and are also able to discover new vulnerabilities?

   A. Elite hackers

   B. Hacktivists

   C. Uber hackers

   D. Advanced persistent threat actors

10. In which of the following threat category the attacks by an attacker or a small group of attackers falls?

   A. Unorganized threat

   B. APT

   C. Singular threat

   D. Hacktivist

11. When the input supplied to the program is more than it can process, what type of vulnerability occurs?

A. Poison Apple

B. Shoulder surfing

C. Smurfing

D. Buffer overflow

12. A user reports that he is unable to connect to the network. When you troubleshoot the issue, you notice that the MAC address for his default gateway is not matching with the MAC address of your company's router. What type of attack is he facing?

A. Consensus attack

B. ARP poisoning

C. Refactoring

D. Smurf attack

13. High traffic load is crashing your e-commerce site. When you look at the traffic logs, you identify that thousands of requests coming from hundreds of various IP addresses for the same URL. You are facing which of the following attacks?

A. DoS

B. DDoS

C. DNS poisoning

D. Snarfing

14. Which of the following can help in cracking the password of a disgruntled user who is fired recently in the least time?

A. Rainbow tables

B. Brute force

C. Dictionary

D. Hybrid attack

15. The attack in which network traffic is captured and retransmitted at a later time by the attacker is known as?

A. Denial of service attack

B. Replay attack

C. Bluejacking attack

D. Man-in-the-middle attack

16. You notice a man in a red shirt standing close to a locked door with a large box in his hands. He waits for someone else to come along and open the locked door, then proceeds to follow him inside. What type of social engineering attack is this?

A. Impersonation

B. Phishing

C. Boxing

D. Tailgating

17. In your company, the desktops are being infected by a malware in a way that more and more systems are becoming a victim of that malware every hour despite the fact that users are not sharing any e-mails, programs, or even files. Which malware is causing this infection?

    A. Virus

    B. RAT

    C. BitLocker

    D. Worm

18. You are not able to open any of the Word document stored on the local system and when a document is forced open for analyzation purpose you see only random characters and there is no sign that the file is still a Word document. You are a victim of which malware?

    A. Virus

    B. Crypto-malware

    C. RAT

    D. Backdoor

19. Some desktops in your company are displaying the message "Your files have been encrypted. Pay 2 bitcoins in order to recover them." These desktops have been affected by which malware?

    A. Zotob worm

    B. Adware

    C. Ransomware

    D. Rootkit

20. A member of your company is facing issues with his laptop. Whenever he opens a browser, he sees various pop-ups after every few minutes and whatever website he visits, the popups appear. His laptop is affected by which malware?

    A. Adware

    B. Virus

    C. Ransomware

    D. D. BitLocker

21. For what reason NAT will likely keep on being used in even IPv6 systems?

    Why will NAT likely continue to be used even in IPv6 networks?

    A. Even IPv6 does not have enough IP addresses.
    B. It is integral to how access control lists work.
    C. It allows faster internal routing of traffic.
    D. It can hide the internal addressing structure from direct outside connections.

22. You are requested to suggest a VPN methodology to a senior management of your company for newly purchased VPN concentrators. For what reason would you firmly recommend IPSec VPNs?
    A. Connectionless integrity
    B. Data-origin authentication
    C. Traffic-flow confidentiality
    D. All of the above

23. Which of the following is the core technology of NIPS on which it relies?
    A. VPN
    B. IDS
    C. NAT
    D. ACL

24. How can security be improved through a proxy server?
    A. They use TLS-based encryption to access all sites.
    B. They can control which sites and content employees' access, lessening the chance of malware exposure.
    C. They enforce appropriate use of company resources.
    D. They prevent access to phishing sites.

25. For encryption keys, the temper protection can be provided by which of the following device?
    A. HSM
    B. DLP
    C. NIDS/NIPS
    D. NAC

26. From the following, which one represents most network tools that detect an attack?
    A. Active

B. Passive

C. Linux based

D. Windows-based

27. The **tcpdump** command-line tool is a category of which of the following?
    A. Network scanner
    B. Password cracker
    C. Protocol analyzer
    D. Data sanitization tool

28. A company was attacked by the bad guys multiple times and that attack results in data violations. Therefore the company set up some vulnerable virtual machines containing fake data that looks exactly like the company's real machines in order to identify how the bad guys get into the system. Which of the following mechanism was implemented by the company?
    A. Passive sensors
    B. Network-based intrusion detection system (NIDS)
    C. DMZ
    D. Honeynet

29. If a worm is going through your company that reaches out to other nodes on port TCP/1337. Which of the following tools would you need to identify the affected nodes on your network?
    A. Protocol analyzer
    B. Advanced malware tool
    C. Network scanner
    D. Password cracker

30. Related to log and event anomalies which principle is valid?
    A. It's important to determine what to log and what not to log.
    B. You should gather and log as much information as you can.
    C. Context doesn't matter much when logging information.
    D. Logs should be actively maintained and never be destroyed or overwritten.\

31. The most likely reason behind access violation errors is?
    A. Intruders are trying to hide their footprints.
    B. The user is unauthorized and is either making a mistake or is attempting to get past security.
    C. A SIEM system will not identify access violations.

D. An APT intrusion won't usually trigger access violations.

32. Which statement is true regarding firewalls?
    A. Firewalls are encrypted remote terminal connections.
    B. Over time, rulesets stabilize and become easier to maintain.
    C. Firewalls are network access policy enforcement devices that allow or block passage of packets based on a ruleset.
    D. Auditing firewall rules is a straightforward process.

33. Satellite communications (SATCOM) usage is most common in which of the following scenario?
    A. In densely populated areas
    B. Rural and remote areas or at sea
    C. As a backup for cell phone coverage
    D. Where line-of-sight issues exist

34. For establishing trust relationship which mechanism is used by the Bluetooth?
    A. Pairing
    B. Kerberos
    C. PKI
    D. Public key

35. From the following which one is not a part of a proper Mobile Device Management (MDM) policy?
    A. The ability to decrypt data on the device
    B. The ability to lock the device if it is lost or stolen
    C. The ability to remotely wipe the device if it is lost or stolen
    D. The ability to wipe the device automatically after several failed login attempts

36. ANT is correctly described by which of the following?
    A. It is similar to Bluetooth enhanced mode.
    B. It operates in the 5-GHz spectrum.
    C. It encrypts HTTP traffic.
    D. It functions well in the crowded 2.4-GHz spectrum.

37. A user is receiving "cannot resolve address" error notes from his browser. Which port is possibly an issue on his firewall?
    A. 22
    B. 53

C. 440

D. 553

38. Which of the following defines the Secure Shell (SSH) protocol?

A. It is an encrypted remote terminal connection program used for remote connections to a server.

B. It provides dynamic network address translation.

C. It provides Software as a Service (SaaS).

D. It provides snapshots of physical machines at a point in time.

39. Which port is used by FTPS?

A. 53

B. 83

C. 990

D. 991

40. Which of the following statement regarding Transport Layer Security (TLS) is correct?

A. It replaces SSL.

B. It extends SNMP.

C. It provides Port Address Translation.

D. It uses port 22 for encryption.

41. Which of the following is the purpose of using Tunneling?

A. Eliminate an air gap

B. Connect users to a honeynet

C. Remote access from users outside the building

D. Intranet connections to the DMZ

42. The defense-in-depth is not supported by which one of the following?

A. Vendor diversity

B. User diversity

C. Control diversity

D. Redundancy

43. Which of the following can result in the highest risk if configured improperly?

A. The operating system on a server

B. Web server

C. Application server

D. Network infrastructure device

44. Why is UEFI preferred rather than BIOS?
    A. UEFI resides on the hardware, making it faster than BIOS.
    B. UEFI is stored in volatile hardware storage.
    C. UEFI has limited ability to deal with high-capacity storage and high-bandwidth communications and thus is more optimized.
    D. UEFI has more security designed into it, including provisions for secure booting.

45. Which of the following is not performed by a Secure Boot?
    A. It provides all approved drivers needed.
    B. It enables attestation that drivers haven't changed since they were approved.
    C. It only allows signed drivers and OS loaders to be invoked.
    D. It blocks malware that attempts to alter the boot process.

46. What is not true about hardware roots of trust?
    A. They are secure by design.
    B. They have very specific functionality.
    C. They are typically implemented in hardware that is isolated from the operating system.
    D. They provide security only at their level, not to higher layers of a system.

47. What is the simple way of improving the security of a system?
    A. Enabling all ports and services
    B. Maintaining comprehensive access control rules
    C. Disabling unnecessary ports and services
    D. Optimizing system throughput

48. Which statement is not true regarding systems on a chip?
    A. They provide the full functionality of a computing platform on a single chip.
    B. They typically have low power consumption and efficient design.
    C. Programming of SoC systems can occur at several different levels and thus potential risks are easily mitigated.
    D. Because these devices represent computing platforms with billions of devices worldwide, they have become a significant force in the marketplace

49. Which aspect is important to remember while dealing with the medical device's security?

A. They are still relatively new in their usage.

B. They can directly affect human life.

C. Security is not related to safety.

D. They are almost exclusively stand-alone devices, without Internet connectivity.

50. Which term describes the loss of control over data during operations?

A. Sandboxing

B. Data exposure

C. Data Breach

D. Runtime release

51. In which testing environment fuzz testing works great?

A. White box testing

B. Gray box testing

C. Black box testing

D. Fuzz testing works equally well in all of the above.

52. Which methodology proceeds through a sequence of stages, with each stage being performed before proceeding to the next stage?

A. Scrum

B. Waterfall

C. Agile

D. Extreme Programming (XP)

53. Which of the following cloud deployment model is finest for the application which is extremely scalable and can be provided on request?

A. SaaS

B. PaaS

C. IaaS

D. None of the above

54. Which model of cloud deployment has the least security controls?

A. Private

B. Public

C. Hybrid

D. Community

55. What is the main drawback of a private cloud model?

A. Restrictive access rules

B. Cost

C. Scalability

D. Lack of vendor support

56. What is the use of Security Content Automation Protocol (SCAP)?

A. To enumerate common vulnerabilities

B. To secure networks

C. To provide automation methods for managing vulnerabilities

D. To define an overarching security architecture

57. Why is automated testing important for configuration validation?

A. It can scale and be used in continuous monitoring.

B. It can compare before and after versions of a given system.

C. It can automatically confirm the validity of a configuration.

D. It can slow the divergence caused by system updates.

58. Complete the sentence with the right answer. Alarms are useful only if:

A. They alert on abnormal conditions.

B. Every entrance is monitored with a sensor.

C. They are not tied to the information systems.

D. They are tuned to provide accurate and useful alerts.

59. Which of the following is the security benefit of a Faraday cage?

A. Prevents attack by EMP

B. Prevents illicit monitoring of Van Eck emissions

C. Works better than anti-scale fencing

D. Prevents stack overflows by EMI

60. Which of the following is the main problem of biometrics?

A. Technically biometrics are difficult to implement

B. The human body changing over time

C. The ease with which biometrics are faked

D. Biometrics can't be loaned or delegated

61. Which account is used to run processes that don't involve human interference to start or stop?

A. Guest account

B. Process account

C. Service account

D. Root account

62. A person who works in the IT department of the bank informs you that the tellers are permitted to access their terminal from 9 A.M. to 5 P.M., Monday through Saturday only. This restriction is an example of which of the following?
    A. User auditing
    B. Least privilege
    C. Time-of-day restrictions
    D. Account verification

63. The process of assigning a computer ID to a particular user is identified as?
    A. Authentication
    B. Validation
    C. Authorization
    D. Identification

64. Which is not a true category of authentication factors to be used if you are developing a new multifactor authentication system for your company?
    A. Something you know
    B. Something you see
    C. Something you are
    D. Something you do

65. Which one of the following passwords seems hardest to break?
    A. An eight-character password based on a common dictionary word
    B. A six-character password using only uppercase letters
    C. A seven-character password using a completely random mix of letters, symbols, and numbers
    D. An eight-character password using only lowercase letters

66. The process of ensuring that every account on a mail server is owned by a valid and active employee is known as?
    A. Recertification
    B. Privilege auditing
    C. Password cracking
    D. Payroll auditing

67. What should occur when a user is no longer authorized or no longer desires to use a system?
    A. Account recovery
    B. Account deletion
    C. Account reset
    D. Account audit

68. For managing identities across corporates and systems, the protocols, policies, and practices are defined by which of the following?
    A. Transitive trust
    B. Single sign-on
    C. Identity Federation
    D. Account management

69. From the following scenarios in which it is acceptable to use a shared account?
    A. On a server maintained by different personnel
    B. On a publicly accessible PC running in kiosk mode
    C. If the account is used only to administer e-mail accounts
    D. If the account is used by the CEO and her assistant

70. For generating a one-time password which algorithm uses the secret key with a current timestamp?
    A. Hash-based Message Authentication Code
    B. Date-hashed Message Authorization Password
    C. Time-based One-Time Password
    D. Single sign-on

71. Which access control system needs to be used in case your company wants a system to restrict access to the files that contain sensitive information?
    A. Discretionary access control
    B. Mandatory access control
    C. Confidential access control
    D. File-based access control

72. Which one is not a form of hardware token?
    A. Proximity card
    B. Common Access Card

C. USB token

D. Iris Scan

73. Your client wants a system that will allow them to authenticate that messages arrived from a particular person. What authenticity providing method you might recommend them to use?

A. Digital certificates

B. One-time passwords

C. Software tokens

D. Fingerprint scans

74. You modify a fingerprint scanner of your company and 1 out of 50 attempts fail despite using a valid finger. The supervisor of the company says that "1 out of 50 is good enough". Which of the following is described by the supervisor for the fingerprint scanner?

A. False rejection rate

B. False acceptance rate

C. Critical threshold

D. Failure acceptance criteria

75. Which protocol can pass a symmetric key securely over the network that is insecure and uses a key distribution?

A. CHAP

B. PAP

C. LDAP

D. Kerberos

76. What is the abbreviation of RADIUS?

A. Remote Application Dial-In User Service

B. Remote Authorization Dial-In User Service

C. Remote Authentication Dial-In User Service

D. Remote Auditing Dial-In User Service

77. Which of the following is allowed by OpenID Connect?

A. A third party can authenticate your users for you using accounts the users already have.

B. Symmetric keys can be shared across unsecured networks.

C. Identity can be confirmed with a single UDP packet.

D. Trusted IP addresses can be used to mitigate brute force attacks.

78. Which service permits authorization across networks & single sign-on & federated identity-based authentication?
    A. PAP
    B. Shibboleth
    C. XAML
    D. OASIS

79. Which one of the following options represents the processes of adding and removing a person to a team or project?
    A. Account creation and account disablement
    B. Intake and outflow
    C. On-boarding and Off-boarding
    D. Account auditing and account review

80. Which authentication factor is not regarded as *"something you are"*?
    A. Fingerprints
    B. Voice
    C. PIN code
    D. Retina pattern

81. The requisite level of performance of a given contractual service is essentially set by which of the following?
    A. Inter-organizational service agreement (ISA)
    B. Memorandum of agreement
    C. Memorandum of understanding
    D. Service level agreement (SLA)

82. Which of the following is responsible for defining the characteristics like privacy, security, and retention policies for specific information?
    A. The data owner
    B. The privacy office
    C. The data security office
    D. An individual specifically is given this responsibility for the organization

83. Which of the following policy describes what a company considers to be the proper use of its resources (like computer policies, internet, network, and e-mail)?

A. Resource usage policy (RUP)

B. Acceptable use policy (AUP)

C. Organizational use policy (OUP)

D. Acceptable use of resources policy (AURP)

84. Which of the following is the step-by-step instruction that describes policies implementation steps in a corporation?

A. Procedures

B. Regulations

C. Standards

D. Guidelines

85. After an incident, the target time that is set for a continuation of operations is described by which of the following term?

A. RPO

B. MTTR

C. RTO

D. MTBF

86. The security control that is used post-event for minimizing the amount of damage is?

A. Corrective

B. Detective

C. Preventative

D. Deterrent

87. A mantrap is an illustration of which of the following security control? (Select all that apply.)

A. Corrective

B. Physical

C. Administrative

D. Preventative

88. From the following, which one is the best explanation of 'Risk'?

A. The damage that is the result of unmitigated risk

B. The level of concern one places for the well-being of people

C. The chance of something not working as planned

D. The cost associated with a realized risk

89. Which term describes the steps that a corporate performs after any unusual/abnormal situation is seen in the operation of a computer system?
    A. Cyber event response
    B. Computer/network penetration incident plan
    C. Backup restoration and reconfiguration
    D. Incident response plan

90. Which step of the incident response process involves eliminating the issue?
    A. Eradication
    B. Mitigation
    C. Recovery
    D. Identification

91. Which of the following site is partially configured (usually contain peripherals & software but not every required thing)?
    A. Hot site
    B. Recovery site
    C. Warm site
    D. Cold site

92. The backup strategy that includes only those files that have been modified since the last full backup is?
    A. Snapshot
    B. Differential
    C. Full
    D. Incremental

93. The process for transferring to the continuity of operation version from a regular operational capability of the business is named as?
    A. Alternate business practices
    B. Continuity of business functions
    C. Failover
    D. Disaster recovery

94. Getting all the team members in a cabin around the table for discussing simulated emergency conditions is known as?
    A. Tabletop exercise

B. Alternate business practice

C. After action plan

D. Incident planning

95. Which one of the following is the most important issue in the process of forensics from the initial step?
    A. Witness preparation
    B. Preservation of the data
    C. Documenting all actions taken
    D. Chain of custody

96. Whose function is identical to the cyclic redundancy check, familiar parity bits, or checksum?
    A. Authentication code
    B. Cryptographic algorithm
    C. Hashing algorithm
    D. Record offset

97. Which of the following is not "personally identifiable information (PII)"?
    A. Customer Social Security number or taxpayer identification number
    B. Customer ID number
    C. Customer birth date
    D. Customer name

98. Whose responsibility is to determine what data is required by the company?
    A. Data owner
    B. Data Steward
    C. Privacy officer
    D. Data Custodian

99. From the following methods which one is perfect for destroying DVD's data at the desktop?
    A. Wiping
    B. Pulping
    C. Burning
    D. Shredding

100.   Which of the following Information discloses the customer's identity?

A. Privacy protected information (PPI)

B. Sensitive customer information (SCI)

C. Personally identifiable information (PII)

D. Customer identity information (CII)

101. Which of the following form of cryptography makes key management less of a concern?

A. Digital signatures

B. Hashing

C. Asymmetric

D. Symmetric

102. What is the finest way to obtain the plaintext from a hash value?

A. Use an ephemeral key.

B. Factor prime numbers.

C. Use linear cryptanalysis.

D. You cannot get the plaintext out of a hash value.

103. Which of the following is the reason behind digitally signed messages distinction from encrypted messages?

A. An encrypted message only uses symmetric encryption, whereas a digitally signed message uses both asymmetric and symmetric encryption.

B. A digitally signed message uses much stronger encryption and is harder to break.

C. A digitally signed message has encryption protections for integrity and non-repudiation, which an encrypted message lacks.

D. There is no difference.

104. If a huge quantity of data in the form of a streaming video file is given, what type of encryption technique will be the best to secure the content from unauthorized live viewing?

A. Hashing algorithm

B. Stream cipher

C. Symmetric block

D. Asymmetric block

105. What does Diffie-Hellman permit us to do?

A. Exchange keys out-of-band

B. Exchange keys in-band

C. Neither A nor B`

D. Both A and B

106. Your corporation wishes to set up a new encryption system that will secure the majority of data with a symmetric cipher of at least 256 bits in strength. What is the rightest option of cipher for the massive amount of data?

A. AES

B. 3DES

C. RC4

D. Twofish

107. In the IEEE 802.1AE standard which cipher mode is employed and accepted by NIST?

A. CTR

B. ECB

C. CBC

D. GCM

108. The boss of your company wants you to initiate the attempt to implement digital signatures in the company and want to get notified about what is required for appropriate security of those signatures. Which of the following algorithm you possibly have to consider?

A. SHA-1

B. AES

C. RC4

D. RSA

109. A hash collision is bad for malware prevention. Why?

A. The hashes are encrypted and cannot change.

B. Two different programs with the same hash could allow malware to be undetected.

C. The hashed passwords would be exposed.

D. Malware could corrupt the hash algorithm.

110. For key exchange protocol why the ephemeral key is important?

A. It increases security due to the usage of a different key for each connection.

B. It adds entropy to the algorithm.

C. It allows the key exchange to be completed faster.

D. It is longer than a normal key.

111. Which of the following is the perfect solution if you are setting up a Wi-Fi network in a company that is meant to be used only by company members (using company's laptops) and must be extremely secure.
    A. WPA2-Enterprise
    B. WPS
    C. WPA2-PSK
    D. WPA

112. Your task is to implement Wi-Fi in enterprise mode and the initial diagram of a network presents only network switches and the updated access points. What is the missing component in the diagram?
    A. Certificate authority
    B. Authentication server
    C. NAC server
    D. Guest wireless

113. Why is it not recommended to enable WPS?
    A. It uses WEP-based encryption.
    B. The use of an eight-digit PIN makes it open to brute force attacks.
    C. The lack of support for AES.
    D. All of the above.

114. What enables RADIUS to scale to a global authentication network?
    A. CCMP-delegated authentication
    B. Two-factor authentication
    C. Strong encryption
    D. Certificate-based tunneling and EAP

115. What is the correct reason for "TKIP enhance security"?
    A. It uses a different key for each packet.
    B. It changes the WEP padding algorithm.
    C. It uses stronger authentication.
    D. It uses SSL VPN tunneling.

116. Which of the following does certificate authority consist?

A. Policies and procedures

B. Hardware and software

C. People who manage certificates

D. All of the above

117. Your boss demands you to examine the corporation's internal PKI system's CPS for applicability and verification and to assure that it satisfies present demands. What are you most likely to concentrate on?

A. Key entropy

B. Trust level provided to users

C. How the keys are stored

D. Revocations

118. To which of the following does the standard X.509 relate?

A. Public key infrastructure

B. Certificate Revocation Lists

C. Digital certificates

D. SSL providers

119. Internet SSL public key infrastructure is best described by which of the following models?

A. Unidirectional trust model

B. Third-party trust model

C. Bidirectional trust model

D. The secure key exchange model

120. A certificate is delivered to you through email but the file does not contain the extension. The email mentions that your certificate, the root CA and the intermediate CAs are all included in the file. What is the format of the certificate?

A. DER

B. PEM

C. CER

D. None of the above

Answers

Chapter 1 Answers

1. Malware
2. Virus
3. Ransomware
4. Ransomware
5. Worm
6. True
7. Rootkit
8. Keylogger
9. Software that displays advertisements
10. Spyware
11. Bots
12. Botnets

Chapter 2 Answers

1. Host-Based Firewall
2. Implicit Deny
3. Inline
4. Omnidirectional Antenna
5. Directional Antenna
6. Nessus
7. HSM
8. It functions well in the crowded 2.4-GHz spectrum.

Chapter 3 Answers

1. Remote access from users outside the building
2. User diversity
3. Network Infrastructure Device
4. UEFI has more security designed into it, including provisions for secure booting
5. If provides all approved drivers needed
6. It blocks malware that attempts to alter the boot process
7. Disabling unnecessary ports and services
8. Programming of SoC systems can occur at several different levels and thus potential risks are easily mitigated.
9. They can directly affect human life

10. Data exposure

Chapter 4 Answers

1. Something you are
2. Time-of-day restrictions
3. Identification
4. Something you see
5. A seven-character password using a completely random mix of letters, symbols, and numbers
6. Recertification
7. Account deletion
8. Identity Federation
9. On a publicly accessible PC running in kiosk mode
10. Time-based One-Time Password

Chapter 5 Answers

1. SLA
2. Data Owner
3. AUP
4. Procedures
5. RTO
6. Corrective Controls

Chapter 6 Answers

1. Asymmetric
2. Exchange keys in-band
3. Two different programs with the same hash could allow malware to be undetected.
4. It increases security due to the usage of a different key for each connection
5. Certificate-based tunneling and EAP

Additional Answers

1. C (User workstation)

Explanation

This device is a stand-alone, single-purpose system that is a component of a larger system.

2. B (DLL Injection)

Explanation

DLL injection is the process of adding to a program at runtime a DLL that has a specific vulnerability of function that can be capitalized upon by an attacker.

3. A (A race condition)

Explanation

A race condition is an error condition that occurs when the output of a function is dependent on the sequence or timing of the inputs. In this case, the application crashes when multiple inputs are submitted at the same time.

4. C (Tripwire)

Explanation

Tripwire detects changes to files based on hash values. Nmap and Zenmap are active tools that generate and send packets to systems being examined. Nessus is a vulnerability scanning tool.

5. B (Using a SQL injection attack to successfully bypass a login prompt)

Explanation

Using a SQL injection attack to successfully bypass a login prompt is an example of initial exploitation. The vulnerability was identified and exploited, but no further action was taken.

6. C (Black box testing)

Explanation

Black box testing is performed with no knowledge of the internal workings of the software being tested. The application is treated as a "black box"—the tester cannot

see what's inside the box.

7. C (Insiders generally do not have knowledge of the security systems in place, so system monitoring will allow for any inappropriate activity to be detected.)

Explanation

Insiders frequently **do** have knowledge of the security systems in place and are thus better able to avoid detection.

8. A, B, C, D, & E (Fraud, Extortion, Theft, Embezzlement, and Forgery)

Explanation

Criminal activity on the Internet at its most basic is no different from criminal activity in the physical world. Fraud, extortion, theft, embezzlement, and forgery all take place in the electronic environment.

9. A (Elite hackers)

Explanation

Elite hackers are the name given to those who not only have the ability to write scripts that exploit vulnerabilities but also are capable of discovering new vulnerabilities.

10. D (Hacktivist)

Explanation

Attacks by an individual or even a small group of attackers fall into the hacktivist threat category. Attacks by criminal organizations usually fall into the structured threat category. The other two answers are not categories of threats used by the security community.

11. D (Buffer overflow)

Explanation

A buffer overflow can occur when more input is supplied than the program is designed to process. If the application doesn't reject the additional input, the extra

characters can continue to fill up memory and overwrite other portions of the program, causing instability or undesirable results.

12. B (ARP poisoning)

Explanation

ARP poisoning is an attack that involves sending spoofed ARP or RARP replies to a victim in an attempt to alter the ARP table on the victim's system. If successful, an ARP poisoning attack will replace one or more MAC addresses in victim's ARP table with the MAC address the attacker supplies in their spoofed responses.

13. B (DDos)

Explanation

DDoS (or distributed denial of service) attacks attempt to overwhelm their targets with traffic from many different sources. Botnets are quite commonly used to launch DDoS attacks.

14. A (Rainbow tables)

Explanation

Rainbow tables are precomputed tables or hash values associated with passwords. When used correctly in the right circumstances, they can dramatically reduce the amount of work needed to crack a given password.

15. B (Replay attack)

Explanation

A replay attack occurs when the attacker captures a portion of the communication between two parties and retransmits it at a later time.

16. D (Tailgating)

Explanation

Tailgating (or piggybacking) is the simple tactic of following closely behind a person who has just used their own access card, key, or PIN to gain physical access to a room or building. The large box clearly impedes the person in the red shirt's ability to open the door, so they let someone else do it for them and follow them in.

17. D (Worm)

Explanation

Worms are self-propagating and don't require any human interaction to spread to additional systems.

18. B (Crypto-malware)

Explanation

If specific file types are no longer usable and seem to be nothing but strings of random characters, then you are a victim of crypto-malware. Crypto-malware encrypts files on a system to make them unusable to anyone without the decryption key.

19. C (Ransomware)

Explanation

The malware has encrypted files on the affected systems and is demanding payment for recovery of the files.

20. A (Adware)

Explanation

This is classic adware behavior. Unwanted pop-ups that appear during browsing sessions regardless of the website being viewed are very typical of adware.

21. D (It can hide the internal addressing structure from direct outside connections.)

Explanation

NAT's capability to hide internal addressing schemes and prevent direct connections from outside nodes will likely keep NAT technology relevant even with the broader adoption of IPv6.

22. D (All of the above)

Explanation

The IPSec protocol supports a wide variety of services to provide security. These include access control, connectionless integrity, traffic flow confidentiality, rejection of replayed packets, data security, and data origin authentication.

23. B (IDS)

Explanation

A NIPS relies on the technology of an intrusion detection system at its core to detect potential attacks.

24. B (They can control which sites and content employees' access, lessening the chance of malware exposure.)

Explanation

Proxy servers can improve security by limiting the sites and content accessed by employees, limiting the potential access to malware.

25. A (HSM)

Explanation

A hardware security module (HSM) has tamper protections to prevent the encryption keys they manage from being altered.

26. B (Passive)

Explanation

The majority of detection tools are passive, in that they wait for something in the environment to change as an indicator of an attack.

27. C (Protocol analyzer)

Explanation

The **tcpdump** command-line tool is a protocol analyzer that allows you to filter and display all the network traffic going to a machine, or save it in files for later viewing.

28. D (Honeypot)

Explanation

A honeynet is composed of several vulnerable machines deployed to purposely be

attacked.

29. C (Network scanner)

Explanation

A network scanner that searches for particular ports can help detect infected machines.

30. A (It is important to determine what to log and what not to log.)

Explanation

A valid principle relevant to logs and event anomalies is that you should determine what to log and what not to log.

31. B (The user is unauthorized and is either making a mistake or is attempting to get past security.)

Explanation

The most likely reason for access violation errors is that the user is unauthorized and is either making a mistake or is attempting to get past security.

32. C (Firewalls are network access policy enforcement devices that allow or block passage of packets based on a ruleset.)

Explanation

Firewalls are network access policy enforcement devices that allow or block passage of packets based on a ruleset.

33. B (Rural and remote areas or at sea)

Explanation

SATCOM usage is most common in rural and remote areas or at sea, where other technologies are not available.

34. A (Pairing)

Explanation

Bluetooth uses pairing to establish a trust relationship.

35. A (The ability to decrypt data on the device)

Explanation

Decryption of data on the device is not an element of a good MDM policy.

36. D (It functions well in the crowded 2.4-GHz spectrum.)

Explanation

ANT functions well in the crowded 2.4-GHz spectrum.

37. B (53)

Explanation

Domain Name Service (DNS) uses TCP and UDP port 53 for standard queries and responses.

38. A (It is an encrypted remote terminal connection program used for remote connections to a server.)

Explanation

The SSH protocol is an encrypted remote terminal connection program used for remote connections to a server.

39. C (990)

Explanation

FTPS uses port 990.

40. A (It replaces SSL)

Explanation

TLS replaces SSL.

41. C (Remote access from users outside the building)

Explanation

Remote access is one of the primary uses of tunneling and VPNs.

42. B (User diversity)

Explanation

Although diversity among users can have many benefits, defense-in-depth isn't one of them. All of the other choices are valid components of a defense-in-depth program.

43. D (Network infrastructure device)

Explanation

When improperly configured, network infrastructure devices can allow unauthorized access to traffic traversing all devices they carry traffic to and from.

44. D (UEFI has more security designed into it, including provisions for secure booting.)

Explanation

UEFI is preferable to BIOS because it has more security designed into it, including provisions for secure booting.

45. A (It provides all approved drivers needed.)

Explanation

Secure Boot does not provide all drivers; rather, it ensures they are signed and unchanged.

46. D (They provide security only at their level, not to higher layers of a system)

Explanation

Hardware roots of trust are built on the principle that if one "trusts" one layer, that

layer can be used to promote security to higher layers of a system.

47. C (Disabling unnecessary ports and services)

Explanation

Disabling unnecessary ports and services is a simple way to improve system security.

48. C (Programming of SoC systems can occur at several different levels and thus potential risks are easily mitigated.)

Explanation

Programming of SoC systems can occur at several different levels and thus potential risks are difficult to mitigate.

49. B (They can directly affect human life.)

Explanation

A very important aspect to always remember when dealing with security of medical devices is that they can directly affect human life.

50. B (Data exposure)

Explanation

Data exposure is the loss of control over data from a system during operations.

51. D (Fuzz testing works equally well in all of the above)

Explanation

Fuzz testing works well in white, black, or gray box testing, as it can be performed without knowledge of the specifics of the application under test.

52. B (Waterfall)

Explanation

The **waterfall** model is a development model based on simple manufacturing design. The work process begins with the requirements analysis phase and progresses

through a series of four more phases, with each phase being completed before progressing to the next phase.

53. A (SaaS)

Explanation

Software as a Service is suitable for delivering highly scalable, on-demand applications without installing endpoint software.

54. B (Public)

Explanation

The shared environment of a public cloud has the least amount of security controls.

55. B (Cost)

Explanation

A private cloud model is considerably more expensive as it is a dedicated resource, negating some of the advantages of outsourcing the infrastructure in the first place.

56. C (To provide automation methods for managing vulnerabilities)

Explanation

SCAP provides automation methods for managing vulnerabilities.

57. A (It can scale and be used in continuous monitoring)

Explanation

Automated testing is an important part of configuration validation because it can scale and be used in continuous monitoring.

58. D (They are tuned to provide accurate and useful alerts.)

Explanation

Alarms are effective only if they are tuned to provide accurate and useful alerting

information.

59. B (Prevents illicit monitoring of Van Eck emissions)

Explanation

A Faraday cage can prevent illicit monitoring of computer systems through Van Eck emissions.

60. B (The human body changing over time)

Explanation

Some biometric features can change over time, or with medical conditions making them less reliable and forcing a re-identification phase to resync users and their biometric.

61. C (Guest account)

Explanation

Service accounts are used to run processes that do not require human intervention to start, stop, or administer.

62. C (Time-of-day restrictions)

Explanation

Time-of-day restrictions are often used to limit the hours during which a user is allowed to log into or access a system. This helps prevent unauthorized access outside that user's normal working hours.

63. D (Identification)

Explanation

Identification is the process of ascribing a computer ID to a specific user, computer, network device, or computer process.

64. B (Something you see)

Explanation

Something you see is not one of the categories of authentication factors.

65. C (A seven-character password using a completely random mix of letters, symbols, and numbers)

Explanation

Of the examples, C would be the most difficult to crack because it is random and is composed of letters, symbols, and numbers—a much larger character set to brute force.

66. A (Recertification)

Explanation

Recertification is the process of ensuring users are still employed and still require accounts.

67. B (Account deletion)

Explanation

Account disablement should occur when a user no longer has authorized use privileges on the system. Account deletion can mess with permissions.

68. C (Identity Federation)

Explanation

Federation, or identity federation, define policies, protocols, and practices to manage identities across systems and organizations. Federation's ultimate goal is to allow users to seamlessly access data or systems across domains.

69. B (On a publicly accessible PC running in kiosk mode)

Explanation

A publicly accessible PC running in kiosk mode is a good use of a shared account, as you wouldn't be able to issue individual accounts to each person who uses the kiosk and tracking specific user activity is not critical.

70. C (Time-based One-Time Password)

Explanation

The Time-based One-Time Password (TOTP) algorithm is a specific implementation of a HOTP that uses a secret key with a current timestamp to generate a one-time password.

71. B (Mandatory access control)

Explanation

Mandatory access control (MAC) is a system used in environments with different levels of security classifications. Access to objects (like files) is based on the sensitivity of the information contained in those objects and the authorization of the user to access information with that level of sensitivity.

72. D (Iris Scan)

Explanation

An iris scan would be considered a biometric technique and is not a hardware token. A hardware token is a physical item the user must be in possession of to access their account or certain resources.

73. A (Digital certificates)

Explanation

A digital certificate is a digital file that is sent as an attachment to a message and is used to verify that the message did indeed come from the entity it claims to have come from.

74. A (False rejection rate)

Explanation

The supervisor just defined the false rejection rate (FRR) for your system. The FRR is the level of false negatives, or rejections, that is going to be allowed in the system. In this case, your supervisor is willing to accept 1 false rejection for every 50 attempts.

75. D (Kerberos)

Explanation

Kerberos securely passes a symmetric key over an insecure network using the Needham-Schroeder symmetric key protocol. Kerberos is built around the idea of a trusted third party, termed a **key distribution center (KDC)**, which consists of two logically separate parts: an authentication server (AS) and a ticket-granting server (TGS). Kerberos communicates via "tickets" that serve to prove the identity of users.

76. C (Remote Authentication Dial-In User Service)

Explanation

Remote Authentication Dial-In User Service (RADIUS) is the abbreviation of RADIUS.

77. A (A third party can authenticate your users for you using accounts the users already have.)

Explanation

OpenID was created for federated authentication that lets a third party authenticate your users for you, by using accounts the users already have.

78. B (Shibboleth)

Explanation

Shibboleth is a service designed to enable single sign-on and federated identity-based authentication and authorization across networks. Shibboleth is a web-based technology that is built using SAML technologies.

79. C (On-boarding and Off-boarding)

Explanation

On-boarding and Off-boarding refer to the processes of adding personnel to a project or team and removing them from a project or team.

80. C (PIN Code)

Explanation

The authentication factor category "something you are" specifically refers to biometrics. These are uniquely identifying characteristics associated with individuals that typically do not change.

81. **D** (Service level agreement (SLA))

Explanation

A service level agreement (SLA) essentially sets the requisite level of performance for a given contractual service.

82. **A** (The data owner)

Explanation

Defining these characteristics is the responsibility of the data owner

83. **B** (Acceptable use policy (AUP))

Explanation

An acceptable use policy (AUP) outlines what the organization considers to be the appropriate use of its resources, such as computer systems, e-mail, Internet, and networks.

84. **A** (Procedures)

Explanation

Procedures are the step-by-step instructions on how to implement policies in an organization.

85. **C** (RTO)

Explanation

The term Recovery Time Objective (RTO) is used to describe the target time that is set for a resumption of operations after an incident.

86. **A** (Corrective)

Explanation

Corrective controls are used post-event, in an effort to minimize the extent of the damage.

87. **B** and **D** (Physical and Preventative)

Explanation

It is possible for a specific security control to fall into more than one category. Because a mantrap is a physical barrier that prevents tailgating, it is both a physical control and a preventative control.

88. **C** (The chance of something not working as planned)

Explanation

The risk is the chance of something not working as planned and causing an adverse impact. The impact is the cost associated with a realized risk.

89. **D** (Incident response plan)

Explanation

The incident response plan is the term used to describe the steps an organization performs in response to any situation determined to be abnormal in the operation of a computer system.

90. **A** (Eradication)

Explanation

Eradication involves removing the problem, and in today's complex system environment, this may mean rebuilding a clean machine.

91. **C** (Warm Site)

Explanation

A one step up site is a warm site that is partially configured. Usually, the hardware is available you just required to bring the operating system and data.

92. **B** (Differential)

Explanation

In differential back up, those files are copied that have been modified since the last time full back up is performed.

93. **C** (Failover)

Explanation

Failover refers to the process of transferring from regular business operation to continuity of operation plan.

94. A (Tabletop exercise)

Explanation

All the key players examine and discuss the actions they would pick up during an incident or emergency and test their plan in order to determine if the plan is viable or not.

95. **B** (Preservation of the data)

Explanation

While all of these are important, from the initial step in the forensics process, the most important issue must always be the preservation of the data.

96. **C** (Hashing algorithm)

Explanation

A **hashing algorithm** performs a function similar to the familiar parity bits, checksum, or cyclic redundancy check (CRC). It applies mathematical operations to a data stream (or file) to calculate some number that is uniquely based on the information contained in the data stream (or file).

97. **B** (Customer ID number)

Explanation

A customer ID number generated by a firm to track customer records is meaningful only inside the firm and is generally not considered to be personally identifiable information (PII). It is important not to use the SSN for the customer ID number, for obvious purposes.

98. **A** (Data owner)

Explanation

The data owner determines the business need. The privacy officer ensures that laws and regulations are followed, and the custodian/steward maintains the data.

99. **D** (Shredding)

Explanation

A desktop shredder can destroy DVDs and CDs. Burning is not wise at a desk. Wiping and pulping doesn't work on DVDs.

100.   **C** (Personally identifiable information (PII))

Explanation

Any information that can be used to determine identity is referred to collectively as personally identifiable information (PII).

101. **C** (Asymmetric)

Explanation

Asymmetric cryptography makes key management less of a concern because the private key material is never shared.

102.   **D** (You cannot get the plaintext out of a hash value.)

Explanation

Hash ciphers are designed to reduce the plaintext to a small value and are built to not allow extraction of the plaintext. This is why they are commonly called "one-way" functions.

103.   **C** (A digitally signed message has encryption protections for integrity and non-repudiation, which an encrypted message lacks.)

Explanation

The digital signature includes a hash of the message to supply message integrity and uses asymmetric encryption to demonstrate non-repudiation, the fact that the sender's private key was used to sign the message.

104.   **B** (Stream cipher)

Explanation

Stream ciphers work best when the data is in very small chunks to be processed rapidly, such as live streaming video.

105.   **B** (Exchange keys in-band)

Explanation

Diffie-Hellman allows an in-band key exchange even if the entire data stream is being monitored because the shared secret is never exposed.

106.   **A** (AES)

Explanation

It can be run at 128-, 192-, and 256-bit strengths and is considered the gold standard of current symmetric ciphers, with no known attacks, and is computationally efficient.

107.   **D** (GCM)

Explanation

Galois Counter Mode (GCM) is recognized by NIST and is used in the 802.1AE standard.

108.   **D** (RSA)

Explanation

Digital signatures require a public key algorithm, so you possibly need to consider RSA to provide the asymmetric cryptography.

109.   **B** (Two different programs with the same hash could allow malware to be undetected.)

Explanation

The ability to create a program that has the same hash as a known-good program would allow malware to be undetected by detection software that uses a hash list of approved programs.

110. **A** (It increases security due to the usage of a different key for each connection.)

Explanation

Ephemeral keys are important to key exchange protocols because they ensure that each connection has its own key for the symmetric encryption, and if an attacker compromises one key, he does not have all the traffic for this connection.

111. **A** (WPA2-Enterprise)

Explanation

WPA2-Enterprise is the correct version of WPA2 for this setup, as it uses enterprise-grade options to establish a shared secret.

112. **B** (Authentication server)

Explanation

Enterprise mode mandates authentication, so an authentication server, typically RADIUS, is required.

113. **B** (The use of an eight-digit PIN makes it open to brute force attacks)

Explanation

WPS uses an eight-digit pin and is subject to brute force attacks.

114. **D** (Certificate-based tunneling and EAP)

Explanation

The use of SSL-based tunneling and EAP packets makes the distributed authentication of RADIUS possible.

115. **A** (It uses a different key for each packet.)

Explanation

TKIP uses temporal keys, so there is a new key for every packet.

116. **D** (All of the above)

Explanation

A certificate authority is a hardware and software that manage the actual certificate bits, the policies and procedures that determine when certificates are properly issued, and the people who make and monitor the policies for compliance.

117. **B** (Trust level provided to users)

Explanation

You are most likely to concentrate on the level of trust provided by the CA to users of the system, as providing trust is the primary purpose of the CA.

118. **C** (Digital certificates)

Explanation

The X.509 standard is used to define the properties of digital certificates.

119. **A** (Unidirectional trust model)

Explanation

SSL PKI is based largely on the unidirectional trust model, where the lower servers in the certificate chain all trust the higher ones in the certificate chain.

120.   **B** (PEM)

Explanation

Because the certificate includes the entire certificate chain, it is most likely delivered to you in PEM format.

References

https://www.safaribooksonline.com/library/view/mike-meyers-comptia/9781260026559/

https://www.safaribooksonline.com/library/view/comptia-security-all-in-one/9781260019292/

https://www.safaribooksonline.com/library/view/comptia-security-review/9781118922903/

https://www.cengage.com/resource_uploads/downloads/1111138214_259146.pdf

http://nvlpubs.nist.gov/nistpubs/SpecialPublications/NIST.SP.800-12r1.pdf

http://bok.ahima.org/doc?oid=300244#.WkzPTN-WaM8

http://www.iaps.com/security-overview.html

http://www.brighthub.com/computing/smb-security/articles/31234.aspx

https://www.kaspersky.com/resource-center/threats/top-seven-mobile-security-threats-smart-phones-tablets-and-mobile-internet-devices-what-the-future-has-in-store

https://us.norton.com/internetsecurity-malware-what-is-a-botnet.html

https://www.safaribooksonline.com/library/view/improving-web-application/9780735651128/ch02s07.html

https://msdn.microsoft.com/en-us/library/ff648641.aspx

https://www.cisco.com/c/en/us/td/docs/ios/12_2/security/configuration/guide/fsecur_c/scfdenl.html

https://www.ietf.org/rfc/rfc3704.txt

www.cisco.com

https://msdn.microsoft.com

www.intel.com

https://meraki.cisco.com

https://en.wikipedia.org/wiki/Computer_network

http://www.computerhistory.org/timeline/networking-the-web/

http://www.computerhistory.org/timeline/networking-the-web/

http://www.thetechnicalstuff.com/types-of-networks-osi-layersrefernce-table/

http://www.utilizewindows.com/data-encapsulation-in-the-osi-model/

http://www.cisco.com/c/en/us/td/docs/solutions/Enterprise/Campus/campover.html#wp737141

http://www.cisco.com/web/services/downloads/smart-solutions-maximize-federal-capabilities-for-mission-success.pdf

http://www.diffen.com/difference/TCP_vs_UDP

http://www.cisco.com/c/en/us/support/docs/availability/high-availability/15114-NMS-bestpractice.html

http://www.wi.fh-flensburg.de/fileadmin/dozenten/Riggert/IP-Design-Guide.pdf

https://www.google.com/url?sa=t&rct=j&q=&esrc=s&source=web&cd=1&cad=rja&uact=8&ved=0ahUKEwih
pKO8lozQAhVDkRQKHeAzA_IQFggnMAA&url=https%3A%2F%2Fwww.cisco.com%2Fc%2Fdam%2Fen%2
Fus%2Ftd%2Fdocs%2Fsolutions%2FCVD%2FOct2016%2FCVD-Campus-LAN-WLAN-Design-
2016OCT.pdf&usg=AFQjCNHwUZXUr3QCKIzXFtBEfV-
HJ7OiVw&sig2=lSO526GEgDoomeEfiSFolA&bvm=bv.137132246,d.d24

http://www.ciscopress.com/articles/article.asp?p=2180210&seqNum=5

http://www.routeralley.com/guides/static_dynamic_routing.pdf

http://www.comptechdoc.org/independent/networking/guide/netdynamicroute.html

http://www.pearsonitcertification.com/articles/article.aspx?p=2168927&seqNum=7

http://www.cisco.com/c/en/us/td/docs/wireless/prime_infrastructure/1-
3/configuration/guide/pi_13_cg/ovr.pdf

http://www.cisco.com/c/en/us/products/security/security-manager/index.html

http://www.cisco.com/c/en/us/about/security-center/dnssec-best-practices.html

https://en.wikipedia.org/wiki/Malware

https://en.wikipedia.org/wiki/Security_information_and_event_management

https://en.wikipedia.org/wiki/Malware

https://ikrami.net/2014/05/19/siem-soc/

http://www.cisco.com/c/en/us/td/docs/ios-xml/ios/sec_usr_ssh/configuration/15-s/sec-usr-ssh-15-s-
book/sec-secure-copy.html

https://en.wikipedia.org/wiki/IEEE_802.1X

http://www.ciscopress.com/articles/article.asp?p=25477&seqNum=3

https://www.paessler.com/info/snmp_mibs_and_oids_an_overview

http://www.firewall.cx/downloads.html

https://en.wikipedia.org/wiki/Threat_(computer)#Threat_classification

http://www.cisco.com/c/en/us/products/security/ids-4215-sensor/index.html

https://en.wikipedia.org/wiki/Brain_(computer_virus)

About Our Products

Other Network & Security related products from IPSpecialist LTD are:

- CCNA Routing & Switching Technology Workbook
- CCNA Security Second Edition Technology Workbook
- CCNA Service Provider Technology Workbook
- CCDA Technology Workbook
- CCDP Technology Workbook
- CCNP Route Technology Workbook
- CCNP Switch Technology Workbook
- CCNP Troubleshoot Technology Workbook
- CCNP Security SENSS Technology Workbook
- CCNP Security SIMOS Technology Workbook
- CCNP Security SITCS Technology Workbook
- CCNP Security SISAS Technology Workbook
- CompTIA Network+ Technology Workbook
- Certified Blockchain Expert (CBEv2) Technology Workbook
- EC-Council CEH v10 Second Edition Technology Workbook
- Certified Blockchain Expert v2 Technology Workbook

Note from the Author:

Reviews are gold to authors! If you enjoyed reading this book and it really helped you through certification, would you consider giving it a review or rate it?

Link to Product Page:

Made in the USA
San Bernardino, CA
02 August 2019